DESKTOP PUBLISHING IN COLOR
MICHAEL KIERAN

DESKTOP PUBLISHING IN COLOR

Michael Kieran

RANDOM HOUSE
ELECTRONIC PUBLISHING

Desktop Publishing in Color

Published in the United States by Random House, Inc., New York, and simultaneously in Canada by Random House of Canada, Limited.

Manufactured in the United States of America

Revised Edition

0   9   8   7   6   5   4   3   2

ISBN 0-679-79039-X

New York   Toronto   London   Sydney   Auckland

Dedicated to
Sheila and Jon,
and to Susan

PRE-PUBLICATION REVIEWS FOR
DESKTOP PUBLISHING IN COLOR

"A definitive book on desktop color which proves to be a useful resource for everyone involved in desktop publishing."

—Paul Brainerd, President, Aldus Corporation

"Clear and concise, this book is an invaluable introduction to the hows and whys of desktop color. We've all been waiting for a book like this."
—Steve Hannaford, Co-editor/Co-publisher, *MacPrePress*

"Michael Kieran has created a well-researched overview of the complex field of color prepress, from a desktop perspective. It should prove valuable for both users and managers in the graphic arts and office publishing environments."
—Chris Dickman, Editor-in-Chief, *Electronic Composition & Imaging*

"Well written and thorough—an excellent overview of this complex topic."
—Peter Fink, Editor, *Desktop to Press*

"Fills many gaps for the neophyte and experienced desktop publisher. Covers the gamut clearly and concisely, from desktop prepress to commercial graphic arts production. A must book for your reference library."
—Steve Abramson, President, TruMatch

"Mr. Kieran has presented a comprehensive introduction to color that both novices and experienced desktop publishers will find extremely useful."
—Mills Davis, President, DAVIS, Inc.

"Michael Kieran has written the definitive resource on color publishing. He starts with the abstract and guides the reader through to the specifics of achieving quality color output from the desktop. Best of all, he names names—he tells his readers what to expect from the software on the market today."
—Anne Galdos, Ventura Software, Inc.

"We would that words become shooting stars, like gods, that they would rise up from the dead page into living forms of light and dark, into fountains of color."

   William Shakespeare

Acknowledgments

In early 1990 it began to occur to me to write a book about desktop publishing in color, and since then I have thought about little else. That I have been able to actually complete this book is a reflection of the commitment of the people around me.

Above all, I thank my wife Jane and children Christopher and Andrew for their understanding and encouragement. They make it all worthwhile.

I have benefited from the editing skills acquired over thirty years by one of the best writers in the business: my mother, Sheila Kieran. Thanks, mom. Technical editor Chris Dickman provided numerous valuable comments and suggestions, and his personable *savoir-faire* helped me bring life to some of the more technical portions of the text. For completeness and accuracy, I thank Steven Hannaford, whose incisive comments led me to include some explanations and technologies that would otherwise have been missed. Michael Roney, desktop publishing editor at Bantam Computer Books, was steadfast and helpful throughout. The color pages were expertly designed and created on the desktop by Donna Chernin and the text was expertly produced Electric Ink, Ltd., of Rochester, New York. Thanks also to Maureen Drexel, Tom Szalkiewicz, Jeff Rian, Rainé Young, and the other professionals in Bantam Electronic Publishing's production department.

The network of supporting people who made this book possible includes my partner Jane England and my other friends at Desktop Publishing Associates in Toronto: Jacquie Graham, Sherwood Fleming, and Judy Horn. My brothers and sisters, Susan, Patricia, Mark, Jon, Frances, and Andrew, also contributed immeasurably, as did Walter Howard, James Oldham, Christine Sutherland, Jim St. Lawrence, Cameron Smith, Lula Faint, and Rudolf Steiner.

Fernando Flores provided crucial distinctions in language and in life that helped me write this book. I also must thank Ted Nace for his commitment to quality, and for suggesting the title. Stephen F. Roth provided valuable suggestions in the book's early stages. The Wit family at Tomtem Farm provided me with a quiet place to work, as did Marg Stewart at the Old Railway Inn in tranquil Meaford, Ontario.

The concept of the beta-tester has become an essential part of quality control in the computer industry, so I enlisted the assistance of numerous beta-readers to help ensure this book is accurate and comprehensive. They include Steven J. Abramson, Rosemary Bach, David Butler, John Cruise, Jennifer Delamare, Ginger Ellard, Klaus Ertle, Mary Frongillo, Lucy E. Garrick, Shawn Greenberg, Jeneane Harter, Jennifer McLeod, John Mitchell, Michael Patterson, Burton Robson, Paul Towner, Darla M. Vernon, and John Willis. A special thanks to Peter Fink, who provided information essential to Chapter 10. To them I offer my thanks, for it is a blessing to know that most of the obvious errors have been caught before going to press.

A number of other people were kind enough to provide information, illustrations, and feedback, among them Dave Bachman, Arlen Bartsch, Suzanne Bertram, Karen Blair, David Butler, Peter Chapman, Laura Childs, Freda Cook, Julius da Costa, Ed Crusciel, Mills Davis, Michael Flores, Julie Gedamanski, Chuck Glassier, James R. Hamilton, Chet Hong, Eugene J. Hunt, Jr., James King, Maire Kushner, Bob Janukowicz, David Leetham, Britt MacKenzie, Susan McKeown, Kathy Melcher, Melodye Mueller, Robin O'Leary, James P.W. Parsons, Bryan Pearson, David Peck, Richard Rollins, Doug Schust, Kel Schwab, Jonathan Seybold, Courtland Shakespeare, Peter Shaw, Helene Smith, Shane Steinman, and Roger Thornton.

Naturally, regardless of who reviewed the text, responsibility for any mistakes rests with me. Please feel free to let me know about them, and I'll make corrections in the next edition of this book. Desktop color is changing rapidly, and I look forward to keeping up with it.

Michael Kieran

Desktop Publishing Associates
1992 Yonge Street, Suite 301
Toronto, Ontario
Canada M4S 1Z7

Phone 416-480-1376
Fax 416-480-0192
CompuServe 71340,310

Contents

CHAPTER 1

The Experience of Color 1

CHAPTER   2

Fundamentals of Color Reproduction   15

C H A P T E R 3

Quality Color—The Eternal Quest 67

CHAPTER 4

Computer Hardware Essentials   97

C H A P T E R   5

Desktop Color Scanning   125

C H A P T E R   6

Desktop Color Graphics   159

C H A P T E R   7

Desktop Color Imaging   195

C H A P T E R   8

Desktop Color Page Layout   239

CHAPTER 9

Color Electronic Prepress Systems 275

CHAPTER 10

Output Service Bureaus   309

A P P E N D I X   A

Vendors   347

A P P E N D I X   B

Introduction

In the past five years, the tidal wave of desktop publishing has washed over the typesetting and publishing industries, as powerful new computer tools enable individuals to gain control over the production of their documents.

Desktop *color* is the next wave.

High-quality color publishing is now on the horizon for every electronic publisher—from desktop and corporate publishers to graphic design studios and service bureaus. The tools to produce color on the desktop have arrived, and the color publishing industry will never be the same.

The transition to widespread color production on the desktop is inevitable—but, undoubtedly, it will be accompanied by many of the same problems, setbacks, and breakdowns encountered in the early days of desktop publishing.

- "The quality's not good enough..."
- "You need a graphics expert, not a computer operator..."
- "Personal computers aren't powerful enough to handle the graphics..."

For those who pioneered the desktop publishing revolution, such complaints have a familiar ring. In the early days of desktop publishing, when a "large" document was one that extended onto the second page, such comments were well founded. What, after all, were professional typographers to make of publishing systems that supported only two typefaces, in just a few sizes and attributes?

But within five years of the release of the first page layout programs for Apple Macintosh and IBM-compatible computers, electronic composition supplanted the old-fashioned way of setting type and laying out a page. In less than 25 years, typesetting has moved from room-sized hot-lead linecasters to electronic machines quietly humming away in the corner.

Desktop publishing programs today are fast and powerful, boasting incredible precision in placing typography, and in providing access to thousands of high-quality typefaces. The microcomputers they run on have achieved performance increases that are impressive, even for the computer industry.

Desktop publishing, initially dismissed by some in the printing industry as a fad, has blossomed into a multibillion dollar industry used to produce everything from daily newspapers to annual reports.

Color publishing moves to the desktop

The primary thesis of this book is that a similar explosion is beginning to occur for desktop color. In the next five years, many, if not most, color documents will be produced on the desktop.

Powerful new tools for desktop color production will spur the growth of a huge new market in short-run color publishing. An entirely new group of users—many with a background in black-and-white desktop publishing—will have the freedom to use color.

And that's the problem: producing high-quality color work requires a set of skills unfamiliar to most desktop publishers. Publishing in color is at least ten times more complex than in black-and-white, with all too many opportunities for technical glitches that can be embarrassing, time-consuming, and very costly.

Learning to produce good color documents takes time, and can easily become very expensive if you do a lot of "on-the-job training" (better known as making mistakes). But it involves skills that can be learned and applied. This book is designed to provide you with the tools and techniques you need to gain competence in desktop color publishing.

Many users will create color documents for production and reproduction in-house. Others will generate documents that are designed, enhanced, color-corrected, and separated on the desktop, but ultimately reproduced by offset lithography or other commercial printing methods.

Are traditional color production tools obsolete?

There are three main factors forcing traditional print and publishing companies to reexamine the way they handle color reproduction.

- First, new technologies such as the PostScript page description language have emerged, resulting in open, standards-based computer platforms.

- Second, the market for color production systems has expanded rapidly, particularly the lower-cost solutions that offer most of the functionality of high-end systems at a fraction of the price.

- Third, there's a general trend toward in-house control of design, thanks to the rapid growth of desktop publishing.

Together, these factors are also pressuring black-and-white desktop publishing service bureaus to offer color services in order to remain competitive.

Corporate publishers are also being swept up in the color revolution, but for different reasons. In the business world, the rationale for increased color use is simple: color sells. Corporate publishers have watched with interest as the tools for desktop publishing have moved ever further into the color prepress world, and they seek to bring more color image reproduction in-house, both to increase their control over the design process and to reduce turnaround times.

The reason for the ultimate success of desktop color systems is evident at any business presentation. Given two proposals of equal merit, an organization is likely to be seduced by the more colorful one.

Thus, in corporate publishing alone, it is easy to predict a healthy future for desktop color. When we include the high-end color prepress market, overwhelming evidence points to a shift to color production on professional systems using desktop computers.

Synthetic and natural color

Most publishers making the transition from black-and-white begin with *synthetic* color—colors produced in graphics and page layout programs—as compared with the *natural* colors found in photographs and paintings.

The main reason is that it is relatively expensive to use traditional color production techniques to add color to a publication—even for something as simple as a three-color tint on all headings and ruling lines. With natural color, even the desktop techniques can be difficult and expensive, whereas desktop production of synthetic color offers tremendous improvements in cost-effectiveness.

Although creating synthetic colors in a graphics or page layout program may not be quite as challenging as separating full-color photographs, it, too, demands care and attention to produce good results. It's very easy to wind up with colors that look blotchy, don't match, and are not in perfect register. Our purpose here is to understand the standard practices that can minimize each potentially harmful variable, and to develop a way of working that maximizes quality and throughput.

Why you should read this book

Because of both its technical complexity and the current pace of change, desktop color has passed the point where any one person can know everything about it. Indeed, people often find uses for a program that its author never imagined.

This book is, first, for people who will actually be using desktop color. It is also for those who, while not working with these tools hands-on, are responsible for managing or supervising the use of these systems. Many readers will have previous hands-on experience with black-and-white desktop publishing, and will be eager to understand and use the new color tools. Others will come from the color prepress and publishing business, wanting to prepare themselves for the new technologies transforming their industry.

The book has been designed as a resource you can use to fulfill two objectives: to assess the possibilities emerging from the rapid evolution of color publishing and prepress technology, and to learn how to apply these possibilities effectively with the new color systems and services.

How this book is organized

This book is structured like a staircase, assuming that different readers will want to progress to different levels. Many people will be interested in color only to brighten a newsletter or brochure with spot color, while others want to create glossy magazines with full-color photography, direct from desktop to final film.

The book begins with the fundamentals of color theory and color reproduction, and examines the factors affecting color quality.

The heart of the book explores three essential aspects of color production:

- First, color graphics, found in drawing programs such as Adobe Illustrator, Aldus FreeHand, Corel Draw, and Micrografx Designer.
- Second, color imaging, found in painting and photo enhancement programs such as Adobe Photoshop, Letraset ColorStudio, and Aldus PhotoStyler.
- Third, color page layout, found in page layout programs such as Aldus PageMaker, Ventura Publisher, and QuarkXPress.

In addition to exploring the color features of each program, the text focuses on how they work together. The suggestions contained in this book are distilled from the wisdom of many experienced designers, publishers, and color house operators.

The final chapters explore color production on high-end electronic prepress systems, the emerging links between the desktop and high-end systems, and color output service bureaus.

Because the desktop color field is so new, all key terms and distinctions are defined, both in the text and in a detailed glossary at the back of the book. Helpful tips are scattered throughout the text to help users get the best possible quality from these new tools and techniques.

Color publishing at the transition point

We are in a moment of transition in which new technologies have challenged traditional methods of color production, and are just beginning to supplant them. This book chronicles that transition and invites you into the fascinating world of color, in which:

- color documents are conceived, created, and beautifully reproduced on the desktop;
- all types of short-run printing jobs routinely include color;
- sophisticated software enables publishers with no experience in color to select the optimal value for each factor that can affect quality.

The emergence of desktop color publishing will alter the fortunes of many companies, both those with significant investments in the traditional methods of color production and those using innovative products and processes.

Only time will tell which of these products, companies, and industries will survive and even thrive. As history shows repeatedly, business opportunities open and close rapidly in any moment of dramatic technological change.

For desktop publishing in color, that moment is now.

The Experience of Color

"Color is the speech of the soul of nature."
JOHANN WOLFGANG VON GOETHE

One fundamental truth shines through in our exploration of color: color is a phenomenon of experience that can be modeled, described, analyzed, and manipulated—but never fully comprehended.

- To the Impressionist painters, color was a bridge to a world of indescribable human experience, a window to the very soul of humanity.

- To a physicist, color is a phenomenon of waves and particles, with one aspect or other emphasized, depending on the properties being observed.

- To a chemist, color is a characteristic of specific molecules and the way their electrons behave.

- To a marketing executive, color is a tool for provoking emotional responses that trigger people to buy things.

In other words, color is a description—or more precisely, an attribute—that changes according to the perceptions of the observer. Therefore, to attempt a useful understanding of color, we must begin with the observer—a human observer.

1

The world is colorful

From an evolutionary perspective, animals developed and refined the ability to distinguish colors because doing so provided them with some competitive advantage over other animals, probably associated with finding a mate, identifying food, or both.

A visit to the caves of south-central France shows that our Magdalenian forebears appreciated the aesthetics of form and color more than 17,000 years ago. Even after all that time, the shadings of color remain vibrant in the paintings that line the cavern walls. (Ironically, these colors have faded most during the past few years, the result of being breathed on by the thousands who flocked annually to see the ancient artworks; in a bid to save them from further damage, most of the famous caves have been closed to the public.)

To our ancestors, color possessed powerful symbolic and magical properties—pure white, evil black, blood red. Since then, color has played a central role in the visual arts, from painting and sculpture to heraldry, weaving, print-making, and the illumination of pages.

From the time of the ancient Greeks, we have interpreted color as an integral part of the object of which it was a part. As civilization developed, it brought with it the urge and the ability to represent, not only the objects of the natural world, but also those of imagination, dreams, and religious aspirations. By the end of the Renaissance, the sophisticated use of color was well established, especially in painting.

Artists such as Leonardo da Vinci spent a great deal of time experimenting with new pigments and special materials in an attempt to produce, not just more pleasing colors, but colors that might resist fading and maintain their brilliance over the years.

The nature of color

In order to use desktop color effectively, it's helpful to understand the basics of color and human physiology as it relates to
color. Those basics did not become evident until the late 1660s,
when Sir Isaac Newton performed many of his original experiments with color that revealed what makes things colorful.

Seeing colors

Newton focused attention on the nature of the spectrum—the
colors seen in a rainbow or in light that has been passed through
a prism. When white light is shone through a prism, it explodes
into a panoply of colors, arranged in the sequence red, orange,
yellow, green, blue, indigo, violet. (The mnemonic Roy G. Biv,
the mascot of a mail-order scientific supply company, makes it
easy to remember this color sequence.)

Some of the subtlety inherent in color can be understood from
Newton's simple experiments, in which two prisms were
arranged to project different colors onto the same spot on a
white background. Combining two such colors will produce a
third color that usually lies between the two source colors in the
spectral sequence. Certain pairs of colors—called complementary
colors—can be combined to create white.

Newton also discovered that by combining blue and yellow
sources, he could create a green that was identical with the
"pure" green in the spectrum. Today, using a color-measuring
device called a colorimeter, we see that these two greens,
although identical to the eye, are quite different in composition.
Such colors—those that look identical but have different spectral
signatures—are called *metamers*.

The visible spectrum extends from infrared to
ultraviolet—only a tiny slice of the overall electromagnetic spectrum, which encompasses everything from ultra-low frequency
to cosmic radiation. (See Color Page 2.)

The primary colors

There are three sets of "primary" colors: the psychological primaries, the light (or additive) primaries, and the pigment primaries.

The psychological primaries are black, white, red, green, blue, and yellow—colors that evoke strong human emotions, but that are not the most important hues in color reproduction. Red, green, and blue, the light primaries, can be combined to create all the colors of radiant light. Physicists identified these three in experiments in which combining balanced amounts of red, green, and violet-blue yielded white light—which is why they are also known as additive primaries. Secondary, or complementary, colors are created from a balanced mixture of two primaries: magenta, for instance, is a mixture of red and violet-blue.

In painting and color reproduction, red, yellow, and blue are known as the pigment primaries because, at least in theory, they can be mixed to produce all other colors. (To complicate matters, the red and blue pigment primaries that are used as colorants in printing inks are different from red and blue light primaries.)

The psychology of color

Color is inspirational; color is evocative; color is emotional.

Color is a subtle, sophisticated phenomenon, with a strong emotional pull that makes the proper use of different colors essential in art, design, and commerce. According to its hue, a color is classified as warm or cool, light or dark, vivid or dull, tranquil or exciting, created or natural.

Many of color's emotional effects are linguistically and culturally determined. People in western civilizations generally experience:

- black as the color of night: evil, chic, cold, elegant, and expensive;

- white as pure, innocent, and peaceful (although it also connotes cold and winter);

- red as passionate, intense, speeding up the metabolism;

- yellow as sunshine, uplifting;

- green as pastoral, suggestive of nature, symbolic of fertility, but also the shade of poison and envy (and frequently considered bad luck);

- blue as light, breezy, dignified, sedate;

- purple as the traditional symbol of royalty, both sophisticated and whimsical;

- brown as rustic, earth-like, natural, and fertile, as well as opulent or sombre.

The physiology of color

The anatomy and physiology of the human eye control our fundamental perception of color. The iris diaphragm regulates the amount of light that passes through the lens to strike the retina, a network of cells and neurons that covers the entire back half of the eye—except the point at which the optic nerve joins the eye: quite literally, the "blind spot."

About 130 million light-sensitive cells—some rod-shaped, some cone-shaped—cover the retina of the eye and respond to light by sending electrical signals to the brain. The rod-shaped cells, which are concentrated on the periphery of the retina, transmit black and white information only, but are more sensitive to dim light. You can't detect color very well after dusk because you're "seeing with your rods." Similarly, astronomers trying to see detail in a faint object will center it in the eyepiece of the telescope, then look away to the edge of the field, in order to point the cones of their eyes at empty space, so the rods can pick out especially dim points of light.

There are three kinds of cone cells, and, according to some physiologists, each has a peak sensitivity to one of the light primaries (red, green, and blue). Whatever the mechanism, all the color we see is the product of the mix of signals coming from the three types of cones.

The temperature of colors

There are a number of simple experiments that show us how elusive and subjective we are in our perceptions of color. The paint chip seen at the hardware store is very different from the paint in the tin, the paint on the roller, the wet paint on the wall, and the dried paint—as any number of frustrated decorators can testify.

While you may be willing to live with what seemed to be subtle peach on the paint chip and turned nasty orange on the wall, integrity of hue is essential to successful desktop publishing in color. Nuances of hue and tone are the key. An understanding of how color scientists make such distinctions will be useful when you're trying to communicate to someone else information about the color you want or have in mind.

Given that each person's ability to distinguish colors from each other is subject to emotion—as well as to ambient light, weather, and other factors—physicists rely on an objective measure, *color temperature*, to define a standard source of illumination. Because it resolves any ambiguities about the lighting conditions under which a colored object is viewed and is not subject to feeling, color temperature makes it possible to calibrate colors as they move through the various stages in the print production process.

Scientists establish the color temperature by specifying the glow given off by an ideal substance, or *blackbody*, as it is heated to various temperatures, measured in degrees Kelvin. (The Kelvin scale matches the Celsius scale, but starts at absolute zero rather than the freezing point of water: 7,000° C is about 6,700 K.)

Take as an example the seemingly simple—but actually complex—problem of defining white light. Ordinarily, we say that white light resembles normal daylight. But daylight changes constantly, varying with the latitude, season, and time of day.

However, using light temperatures, we know that at 5,600 K, an ideal sample glows with a light that has spectral qualities approximating direct sunshine on a June day in the temperate latitudes. Open, north-facing sky contains more blue wavelengths and has a color temperature of about 7,500 K, while morning or evening sky is redder and has a correspondingly lower color reading.

In order to minimize variations in perception, the North American graphic arts industry has established 5,000 K as a standard light source for viewing color originals, proofs, and printed samples; today, virtually all printing companies and film separation houses use viewing booths outfitted with 5,000 K lamps. (In Europe, both 5,000 K and 6,500 K sources are used.) Viewing booths are used when comparing a color original to the color proof or printed piece.

Some color professionals will argue that even more control over viewing conditions is necessary. For example, the 5,000 K tubes produced by different manufacturers are visibly redder or bluer than one another. Also, the tubes change color over time, so they must be replaced on schedule or their effectiveness is limited.

Color perception

The effects of color are influenced by the context, or surroundings, against which it is viewed; therefore, color matching should always take place against a standard background and with an illuminant of known color temperature, such as the lights and gray background used in viewing booths. Also, it takes a few minutes for the human eye to fully adapt to changes in the intensity of illumination, so wait for your eyes to adjust to the ambient light before assessing whether two colors match.

There is one other perceptual limitation: densities in a typical transparency range widely between the highlights (the least dense areas) and the shadows (those that are most dense). But when color appears on the printed page, it simply cannot show those vast differences, that wide a "dynamic range" (a problem we'll discuss in more detail in Chapter 3 on Quality Color).

Color models

A color model is a way of representing colors as data. As mentioned earlier, color is affected by perception and, therefore, color models are imperfect. Nonetheless, people who use color in publishing must have a consistent way of describing it, which is why attempts to create color models go back hundreds of years, if with limited success.

Today's color models fit into three categories:

- *Subtractive color models, such as CMYK* (Cyan, Magenta, Yellow, Black). The printing process relies on light reflected from the image on the page to the eye, as determined by the light-absorbing properties of the ink. In other words, the color of the object is established by the frequencies of light that are absorbed or subtracted. In a subtractive model, a white surface reflects all the wavelengths of visible light; a black surface absorbs all of them; and a green surface absorbs (subtracts) all but the green wavelengths.

- *Additive color models, such as the RGB model used for a computer screen.* These combine red, green, and blue light to create what are sensed by the human eye as a multitude of colors. The human eye can detect very subtle changes in the form and color of reflected light—from which we get almost all our daily sensory experience—but is less well designed for a screen's radiant light.

- *Perceptual color models, such as the CIE system.* These are not related to any particular printing process or display, but are based on measurements derived from the perceptions of large numbers of people. These perceptual models become increasingly important as responsibility for color production shifts to less skilled operators of desktop hardware and software.

When people match colors visually, they are often trying to transform the additive colors produced on a computer screen into the subtractive colors produced by the printing process. And, of course, everything is perceived by the viewer. Therefore, it is important for color publishing to know something about the most commonly used color models—CIE (and its variations), HSL, RGB, and CMYK.

CIE

All computers, software, and peripherals must use a color model internally for specifying color. Color research has been directed toward finding a color model, one independent of any particular device, and based on the way the human eye perceives color, rather than the way color is interpreted by an input scanner or rendered by a particular output device.

Figure 1-1
The original 1931 CIE diagram

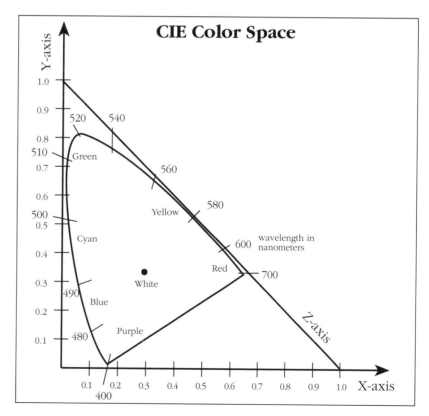

The concept of device-independent color was developed in the 1920s by an international scientific commission on illumination, the Commission Internationale de l'Eclairage, or CIE. Its 1931 model is based on the notion of a "standard observer" whose color vision is described in terms of the spectral sensitivity of the red, green, and blue receptors in his or her eyes.

Under the original CIE system, known as CIEXYZ, it was impossible to tell from the numbers how similar two colors were, and the system lacked perceptual uniformity (my bluish-green is your greenish-blue). Later improvements, known as CIELUV and CIELAB, corrected this deficiency. This gives them the potential to be very useful in desktop color publishing.

In the CIELUV system, the various hues are plotted on a pair of axes, known as v^* and u^*, with a third dimension, L, used to specify the lightness or darkness (luminance) of a color. A high positive v^* value indicates yellow, while a large negative value indicates violet. Similarly, a high positive value of u^* indicates a magenta or red hue, while a negative value indicates cyan or green. If both values are zero, a neutral gray is indicated, with colors becoming more intense (saturated) as the numbers increase.

In the CIELUV model, color changes that appear as equal steps to the eye will be reasonably equally spaced on the CIELUV diagram, and mixtures of colors will always fall on a reasonably straight line between the two source colors. Both factors are useful when mixing colors or when trying to match color samples. CIELAB is a modification of CIELUV and makes the color steps even more like the visual perception of a standard observer.

To date, no one has discovered a completely satisfactory way of specifying device-independent color, but a great deal of research continues to be directed at the problem. When such a system is developed (as seems likely), scanners will be calibrated to produce image files codes based on visual perceptions, so that any properly calibrated monitor or output device could render the image without having to be concerned about its source.

Adobe has selected CIEXYZ as the internal color model in PostScript Level 2, with built-in conversions to most of the other leading color models.

RGB

In the RGB (red, green, blue) system, the red, green, and blue components of each picture element, or pixel, in the image are assigned a number, usually an integer between 0 and 255. The RGB model is used in virtually all television sets, computer displays, and color film recorders. In a cathode ray tube, the numbers are fed to digital-to-analog converters, which produce a voltage proportional to each number, and the voltage is used to drive the monitor's red, green, and blue electron guns. Although it is widely used, RGB remains device-dependent (and, because there is no single standard used by all manufacturers, this can mean variations according to brand).

A major limitation of the RGB system is that because it's based on adding colors together, it works for devices that radiate light, such as monitors, but not for objects that reflect light, such as the printed page. It's impossible to simulate on paper the infinite number of colors in nature by printing with just red, green, and blue inks. There are many shades of yellow, for instance, that can't be constructed from any combination of red, green, and blue.

In other words, although the RGB model is well suited for use in display monitors, it is not appropriate for printing devices. Given that monitors made by different manufacturers, and even individual units made by a given manufacturer, differ in their response to specific voltages, and that colors change depending on the monitor on which they are displayed, RGB cannot be considered a color "standard."

A number of vendors have attempted to calibrate the RGB model, usually to the CIE model or one of its derivatives. In the movie world, the Society of Motion Picture and Television Engineers (SMPTE) has developed such a model—although, to date, it has not been widely accepted in the graphics art industry. PostScript Level 2 goes a long way toward providing a consistent way of converting between different color models, though technical and standardization problems remain to be solved.

HSL

The HSL (hue, saturation, luminance) model is similar to RGB, as are variants in which saturation is labeled chroma (HCL), or luminance is known as value (HSV). Although they make color adjustments somewhat easier, these models are also not standardized.

Another derivative of HSL is HSB (hue, saturation, brightness), in which the linear luminance value, which does not correspond to human perception, is replaced by a nonlinear brightness value that more closely relates to perceived color. (A further confusing factor is that some companies use the word "lightness" to describe the brightness value, resulting in another model called HSL.) While these various terms and labels may seem confusing, they provide a background against which the person eager to desktop publish in color can appreciate the complexity of color models and can exercise the care necessary to ensure reasonably reliable and consistent high-quality color.

CMYK

Practically speaking, the CMYK (cyan, magenta, yellow, black) model is among the most important color models, because it is the basis of almost all color reproduction processes. Combining percentages of the four process color inks (cyan, magenta, yellow, and black) on a press produces the appearance of millions of colors— enough to reproduce even color photographs.

In theory at least, we should be able to print full-color images with only cyan, magenta, and yellow inks, the complements, or opposites, of red, green, and blue. In reality, however, the inks, papers, and presses used do not make this possible; a combination of pure cyan, magenta, and yellow (such as that produced on a low-end color printer with no black ribbon) does not produce a solid black but, rather, a muddy brown, the result of both imperfect color pigments and lack of density.

These problems are resolved, to some extent, in the color separation process. To increase density, especially in the dark areas of the image, black ink is added to cyan, magenta, and yellow.

In full-color imaging, the problem of nonideal pigments is solved by having the scanner operator key in adjustments to the relative strengths of the different inks. Similar compensations have to be made in desktop color separation programs. For instance, to compensate for the fact that cyan often appears more blue than it should, the operator may want to decrease slightly the magenta content of any area containing cyan, and increase cyan approximately 10 percent in any neutral areas.

PhotoYCC

The most recent color model to be unveiled is the PhotoYCC model developed by Eastman Kodak for use in their new consumer product, Photo CD. Photo CD could represent the future of home photography. Pictures are taken with a regular camera, and the film is developed conventionally. The finished negatives or slides are then scanned into the Photo CD system, from which they can be transferred to a compact disk (CD) for viewing and editing via an ordinary television set.

PhotoYCC is of importance to color publishers because it has potential to provide color calibration between video signals and desktop publishing. Indeed, PhotoYCC is one of the color models supported by PostScript Level 2.

In addition to the CIE, RGB, HSL, CMYK, and PhotoYCC color models, there are also a variety of color *specifying* systems, all based on carefully printed samples, or *swatches*, of each color. Color swatch systems, such as the PANTONE MATCHING SYSTEM®,* Focoltone Colour System, and Trumatch Swatching System, are discussed in Chapter 2.

*Pantone, Inc.'s check-standard trademark for color reproduction and color reproduction materials.

Working with appropriate color models

Because of the differences between the various color models, it is important that you work in the model that will provide the best color fidelity. For example, when the project being created in a publishing or graphics program is going to be reproduced using process colors, be sure to specify the colors in the software according to their CMYK values. (These are the values that will be used to create a prepress proof, as well as the printing plates themselves.)

If, on the other hand, you are designing a brochure that will be printed as black plus one spot color, that color will be specified according to its PANTONE Number, which your printing company needs in order to mix the correct ink for your specific print run. Again, keep in mind that the PANTONE Colors displayed on screen will not match those printed on paper. This holds true for any of the previously mentioned color systems.

As of 1991, the electronic publishing industry is moving rapidly toward establishing standards for unambiguously defined color, although many complex technical and commercial issues remain to be solved. We look at this issue in more detail in the next two chapters, first at color reproduction, then at maintaining quality throughout the entire design-to-print process.

Before moving on, remember the key point: color is a subjective experience, a phenomenon of perception. With practice, you may eventually grow to be quite adept at recreating nature's colors with reasonable fidelity on the printed page. But you are more likely to do so if you remain conscious of the infinite variety and mystery that is color.

Fundamentals of Color Reproduction

"Colors speak all languages."
JOSEPH ADDISON

With the advent of desktop publishing, it's now a lot easier to produce documents, but not necessarily easier to reproduce them. The distinction is crucial because different machines, processes, and people are used for creating documents than for replicating them.

A designer, who sits in front of a computer running a powerful graphics package filled with all the latest bells and whistles, having worked for months to learn how to produce great-looking graphics, is still usually limited to a press run of a single copy.

Whether in black-and-white or color, the single page is relatively cheap and easy to produce. If 500 black-and-white copies are required, they can be quickly and inexpensively duplicated on a photocopier. Until now, making hundreds of color copies has been prohibitively expensive, but this is likely to change rapidly during the next few years.

If thousands of copies are required, then photocopy technologies no longer make sense (for either black-and-white or color); offset lithography or some other printing method is more appropriate.

Composite color versus separated color

This chapter explores two different ways of reproducing color documents: by color photocopier or color desktop printer (which uses toner) and by traditional printing press (which uses ink), the new technology and the old. Both require the concept of color separation, although only the printing press processes use actual separation films.

In using separated color, films for each process color are created, and a plate is made from each piece of film. The four plates are run in sequence on a multicolor printing press to simulate the color in the original. There are a variety of printing methods available, including lithography, gravure, flexography, and letterpress, but litho is by far the most common. Our discussion will refer specifically to lithography, but much of this information is relevant to other major printing methods as well.

Thermal printers, color copiers, and other new digital devices produce what can be called composite color, because the colors cyan, magenta, yellow, and black are combined together on the page inside the printer. It works with the same digital separation data, but prints each process color internally, without the photographic film stage.

The difference between these two technologies may be interpreted as the shift from analog technology (photography) to digital technology (computers) or as the difference between short-run color duplication and long-run multicolor printing.

Producing a document is different than reproducing it

When you create a document at your desk, whether in black-and-white or color, it's usually cheapest and fastest to print a single original and have it copied on a photocopy machine.

The desktop laser printer is ideal for producing the original of a 100-page report in black-and-white, but far from ideal for reproducing 50 copies (5,000 pages!) of the same document.

Nowadays, relatively small runs (fewer than about 500 copies) are usually duplicated on a photocopier, or xerographic device.

Larger quantities are usually produced with offset lithography. A similar situation is developing in color: color printers are being widely used for producing documents published by desktop.

Xerography and litho: the major methods of duplication

When more than a few copies of a color document are needed, xerography and lithography again become the main duplication methods. If you need more than a few copies of each original page, it is probably faster and cheaper to have them duplicated with a color photocopier, than to print them one at a time on a color printer.

It's worth noting that a vast new market—short-run color—is opening up as a result of the proliferation of color xerographic and thermal transfer tools—which are both color printers and color copiers. These new machines are the enabling technologies of the emerging age of color publishing, just as the first PostScript printers signaled the emergence of desktop publishing itself.

Until very recently, it was rarely cost-efficient to produce fewer than 5,000 copies of a printed color piece. The spread of low-cost color printers and copiers is changing all that, resulting in an increased use of color in all kinds of business documents:

- a training company can now produce course manuals that combine color covers and a dozen pages of color charts and graphics with about 100 pages of black-and-white text and pictures;
- a real estate agent can take color photographs of a house and use a template of standard presentation formats to desktop publish custom brochures that are mailed to selected clients or kept on hand for new prospects;
- a catalog production team can produce many kinds of page designs and exchange them with one another for various stages of approval, while working with type and pictures whose colors will closely match those in the millions of pages that ultimately come off the huge web presses.

The convergence of software and hardware now makes it possible to create even a few hundred copies of any kind of full-color document relatively cheaply and easily. (For larger quantities, however, offset litho or other large-scale production methods will continue to prevail for the foreseeable future.)

The important difference between offset litho and xerography is that the former is far more complex than the latter, but is the only way when thousands or millions of copies are needed. Moreover, once the make-ready phase is complete and actual production begins, offset is fast and xerography is s-l-o-w.

Xerography—the enabling desktop technology

The laser printer is a form of xerography that led to the birth of desktop publishing; the two other crucial innovations, the PostScript language and the PageMaker page layout program, are software. As such, the laser printer is part of a tradition of improved printing technology dating back almost exactly 100 years.

During the late 1880s, Otto Mergenthaler, one of the inventors of the typewriter, decided to apply the same principle to the task of typesetting, which until then had changed little since the days of Johann Gutenberg. The result was the first Linotype machine, which allowed the operator, using a keyboard, to compose an entire line of type at once, rather than assembling it one character at a time on a manual composing stick. These linecasters came to completely dominate typesetting during the first half of this century.

The hot metal type characteristic of linecasting machines was gradually supplanted in the 1970s by phototypesetting, in which a bright light source is used to selectively expose the character shapes onto photosensitive paper. In some phototypesetters, the conventional light source was replaced by a laser beam, which emits pure, highly concentrated light.

How laser printers work

In the early 1980s, the technology of laser phototypesetting was married to the technology used by the everyday office photocopier. The result was the low-cost laser marking engine, in which a laser beam scans across a photosensitive drum. At each point, the computer tells the laser whether the particular picture element, or pixel, is on or off.

A piece of paper is wrapped around the drum and the charge passes from the drum to the paper, following which it passes over a hopper of toner particles, causing the toner particles to stick electrostatically to the paper. The paper then passes through heated rollers, which melt the toner particles into the fibrous structure of the paper, and it emerges from the printer as a (literally) hot new page.

This mechanism is virtually the same whether you are making a photocopy or printing a page on a laser printer. The major difference is that the laser printer's original signal comes directly from a computer, while the copier's is from its built-in laser page scanner.

Color desktop printers

Desktop color is a cost-effective way to create beautiful prints of graphics and documents. And nothing matches the impact of color on documents you've grown used to seeing in black-and-white.

There are a variety of output devices that can take a signal from a microcomputer and render it in living color. They vary tremendously in quality and price, and use a diverse assortment of technologies to produce a hard-copy version of color information.

Starting with the least expensive printers and moving upwards in both cost and quality, the choice of color output devices includes:

- color-capable *dot matrix printers,* costing as little as $500, used for charting and presentations in the office;

- low-end *ink-jet printers*, starting at about $1,000, that are also designed for charts and graphs;

- *thermal transfer printers*, the largest category, suitable for desktop publishing and costing from $5,000 to $30,000;

- *solid ink printers*, which produce vivid colors that feel embossed on the page, and cost about $10,000;

- *phase-change printers*, costing $10,000 to $15,000, that offer vivid color and can print onto plain paper;

- *dye sublimation printers*, costing $10,000 to $70,000, which produce continuous-tone prints of a quality that is not quite photographic but is pretty darned good;

- high-end *ink-jet printers*, which cost more than $60,000 and are finding increased acceptance as direct digital color proofers (DDCPs);

- high-end *direct digital color proofers* costing well over $100,000, used as part of large-scale color electronic pre-press systems.

Thermal printers

Thermal printers, most containing the PostScript language, are by far the most common output devices for color desktop publishing. In the next few years, sales are expected to rise substantially as costs continue to decline.

The color thermal printer works much like the original black-and-white laser printer, although it uses heat to melt colored material (usually a chemical polymer) onto paper, rather than containing a laser. A colored ribbon (cyan, magenta, yellow, or black) is placed against a metal drum, that has been divided into a grid of tiny pixels, 300 to the inch, each of which can be addressed by the computer. Each pixel for a given color heats up, melting the colorant into the paper.

Many printers move the sheet of paper in and out four times, once for each process color. This limits the repeatability, and therefore the quality, of the resulting pages, and has been dealt with in the newer models that require only a single pass.

As with black-and-white printers, the availability of the PostScript language has been an important factor in the success of thermal printers. Right now, color PostScript printer buyers are benefiting from both a steady decline in prices and an increase in the machines' capabilities. First introduced in 1988 at a cost of more than $30,000, within two years they broke the $10,000 barrier; today, $5,000 color PostScript printers are available.

Before getting too carried away with thermal printers, keep in mind the per-page costs (which typically range between $1 and $4), and the fact that it can take a long time to print out multiple copies of a single page.

Moreover, there is little if any calibration between the colors produced by a thermal printer and the original colors specified in the graphics or publishing program. For most applications, the thermal printer provides proof that some color is on the page, but there is no guarantee as to which color.

Color copiers

The high-speed black-and-white copier has been a major factor in the explosive growth of printed business documents for the past 20 years—one of the reasons we're all drowning in paper, despite the fact that there are a number of applications in which data can be processed and exchanged electronically, without ever appearing on paper. Some large organizations have moved toward electronic data interchange (EDI) for invoices, purchase orders, statements, and even payments. But there are many situations in which the printed word must be just that: printed. It is, after all, portable, browsable, and reusable. And with the recent surge in desktop publishing and photocopying, the printed word is everywhere (unfortunately, in the same 35 fonts).

Just as desktop laser printers are used to create an original page that can then be duplicated with a black-and-white photocopier, color thermal printers can be used to create a color original that is duplicated on a color copier.

At a time when many companies were still insisting that it couldn't be done, wouldn't look good enough, and would cost too much, Canon staked out turf in the color copying market. Since then, it has been joined by Kodak, Xerox, Sharp, Ricoh, Savin, Panasonic, Brother, Minolta, and others.

Color copying is used by in-house reprographic centers, copy shops and quick print shops, advertising and public relations firms, graphic art and design companies, sales and marketing organizations, and real estate agencies, as well as packaging, fashion, and interior designers. Many of them still use black-and-white copiers as well, not only because they produce a better solid black, but also for speed, economy, and paper-handling options missing from the color versions.

Although there are desktop models that cost one-tenth as much, high-quality color copiers can cost more than $100,000, depending on the quality of their output and the speed with which they operate. (The type of paper required is another important factor. In general, the more expensive and processed the paper, the plainer and less costly the machine; the high-end machines tend to use less costly paper and supplies.)

Color copier technologies

There are three main kinds of color copiers:

- thermal transfer copiers use a four-color ink ribbon, and are the least expensive;

- photographic copiers produce the best results, but have the highest per-copy cost, because of the chemicals and special paper required;

- color copiers based on xerography or electrophotography have the highest initial cost, but, because they use plain paper, toner, and developers, have the lowest per-copy cost.

There are a number of important factors to remember when purchasing a color copier. The major considerations are:

- the overall costs of reproduction, including both initial and per-copy costs;
- speed;
- image resolution—the color produced with specially treated photographic paper will exceed the quality of color created with the xerographic (photocopy) process;
- the versatility of the copier;
- the cost of supplies and service.

Color copiers could become crucial to the proliferation of color publishing, because the per-page copy is low enough to enable users to freely include color graphics and pages in a document. They could quickly usher in an age when color business documents will be the accepted standard.

Color printers merge with photocopiers

Canon sells an Intelligent Processor Unit (IPU) containing an Adobe PostScript interpreter that interfaces with its Color Laser Copier 500 to transform the copier into a color PostScript printer. In addition, Canon recently licensed an even more powerful controller for the CLC 500, the Fiery controller from Electronics For Imaging (EFI). The Fiery controller contains 64Mb of RAM, and can address up to 256 levels of each of the copier's cyan, magenta, yellow, and black toners. This creates continuous-tone colors, rather than *dithered* colors.

Dithering is a way of creating different colors by grouping various proportions of cyan, magenta, yellow, and black pixels. Because each pixel has only two possible states (on or off), rather than 256, dithered colors are far less realistic than continuous tone colors.

The emergence of high-speed low-cost color copiers signals a new era in color publishing, in which relatively large quantities of color documents can be created directly from the original data, without a single intervening prepress stage. This development is already having an impact on color publishing, through the proliferation of service bureaus that will take a color illustration on disk and provide quick, relatively inexpensive output. Although they are called color copiers, these machines produce pages that are all originals—created directly from the digital data, rather than a thermal print.

Over the next few years, it will become ever cheaper and easier to make use of color printers/copiers, leading to an explosion in short-run color for all kinds of applications, both in business presentations and in the prepress approval process.

Methods of color reproduction

Although we have so far concentrated on the new composite-color technology, and said little about traditional printing presses (which work with color separation films), the vast majority of the color documents being used every day came off a printing press, not a copier.

This section explores the major current printing technologies, with emphasis on the most popular one, offset lithography. For most desktop publishers, it will produce the output for which all color prepress work performed on the desktop is the input. Knowledge of the underlying principles of offset litho is essential: producing high-quality color separations from the desktop requires a firm understanding of the reproduction process in which those pieces of film play such a crucial role.

To understand the challenge inherent in any printing job, keep in mind that the dynamic range (the difference between the lightest and darkest perceivable areas in an image) of the human eye is much greater than that of a printed page. Humans have a dynamic range of about 1,000,000 to one, which means that we can see shadow details that are one millionth as bright as highlight details in the same scene.

By comparison, the dynamic range of high-quality slide film is about 1,000 to 1, which means that it is incapable of registering much of the detail in the highlights and shadows, detail that can be seen by the eye. Worse still, the dynamic range of offset lithography onto high-quality coated stock is about 300 to 1, while onto newspaper stock it is only 30 to 1.

Sheet-fed versus web

Before discussing how ink is put to paper, it's necessary to clarify the way paper moves through sheet-fed or web printing presses.

Sheet-fed is the older technology, dating back to the earliest days of printing and is still the basis of most printing presses operating today. Most modern presses are sheet-fed rotary: the printing plate surface is fixed around a cylinder and is fed with single sheets of paper. Sheet-fed printing is used for one-color business cards, glitzy full-color magazines, and everything in between.

By comparison, the web-fed or web presses are fed from a large roll of paper. They take longer for make ready and have traditionally been appropriate only for long-run printing jobs, such as national magazines or catalog mailings. (On some huge web presses, such as those used for producing daily newspapers, the machine automatically splices the reels of paper to maintain a non-stop flow of printed newspapers at speeds of more than 100 feet per second.) However, during the late 1980s a variety of mini-web and half-web presses made this method more economical for smaller runs as well.

Other printing processes

Other than xerography, there are five major processes used in printing today: lithography, gravure, flexography, letterpress, and screen. In 1990, the breakdown of pages produced using these five processes for printing, publishing, and packaging was approximately:

- 45% lithography;
- 20% gravure;
- 17% flexography;
- 11% letterpress;
- 7% screen and other processes.

Offset lithography

Why is lithography the most widely used method? Because it provides the most acceptable compromises between cost and quality for the bulk of books, magazines, newsletters, price lists, catalogs, directories, annual reports, and the like.

The process takes its name from the Greek word *lithos*, meaning stone, because flat stones were originally used in the process (and still are for some kinds of fine-art prints).

Litho presses are well suited to color production, because it is easy to construct high-speed presses with multiple color impression stations, called towers. A six-color offset press, for example, can print a job with the four process colors plus two additional inks—with only one pass through the press. Some presses, called *perfecters*, can even print both sides of the paper at the same time.

Lithography is described as a planographic method of printing, because the image and nonimage areas are essentially on the same plane of a thin metal plate, with the distinction between them maintained chemically. The most common form of lithography is called offset lithography because the ink is offset from the plate to a rubber blanket, and then from the blanket to the paper. Because the plate does not come in contact with the abrasive surface of the paper, it holds an image through many more impressions. Without the blanket, the plate would wear out after as few as 1,000 impressions.

The printing plate is designed so that the image area is receptive to grease and is water-repellent, while the nonimage areas are rendered water-receptive and grease-repellent. When the plate is mounted on the press, it comes in contact with rollers wet by a dampening solution, then by rollers wet by ink.

Figure 2-1
The lithographic process is based on the principle that oil and water don't mix.

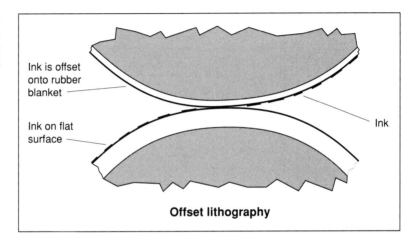

Ink is offset onto rubber blanket

Ink on flat surface

Ink

Offset lithography

The nonimage areas pick up the dampening solution and repel ink. The image areas are coated with ink, and transferred to the rubber impression blanket cylinder. The ink is transferred to the paper as it passes between the blanket cylinder and the impression cylinder. The result—a major advantage of the offset method—is that the soft rubber surface of the blanket creates a crisp impression on a variety of papers and other surfaces, both rough and smooth.

Letterpress

Letterpress is the oldest method of printing, based on cast metal type or plates on which the image or printing areas are raised above the nonprinting areas. Ink rollers contact only the top surface of the raised areas, and the inked image is transferred directly to paper.

When viewed under a magnifier, letterpress can be distinguished by the slightly heavier edge of ink around each letter. This is the result of the ink spreading slightly as the result of the pressure of the plate on the printed surface. Despite this effect, the letterpress image is usually sharp and crisp. The major advantages of letterpress, compared with lithography, are better print consistency and a thicker ink film. The major disadvantage is the cost of creating plates.

Figure 2-2
The letterpress process

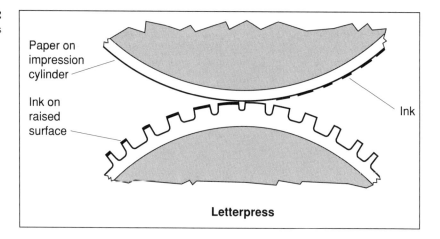

Paper on impression cylinder

Ink on raised surface

Ink

Letterpress

Flexography

Flexography is a form of letterpress based on flexible rubber plates and is used for printing in color on just about anything that will go through a press: cellophane polyethylene, gift wrap, foil, shopping bags, toilet paper, milk containers, drinking straws, and shower curtains, among other things.

Flexography produces brilliant colors, making it ideal for packaging, and has recently made inroads into the newspaper and magazine printing fields.

Gravure

Gravure printing is based on the intaglio principle: the image areas consist of cells or wells etched into a copper cylinder or wraparound plate, and the cylinder or plate surface is the non-printing areas. The plate surface rotates through a vat of ink, following which excess ink is scraped off; the ink remaining in the countless recessed cells forms the image by direct transfer to the paper as it passes between the plate cylinder and the impression cylinder.

Gravure plates are more expensive than those needed for most other printing systems, and gravure is therefore usually limited to jobs with large print runs, often a few hundred thousand copies or more. The advantages include excellent reproduction of photographs, especially on relatively cheap (uncoated) paper, and the fact that gravure plates last much longer than conventional ones.

Figure 2-3
The gravure process

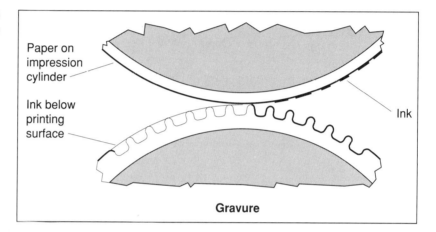

Screen printing

This method uses a fine silk, nylon, or steel screen mounted on a frame. The screen contains a stencil of the image, created either manually or photomechanically, so that nonprinting areas are protected by the stencil. Ink with a paintlike consistency is pushed through the screen with a rubber squeegee, forcing it onto the paper below.

Screen printing can sometimes be distinguished by the thick layer of ink, and sometimes by the texture of the screen, on the printed surface. It is used primarily in the textile and packaging industries. (Without screen printing, the world would never have known the printed t-shirt!)

Before the presses roll

Despite the differences between the various methods, much of the work leading up to actually producing a document is identical. In fact, most of the crucial work is done in the prepress stage and it is there that the potential for desktop tools is the greatest.

Therefore, it is necessary to shift our attention from the printing presses themselves to the many tools and techniques used in preparing the pages for printing.

Spot color and process color

An essential distinction in color printing can be made between the two different ways color can be added to a document:

- spot color involves printing a specific color, often in addition to black, in which the spot color is solid and flat, and has been specified according to some standard matching system, such as the PANTONE MATCHING SYSTEM;

- process color involves separating the original image into its cyan, magenta, yellow, and black components, then printing the four together to recreate all the original shadings of color.

For example, if you currently print your newsletter in black and white and want to give it some zing, you specify spot color printing for certain headlines, ruling lines, logos, and other elements. The spot color is usually specified in terms of its PANTONE MATCHING SYSTEM number. However, if your company logo is always printed in a specific PANTONE Color, running an ad in a full-color magazine could be a problem—although some PANTONE Colors can be reasonably well matched by combining cyan, magenta, yellow, and black, the PANTONE MATCHING SYSTEM defines other colors that simply can't be duplicated.

If your company color can't be approximated with process inks, you can always get them to print the entire magazine run one extra time to add your spot color (or use a press with one additional color tower); but, because this can be prohibitively expensive, it often makes more sense to change the design. Some applications, such as high-quality maps or product labels, may involve ten or more spot colors, in addition to the four process inks.

The PANTONE Process Color Imaging Guide, as shown on Color Page 5 gives the closest cyan, magenta, yellow, and black equivalents for each of the 747 PANTONE Colors, and shows at a glance which PANTONE Colors can't reasonably well approximate process colors.

One useful way to think about the difference between spot and process color is that spot colors are like overlays—each color is placed by itself on the page whereas the process color method creates different hues through combinations of the four process ink screens.

The important thing about spot color is that it has made it possible for many people to create colorful documents for which the cost of full four-color printing would be prohibitive; as long as documents are reproduced on multicolor printing presses, it will be cheaper and easier to use spot color, rather than process. However, the proliferation of PostScript thermal color printers and color copiers may lead to a rapid decline in spot color work.

Knockouts and overprints

When working with spot color, it is necessary to pay careful attention to the order in which the different inks are overlaid, or weird color effects can result. For instance, a yellow square printed on top of a blue background will result in a green square rather than in one that is the intended yellow. The solution is to knock out the square from the blue background, so the yellow square prints on a white background, and stays yellow. These knockouts have traditionally been created manually, and they can be produced today within most graphics and page layout programs.

(Chapter 3, Quality Color, examines how knockouts solve one problem while creating another: the inevitable gaps of white space between the overprint and the background color, caused by slight registration errors on press.)

In a spot-color job that includes black, the black ink is always printed last, and overprints the other inks where needed.

Combining spot and process color

There are many reasons for running a print job in process plus one or more spot colors. A full-color brochure might use process color for the tints and photos, but use spot color for the corporate logotype or to add a special metallic ink or fluorescent ink. Spot inks might also be added to precisely match a paint or fabric sample.

Color matching systems

PANTONE MATCHING SYSTEM®

Strictly speaking, the PANTONE MATCHING SYSTEM and others like it, such as the Focoltone, Trumatch, Munsell, Ostwald, and DIN systems, cannot be considered color standards because they are based entirely on visually matching a known color to a carefully printed standard, rather than on colorimetric measurements. However, the PANTONE MATCHING SYSTEM is widely used in the graphic arts industry worldwide as a way of attempting to maintain fidelity of color in the finished printed piece.

The PANTONE MATCHING SYSTEM is based on a series of books of color swatches, printed on coated and uncoated stock, and a set of ink formulations for creating such colors on a printing press.

Using the system, a graphic designer can specify that the logotype on a client's letterhead be printed as PANTONE 314, and be reasonably sure that the resulting color will be the same deep forest green shown on the PANTONE Color swatch—whether it's printed in Los Angeles or Leningrad.

Most jobs printed with PANTONE Color inks are one-, two-, or, occasionally, three-color jobs, to provide some color when the budget does not allow the full four-color treatment. Some really expensive print jobs run with five, six, seven, or eight colors—the four process inks plus one or more PANTONE Color inks.

It's important to understand the relationship between PANTONE Colors and CMYK inks. CMYK inks build up colors by combining them in various percentages. PANTONE Colors allow the user to choose the color and the printer to use the matching ink on the press. Moreover, PANTONE Color inks include colors that are impossible with process inks, including silver, copper, and creamy, saturated slate blue.

While some PANTONE Color inks can be matched, almost identically, with process inks, others will vary radically. In the example shown on Color Page 5, the green solid color appears very similar to its CMYK equivalent, while the two orange colors are distinctly different. (The color pages in this book were printed using process inks, so the examples on Color Page 5 are simulations only, intended to show the variability between solid and process inks.)

You should also be aware that, as in the case of process colors, you can overlay percentages of PANTONE Color inks to produce totally different colors—a great way to add variety to a two-color job. However, this won't work until you have a thorough knowledge of color mixing.

A great many ink manufacturers and software developers advertise their products as complying with the standard PANTONE Colors, thereby providing publishers with some measure of certainty that color graphics and documents will print in the desired shades. In practical terms, it means that the artist or designer can specify a colored graphic element within a desktop program, knowing the on-screen representation need not exactly match the sample in the swatch book, yet secure in the knowledge that the printed piece will come reasonably close to the intended color.

**Process color
guides**

The major limitation of the original PANTONE MATCHING SYSTEM is that it is based on specially mixed inks, rather than on the four process inks. This has made it difficult to specify colors that were being reproduced with process color, until the recent release of three new matching systems, all based on CMYK inks: PANTONE Process Colors, the Focoltone Colour System, and Trumatch. The advantage of all three systems is that they enable designers to select colors efficiently, without *ever* choosing a color that falls outside the range of four-color process reproduction. (See Figure 2-4.)

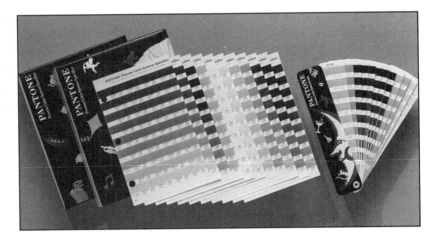

Figure 2-4
The PANTONE Process
Color System relies on
swatch charts showing
sample colors on
coated and uncoated
stocks. Photo courtesy
of Pantone, Inc.

**PANTONE Process
Colors**

Pantone recently announced the release of a new CMYK-based color specification system, designed to fill the gap for those working with process rather than solid colors. The PANTONE Process Color System specifies more than 3,000 colors in CMYK percentages. All screen values are specifically chosen to perform within the quality control tolerances and capabilities of today's printing presses. The new system is also available in Pantone-licensed software applications, and has been formulated in both SWOP (Standard Web Offset Press) and Euroscale versions for international use.

The PANTONE Process Color System Specifier is a two-book set that presents the same process color values in a tear-out chip format. Each chip is identified with its corresponding CMYK percentages.

In an attempt to cross media boundaries, PANTONE has also developed the PANTONE Broadcast Color System for digital video, and the PANTONE Presentation Color System for "point and click" color presentations.

Focoltone Colour System

The Focoltone Colour System, invented in Wales, is an innovative way of selecting and matching process colors. Focoltone is designed to help everybody involved in *process* color reproduction—print buyers, designers, prepress houses, and printers. The Focoltone colors (shown on Color Page 5), are printed on swatches, specifier sheets, and charts, showing not only the specified color but all the (process) colors used to produce it. This enables the printer to follow the progressions in the charts, matching them to the press sheet as each new process color is added.

Figure 2-5
The Focoltone Colour System. Photo courtesy of Focoltone U.S.A., Inc.

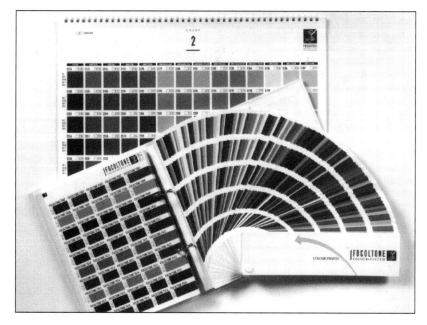

The Focoltone Colour System is supported by QuarkXPress 3.1, Adobe Photoshop 2.0, Adobe Illustrator, Aldus FreeHand, and PageMaker.

The Focoltone color range consists of 763 four-color combinations containing single tints of all four process inks from 5 to 85 percent. By selecting colors from this palette, the designer can be confident that the specified colors will be closely approximated on press.

Focoltone specifications refer to colors printed on single-sheet rotary presses with industry average dot gain and ink density levels (these are discussed in Chapter 3). From these conditions the standard specification lets you quickly match to the reference color by normal press adjustments.

Different printing conditions, such as web offset, will print different colors from the standard specification. Focoltone uses a software program to recalculate each of the color percentages every time a new dot gain is entered, thereby changing the specification so that the color remains the same. A special set of charts are available for printing color newspapers.

Once a color specification has been chosen, all the other colors are generated from it. Each line on the Focoltone chart begins with a four-color process color and continues by showing the 14 colors that can be accessed from it—four single colors, six combinations of two colors, and four combinations of three colors. This provides the printer with an excellent progressive proof to follow for each color, as it shows not only the single colors but also every combination of them.

Trumatch

The Trumatch Swatching System from Trumatch takes a similar approach, and is also designed specifically to improve the accuracy of color specifications for process color. It offers more than 2,000 computer-generated colors that specify exact percentages of cyan, magenta, yellow, and black for process inks.

The Trumatch system is supported by Quark (in QuarkXPress 3.1) and Scitex, as well as by-products such as SuperMac Technologies' SuperMatch ColorPicker, and the RIPLINK system from Screaming Technology. By adding device-specific color lookup tables, color publishers will be able to specify Trumatch colors by name or number, as well as by CMYK percentages.

Typical commercial printers' process tint guides display colors as combinations of cyan, magenta, yellow, and black in 5% or 10% increments. Trumatch provides proportional gradation of color using the computer's ability to produce CMYK in increments of 1%. This results in smooth steps of color without color gaps, and without changing color cast.

The color separation process

Throughout this book, there are frequent references to the process of color separation, and to the separated film that is the end product of the process. Therefore, a thorough understanding of the principle governing color separation is essential for all that follows.

Color printing is based on an illusion: that a few colors in combination appear to contain all the colors of the rainbow. This illusion is reversed when a colorful original is separated and the purpose is to create four pieces of film, one for each of the process colors, so they can be combined during the printing process to create all the other colors.

Ideally, four colors simulate all the others

A color graphic created in a paint or draw program can be separated easily if its colors have been specified according to their cyan, magenta, yellow, and black values. With a little more work and a handy set of conversion tables, colors can be separated that were originally specified in another color model.

It is thus possible to create a graphic in an illustration package, specify its colors according to their CMYK values, and import it into a page layout program for integration with type and other graphics. This practice of building up colored areas in a drawing through the use of tints is among the most important current applications of desktop tools for color production. It provides a much more powerful set of tools than traditional marker renderings.

The practice of separating a colored original artwork or photograph is more complex, although the process itself is analogous to the way the eye sees. The original is photographed using three filters, each corresponding in color to one of the additive primaries: red, green, and blue.

Placing a red filter over the lens produces a negative recording of all the red light reflected or transmitted from the subject—a red separation negative. When a positive (print) is made from this negative, the silver in the film will correspond to the blue and green areas that absorbed red.

One way to think of this is that the negative has subtracted the red light from the original subject, and the positive is a recording of the blue and green in the scene, the color cyan. The positive is the *cyan printer.* Similarly, shooting through the green filter creates a negative recording of the green in the original scene. The positive is a recording of the other additive primaries, red and blue, which is called the *magenta printer.*

Likewise, the blue filter produces a negative recording of all the blue in the subject. Its corresponding positive records the red and green, which add together to produce the *yellow printer.*

In reality, only certain colors can be printed

Ideally, we should be able to print an accurate rendition of any color by combining and printing the cyan, magenta, and yellow positives. In reality, it isn't that easy: these three colors together define a gamut of possible colors that can be formed by combining them in varying proportions. There are some colors outside the gamut of CMY printing that simply cannot be printed with just these three inks.

Also, when the three subtractive primaries are printed together, most of the colors other than yellow and red are slightly dirty and muddy. There is often too much magenta in the greens, blues, and cyans because of unavoidable limitations in the pigments used in the inks.

Even with compensations made in the color separation negatives and positives to overcome limitations in ink colors, the final result usually lacks full contrast. A fourth black printer is added to increase the contrast of the grays and deep shadows, and other colors are reduced proportionately so that inks transfer properly on the press.

Once the color separations are complete, there are problems inherent in trying to reproduce these wonderful colors on thousands or millions of pieces of paper. But before examining those, we must explore in more detail how the infinite shadings in a color tint or photograph can be approximated on the printed page.

Figure 2-6
The gamut, or range, of colors you can print is smaller than the gamut of the colors you can see.

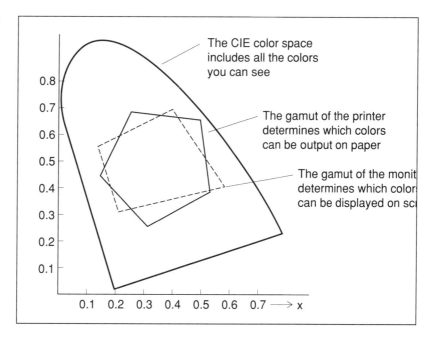

Understanding halftones

The hallmark of fine printing is the reproduction of photographs. In color and black-and-white, screened tints are an essential part of many illustrations and designs. Unfortunately, neither of these can be printed on a press without the use of a halftone.

Halftoning is a process long used by offset printers, in which a finely etched screen is placed between an image and a piece of photographic paper or film, then exposed. This recreates the image as a pattern of black dots or spots on the photographic medium. The halftone dots are larger in dark areas of the image and smaller in light areas.

The color separation process requires that a halftone screen be created for each of the four process colors. When the process colors are printed, the cyan, magenta, yellow, and black inks will overprint in various combinations, depending on the density of each halftone. It is the blending of these multiple screened inks that creates, in the perception of the viewer, the appearance of countless colors.

A halftone is really an illusion, a precise grid of dots that the eye converts into the appearance of objects and levels of gray. (Some of the greatest of the Impressionist painters—Van Gogh, among them—relied on the same visual response to create their pictures.) As shown in Figure 2-7, the halftone illusion is revealed by enlarging the reproduction to show the individual dots that make up the image.

Figure 2-7
The halftone illusion works because the eye interprets different densities of dots as varying intensities of gray.

Why not print the photograph directly on the page? Because you can't. Printing is an all-or-nothing process: either the press puts down ink at a given place on the paper, or it doesn't. A printing press (or laser printer or photocopier) has no innate way of distinguishing tones or densities of black, no way of representing the shades of gray in the original photograph. It can make an area black or white, but not gray.

This is why the halftone process was invented. It permits the dot pattern and the size of the dot, and even the shape of the dot, to be controlled and thereby give the illusion of a shade of gray.

To prove this, look at a photograph in a newspaper through a magnifying glass. You will notice how the small dots make up the image. You can also see:

- how the bright areas (highlights) consist of a few small black dots totally surrounded by white space;
- how the middle gray areas (midtones) consist of dots in the same position on the grid but with increased diameter;
- how the darkest (shadow) areas consists of dots that are so large they overlap, with very small white areas between.

The halftone principle applies equally to black-and-white photographs and to tints of gray: by controlling the size of the dots, it is possible to achieve a full tonal range from white through the gray scale to solid black. This overcomes the inherent limitation of the press in reproducing a range of tonalities.

The screening process creates patterns that are made up of dots, and although the dots are usually square, round, or elliptical, they can be any other shape. The key concept is that, while the size of the halftone dots changes within an image, the basic pattern of the dots remains the same.

There are three variables that can affect gray screens:

- frequency—the number of cells per inch;
- angle—the orientation of the cell pattern (in degrees);
- dot—the shape of the halftone dots.

By adjusting these three, it is possible to create a variety of screen effects, from a coarse stubble for special effects to a fine gray fill that approximates a photograph. Using traditional photographic methods, all three are easily altered. A variety of different screens make it possible to change the frequency and dot shape, though that can be costly.

Figure 2-8
Halftone screens with round, elliptical, square, and cross-shaped dots

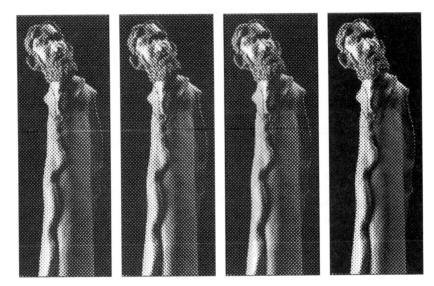

Halftone screen frequencies are specified in lines per inch (lpi), even though the screens usually have dots rather than lines. Newspapers commonly use 75- and 85-line screens, while most magazines use 120-, 133-, or 150-line screens, and high-quality art books often use 175- or 200-line screens, or above.

The problem with photographic halftones is that they can't be changed: a halftone produced as a 133-line screen for a magazine can't be converted easily to an 85-line newspaper screen. Attempting to photographically enlarge or reduce the image causes changes to the screen frequency and the halftone pattern breaks down. Enlarging it makes the dot pattern become apparent; reducing it makes the dark areas fill in and go black. The only option is to rescreen the image to the desired size and frequency.

Photographic halftones are important to the world of electronic publishing because laser printers and imagesetters, like printing presses, are unable to reproduce shades of gray. The solution is to create an electronic equivalent of the photographic halftone—the digital halftone.

Figure 2-9
Halftone screen frequencies are specified in lines per inch or lpi, even though we usually work with dots, rather than lines. Newspapers commonly use 75- and 85-line screens (left), while most magazines use 120-, 133-, or 150-line screens (center), and high-quality art books often use 175- or 200-line screens, or above (right).

Digital halftoning

As we have seen, halftones create the impression of gray by using black dots that vary in size depending on how dark an area is. But a laser printer or imagesetter can't vary the size of the laser pixels, and therefore must group them together to produce halftone dots of different sizes.

Digital halftoning achieves the halftone effect used for photographs by grouping many printer pixels together to form a halftone cell, such as the 75 percent gray cell in Figure 2-10.

Switching on and off individual laser pixels within the halftone cell can effectively change its size.

The more pixels in the halftone cell, the more shades of gray that can be obtained. A group of 25 laser pixels in a 5-by-5 matrix produces 24 different shades of gray, plus black (all pixels on) and white (all pixels off). All the pixels black gives 100 percent black area; if one pixel is white, the result is 96 percent black, and so on.

Figure 2-10
Digital halftones group many printer pixels together to form a halftone cell, such as this 75 percent gray cell.

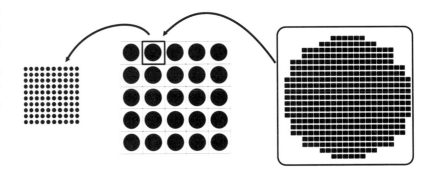

Using a larger matrix of laser pixels for the halftone cell makes it possible to create more shades of gray: a 16-by-16 matrix contains 256 pixels and can represent 256 levels, plus black and white. The inevitable trade-off in digital halftoning is that there are a limited number of gray tones that can be created for a given combination of output resolution and screen frequency.

Higher resolution to the rescue

Using a 5-by-5 halftone cell matrix and outputting on a 300 dpi (dots-per-inch) laser printer produces 60 cells per inch (300 divided by 5) or a 60-line screen. But it results in only 24 gray levels, while the human eye can detect hundreds of levels and requires at least 60 for the illusion of continuous gray tones, depending on the image.

The answer is to print on an output device with higher resolution, making it possible to get all the gray levels needed, at a sufficiently high screen frequency. An imagesetter at 2,400 dpi, for example, can use a 16-by-16 matrix to produce 256 shades of gray with a screen frequency of 150 cells per inch (2,400 divided by 16), but no higher.

To summarize, a high-resolution output device allows you to create digital halftones suitable for reproduction, while a low-resolution device (such as a desktop laser printer) requires trade-offs between screen frequency and number of gray levels.

Figure 2-11
Halftone dots created with a larger matrix can represent a greater number of shades of gray.

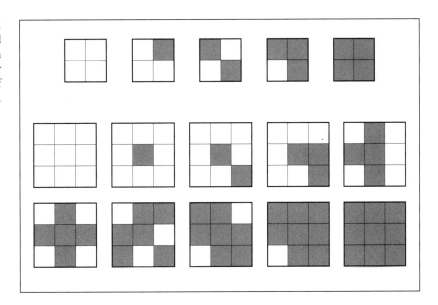

The PostScript language

While the concepts on which digital halftone are based are fine in theory, it is necessary to grasp how they work in practice. In the desktop publishing world, that means knowing about PostScript.

PostScript is based on a wonderfully simple idea that allows the desktop publisher to do some very complex things, including digital halftones. It is a programming language, known as a page description language, that treats the vector graphics and textual elements on a page as if they were composed of lines and curves rather than dots.

Most of the original laser printers, such as the Hewlett-Packard LaserJet, created type from bit-mapped font files, one each for every variation in typeface, size, and weight. These files took a long time to generate and to download from computer to printer. They can quickly overrun a hard disk, taking up many megabytes.

By contrast, every PostScript typeface is stored as the outlines, or vectors, that make up each character. They can be quickly scaled to any size, so that every PostScript laser printer comes with 237 1/2-point Palatino bold italic built in, whether or not it's ever needed. PostScript laser printers (and monitors with Display PostScript) take advantage of typographic hints built into each font, or more precisely, into each Type 1 PostScript font (in contrast to older Type 3 fonts).

These hints cause PostScript printers to modify the shape of each character as it increases or decreases in size, thereby improving typographic quality, especially for smaller type sizes and at lower resolutions.

Figure 2-12
PostScript fonts change shape as they change size, which ensures optimal quality regardless of the resolution of the output device.

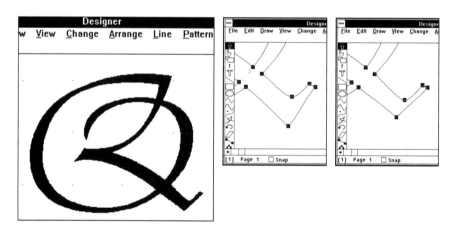

There's another advantage of PostScript, one that has been crucial to its success. It's called device independence, and it means that, at least in theory, a graphic or document created as a PostScript file by any application will be printed identically (except for resolution) by any PostScript output device.

The user who reads or proofs a document on a 300 dpi PostScript desktop laser printer can be confident that (in most cases) plate-ready film of the document created on a 2,400 dpi PostScript imagesetter will look the same, except that it will be at increased resolution. PostScript graphics or documents created on an IBM-compatible system can (with limitations we'll examine later) be viewed and printed on Macintosh computers, minicomputers, mainframes, and dedicated color prepress computers that also support PostScript.

Although typographic flexibility, typographic quality, and device independence were crucial to the initial success of PostScript in desktop publishing, its success in color publishing is directly linked to its ability to generate good halftone screens.

Digital halftoning with PostScript

There are three parameters in the PostScript language, equivalent to the three variables for traditional halftones, that control the creation of halftone cells: frequency, angle, and a spot function that controls the shape of the digital halftone dot within the cell.

An important characteristic of PostScript is that its halftoning machinery operates independently of its scaling and rotating commands, so that gray-filled objects and halftoned images can be scaled and rotated without affecting their screen angle, frequency, or cell shape.

One technical constraint on PostScript's production of digital halftones is that it is limited to 256 levels of gray. At the same time, the human eye can scarcely distinguish such fine variations, except in ramped color tints or gradient fills.

There's another important limitation on PostScript Level 1 printers and imagesetters: the screen angles and screen frequencies PostScript creates are unlikely to be exactly those you request, especially on low-resolution devices, because, at any given resolution, only certain patterns of printer dots will form repeatable patterns for a given frequency or angle. PostScript Level 2 and some high-end Level 1 imagesetters use accurate screening to eliminate this problem.

The key word is "repeatable." One of PostScript's real strengths is its ability to produce seamless gray screens, in which each halftone cell uses a matrix exactly the same size as its neighbor; each adjacent cell must tile seamlessly with its neighbors. At any given angle or frequency, especially at low resolutions, there are only a limited number of matrix patterns that will repeat seamlessly.

The color separation process involves preparing halftone screens for each of the four process colors. When these process colors are printed, the cyan, magenta, yellow, and black inks may all overprint the same area in many combinations and in various densities. The interaction of these multiple screened inks sometimes results in coarse moiré patterns forming in the printed piece.

Figure 2-13
Digital halftone cells created with PostScript must seamlessly align with their neighbors in a tiling pattern, thus limiting the screen angles and frequencies available for small cells.

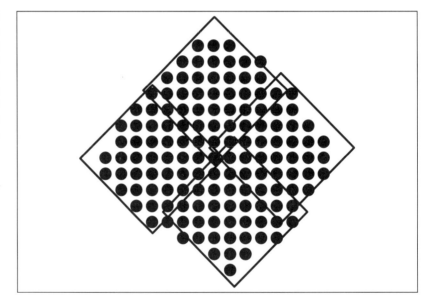

Adobe recommended angles

In the early days of PostScript imagesetting, many service bureaus discovered that serious moiré patterns were more the rule than the exception when working with black-and-white halftones or color tints and images. By analyzing the mathematics of these interference patterns, in 1989 Adobe was able to devise new halftone screen frequency and angle values which reduced moiré when offset printed.

These new screening parameters were incorporated into existing PostScript Printer Description (PPD) files, which are used by applications and printer drivers to access specific features of a device, and to provide printer-specific information such as ROM font lists. Every PostScript printer has a PPD.

Figure 2-14
Chart of 1989 Adobe recommended screen values. PostScript Level 1 Screen Values are reproduced from Advances in Color Separation Using PostScript Software Technology Copyright. © 1989 Adobe Systems Incorporated. All rights reserved.

Screen Values

color	frequency	angle	color	frequency	angle
2540 dpi			**2400 dpi**		
C	100.402	71.5651	C	94.8683	71.5651
M	100.402	18.4349	M	94.8683	18.4349
Y	95.25*	0.0	Y	90.0*	0.0
K	89.8026	45.0	K	84.8528	45.0
C	133.87	71.5651	C	126.491	71.5651
M	133.87	18.4349	M	126.491	18.4349
Y	127.0	0.0	Y	120.0	0.0
K	119.737	45.0	K	113.137	45.0

A halftone screen is defined in PostScript as a grid of halftone cells laid upon the device pixels. The halftone dot is composed of the device pixels contained within a cell; these pixels are at a fixed location on the output device. The number of halftone cells per inch determines the frequency of a screen, while the rotation of the cell determines its angle. The calculations of a screen's angle and frequency take place in device space, which means that the halftone screen characteristics are dependent upon the device resolution.

For a given device resolution, the halftoning mechanism allows a fixed set of screen frequencies and angles; it is not always possible to reproduce a requested angle or frequency on the output device. The actual values used may be shifted in frequency or angle from those requested. Because the traditional screen values used in color separation are sensitive to any slight deviation in angle, this shifting often leads to coarse moiré patterns. In fact, the angles must lie very close to 30° or 60° (within 0.01°) or visible moiré is likely.

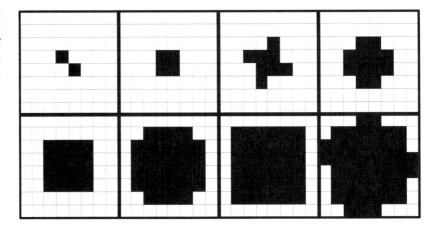

Figure 2-15
PostScript defines a halftone as a grid of halftone cells laid upon the device pixels.

The improved Adobe screen values, which are known as RT Screening, use an unusual set of angles—the black and yellow screens stay at zero° and 45°, but the cyan and magenta move to 71.5° and 18.5°, respectively.

PostScript Level 2

The emergence of PostScript Level 2 has significantly increased the quality of halftones by allowing more precise control over screen angles. In the original PostScript specification, a user of an application program could request a certain angle, a certain frequency, and a spot function. The PostScript interpreter within a specific device would often have to modify the requested angles and frequencies to accommodate the resolution of that particular device. However, the user might not discover a problematic shift in screen frequencies until it showed up later, sometimes in the proof, sometimes in the printed piece as a hideous moiré pattern.

PostScript Level 2 adds a new method for specifying screens and constructing dot shapes, and is based around the idea of halftone dictionaries that gather all the various parameters into a single package. Indeed, virtually any kind of halftoning algorithm can be loaded into PostScript Level 2 as a dictionary.

Figure 2-16
Moiré effects are coarse patterns caused by interference between halftone screens.

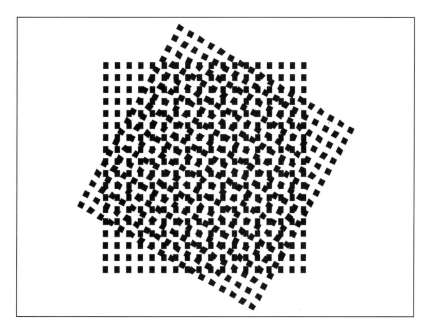

The dictionaries contain values for the screen frequency, screen angle, and spot function, just as they were defined in PostScript Level 1. But they can also contain options, such as a request for Adobe's new accurate screening algorithm.

Adobe accurate screen technology

The basic idea behind Adobe's new accurate screen technology is that by considering a large number of digital halftone cells as a single supercell, it becomes possible to create repeating patterns at ever finer angles. When accurate screening is enabled, the

PostScript interpreter can achieve, within very small tolerances, the exact frequency and angle requested. The degree of accuracy to which the requested values are achieved is dependent mainly on the amount of memory that's available for their use, although resolution is also an important factor. In Level 2, the memory is managed dynamically, so that when memory is not being used for halftoning, it can be used by other parts of the system.

Figure 2-17
By creating a sufficiently large supercell, the Adobe accurate screen algorithm can create a digital halftone screen of any frequency, precise to a thousandth of a degree.

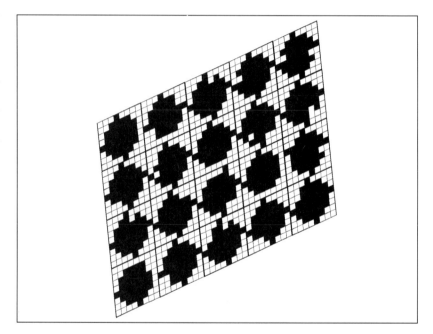

In addition to Accurate Screens, Level 2 has parameters called ActualFrequency and ActualAngle, which show you exactly what angles were achieved. One potential drawback to the accurate screen method is that in some cases it takes more time and memory than previous screening technologies, and is thus best suited to high-resolution imagesetters with fast RIPs.

PostScript Level 2 provides other benefits to color publishers, including:

- data compression, which improves performance by reducing transmission times and conserving disk space;

- new color models, including both those that incorporate industry-standard color spaces for device-independent color, such as CIEXYZ standard, CIE Y, CIELAB, and CIE L, and those that are calculated from lookup tables, such as indexed color, device gray, device RGB, device CMYK, and device separation;

- color extensions, including CMYK-model support, black generation and undercolor removal functions, screen and transfer functions for four separate color components, and a colorimage operator for rendering colored sample images.

All programs that print to conventional PostScript printers (which we can now think of as Level 1 printers) will print to Level 2 printers. In other words, PostScript Level 2 is upward-compatible with existing PostScript language programs and print drivers.

Building color tints

High-quality digital halftones are important because they are essential for reproducing color tints, such as those created in graphics programs like Aldus FreeHand, Adobe Illustrator, Corel Draw, and Micrografx Designer, and in page layout packages like PageMaker and QuarkXPress.

In fact, the vast majority of color documents produced on the desktop contain color tints but not color photographs. Because reproduction of color photographs is the most demanding aspect of printing, many designers have relied on color professionals to take care of color prepress and production work, but that's changing rapidly now. Meanwhile, the type component has been almost completely taken over by desktop tools, as have color tints or *tint builds*, as they are sometimes called.

Tint builds provide the artist or designer with tremendous flexibility, because of the wide variety of colors that can be specified in graphics and publishing programs according to their CMYK values. The CMYK system has a very wide range, or gamut, of possible colors. There are countless possible combinations of these four inks, producing virtually all the colors of the rainbow.

The prepress process

Traditionally, artists and designers considered the original artwork for a color illustration or layout to be the final product. But for a printing company, the raw material is often four-color film separations, ready to be made into plates and installed on the press.

Between these two worlds is the prepress process, in which original art, photography, and typography are transformed into color separations. The central problem in prepress is that the exact color values found in the original graphic or image will often produce printed colors that look wrong to the eye. Therefore, a skilled technician must subtly shift the specific content of the original to produce accurate-looking colors.

As discussed earlier, the color-separated films allow reproduction of the diversity of colors found in the original images, provided the color information is captured accurately and separated properly. High-quality results are within reach only if the separation negatives have been properly generated, with careful attention to screen angle, screen frequency, and halftone cell shape.

There are two main ways of producing color separations: the conventional photographic method and the newer electronic method that requires scanning. Although both ultimately record images on four separated halftone negatives, they do so in completely different ways, as shown in Figure 2-18.

In the photographic method, light from all points of the color original passes through the lens of a camera onto a sheet of film simultaneously. In the electronic method, each tiny segment of the original is pinpointed by a light source and recorded instantly, after which the scanning laser moves to the next segment.

Figure 2-18
Traditional photographic color separation and the newer scanner color separation technology.

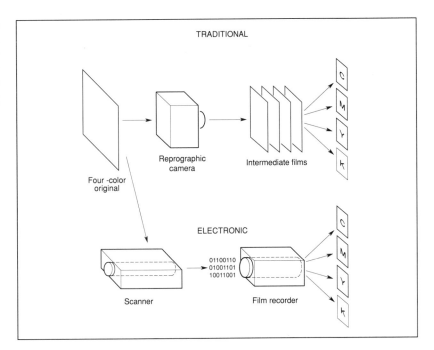

The photographic method dominated color production for many years, but it is now being supplanted by the electronic method. Both methods can produce high quality if they are used by a knowledgeable operator, and it's impossible to say that one is unequivocally better than the other. The factors that point to the eventual domination of the field of color separation by desktop tools involve economics and user control rather than just quality.

Photographic color separations

In traditional separations, a photographic halftone screen is created for each of the four colors. This is simple enough in theory, but in practice, it can result in many pieces of film being used for color correction, image sharpening, and color cast removal, prior to making final film.

Although low-cost commercial color printing makes use of a direct photographic separation in which the halftones are exposed directly from the original artwork, most high-quality work uses an indirect method in which halftone positives are made from intermediate continuous-tone negatives. The advantage of the continuous-tone negative is that it offers greater control of tones and colors, through the use of photographic masks.

Color correction masks

One of the realities of color printing is that for a variety of technical reasons, the basic inks, especially the cyan and magenta, cannot be produced in a completely pure form. Without some kind of color correction, most colors—especially blues, reds, greens, oranges, and purples—will reproduce poorly, appearing muddy or discolored.

It is essential that the negatives be properly exposed and developed, in order to maintain control over the tonal structure of the image. A balanced set of separations produces all tones of gray as neutral gray, without any color cast. In practice, however, equal combinations of cyan, magenta, and yellow will reproduce as a brownish gray color, which must be compensated for deliberately by making the separations out of balance, with slightly stronger cyan.

Even after color correction, there will sometimes be specific areas of the image in which negatives lack the proper balance or correct tonal detail. In such cases, a technician known as a dot etcher will make the appropriate corrections, either with a custom mask or by applying a density-reducing solution by hand.

The masks are relatively faint negative images that have been made from each of the separation negatives. To color correct the image, they are positioned back in the focal plane of the camera, one at a time, and the four continuous-tone negatives are exposed to the artwork, each through a primary color filter and the appropriate mask.

Figure 2-19
A mask enables the user to isolate any area and modify it, independent of the rest of the image.

When the corrected negatives are satisfactory, a halftone positive is created by projecting the continuous-tone negative in the camera to the final reproduction size, through a halftone screen with the appropriate number of lines per inch.

High-end imaging computers and desktop imaging programs, such as Adobe Photoshop or Letraset ColorStudio, perform the same kinds of adjustments and improvements by manipulating the individual bits making up an image.

**Electronic color
separations**

The main similarity between electronic scanning and the photo-graphic method is that both ultimately depend on the subjective skill of the person adjusting the controls. The main difference is that in electronic scanning, virtually all the steps take place inside the computer, rather than on the film.

Almost all high-quality scanning is performed with drum scan-ners, which are currently large and expensive devices, used mostly by professional color houses. However, desktop rotary drum scanners costing less than $70,000 are now available, and these will continue to drop in price until they become routine peripherals in the not-so-distant future.

At the input end of the scanner, the color original is wrapped around a transparent drum, which revolves around the light source. The light source can also be located outside the drum for reflective art (photographs and prints). To color separate the original, a light beam is split into three beams after passing through, or being reflected from, the original. The intensity of each beam is measured by a photocell covered with a filter that corresponds to one of the red, green, and blue additive primaries, thus separating each area of the image into its three RGB color components.

Because the scanner input is in RGB space and its output signal is CMYK data, the conversion from one to the other is a central issue in color scanning. Because red, green, and blue are the complements of cyan, magenta, and yellow, respectively, the conversion from RGB to CMY is a straight linear transform, one that is easily handled by microcomputers. But calculating the black channel is extremely compute-intensive, requiring the processor to solve complex mathematical problems known as *17th-order polynomials*. Different scanner vendors have their own proprietary algorithms for effecting these conversions, and it seems unlikely at this late date that the high-end color industry will make any serious progress toward widespread technical standards.

In many cases, color separations are created directly from the original to film, without the data being stored on a hard disk or magnetic tape. When the image will be used just once, it is faster and cheaper to generate the separations directly from the original data, rather than through an intermediate storage medium.

Most high-end scanners used today have the ability to generate the halftone dots directly, without a screen. They also provide fine control over the screen frequency and angle.

In recent years, the scanners have been combined with page layout stations so that all the elements of a page, including color images, can be scanned at once, which reduces separation costs. Most scanners also provide built-in control for two variables that significantly affect print quality: undercolor removal and gray component replacement.

Controlling ink coverage—undercover removal

One of the physical constraints of the printing process is that it is difficult to stack four wet layers of ink on top of one another. Although it might be possible to specify nice bright colors by heavily saturating all four process colors, the resulting film cannot be printed. In theory, printing 100% of each of cyan, magenta, yellow, and black would result in 400% coverage. In reality, it is difficult to print jobs that have more than 300% ink coverage, and most printers feel more comfortable with 260% coverage.

As discussed earlier, the original RGB data from the scanner can be converted to CMY data with a simple mathematical formula, but the tricky part is to add the appropriate amount of black and interpolate the correct amounts of each process color. The combination of cyan, magenta, and yellow produces muddy brown, and black is added to produce a true black.

The traditional solution to the problem of excess ink coverage is to incorporate undercolor removal (UCR) into the color separations, by reducing the yellow, magenta, and cyan dot values wherever black is going to print—in effect, removing color from the neutral scale.

Undercolor removal partially solves the problem of printing four solid layers of ink, one on top of the other, while each preceding layer is still wet. Proponents of UCR claim that reducing the ink coverage improves ink trapping (the ability of paper to firmly hold each layer of wet ink).

Separations produced with UCR result in more detail and better color saturation, especially in shadow areas. The bottom line is that UCR tends to control dot gain and minimize registration problems. Note that black ink is being used not only to create solid black, but also for adding detail and deepening shadow areas.

The major drawback is that as UCR is increased, the maximum density of the printed sheet decreases, resulting in reduced contrast and quality. Critics of UCR suggest that when good-quality paper and ink are available, and the press has been set to minimize dot gain and to maximize ink trapping, UCR should not be needed.

Figure 2-20
You have complete control of black generation in programs such as Barneyscan Color Access.

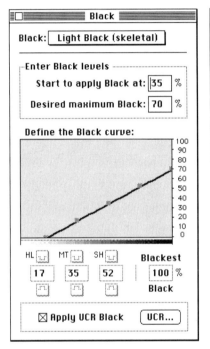

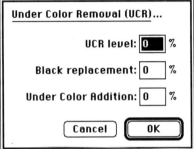

Gray component replacement

A variation on undercolor removal, known as gray component replacement (GCR), has become more popular recently, and is built into most color scanners. The theory behind GCR is that whenever dots of cyan, magenta, and yellow are present in the same color, that color also has a gray component. Some or all of this gray component can be printed with black ink, thereby reducing the amounts of colored ink required. Taken to the extreme, it is possible to print almost any given color by using two of the three colored inks plus black.

The major advantage of GCR is that it reduces the effects of variations on press, so that when ink coverage varies, the colors becomes slightly lighter or darker, rather than changing hue. Moreover, GCR allows the printing company to use a somewhat higher proportion of black ink, which costs less than colored inks.

However, when black ink replaces the gray component in a three-process color combination, different colors will respond in different ways. The changes are most noticeable when the yellow component of the image is swapped out for black.

And when black is added, the color technician (and the software) must take into account the potential ink buildup of the separated image. The standard range for ink coverage at any point in the image varies between 240% to 280% (where 400% ink would be 100% coverage of each process color). For most color houses, 300% coverage would be an absolute upper limit.

Leave it up to your color house to decide whether to use GCR or UCR on a given separation. Although the technical controls for these are appearing in an increasing number of desktop color programs, they still require the judgement of an experienced color professional.

The major problem with GCR, as with UCR, is the reduced density of darker colors, which will be more of a concern in some jobs than in others. For example, the amount of GCR and UCR should be limited whenever large areas of strong, dense blacks are required. High GCR levels also limit the press operator's ability to adjust the inks to attain a particular color balance. To help correct for excessive color reduction, many scanners include a feature for undercolor addition, adding color selectively to dark tonal areas.

Desktop color separation programs are now including UCR and GCR, or variations thereof such as the black generation features in Adobe Photoshop, Letraset ColorStudio, or Aldus PhotoStyler.

Ink Sequence

Although four-color process printing is commonly described as "YMCK" or "CMYK," the sequence of inks is usually KCMY. Because yellow is the most transparent of the process colors, printing it last provides more gloss to the printed image. On the other hand, when printing a spot color job with black and one or more other colors, black is usually printed last.

Film assembly and imposition

Film assembly is the integrating of page images for printing, and is required for all jobs prior to the manufacture of printing plates. For multipage publications, the page sequence must be coordinated with the layout of the printers' flats, so that pages appear in the correct order. This imposition is worked out by the color house in consultation with the bindery, to ensure the sheet is printed, folded, and trimmed so that pages appear in proper sequence.

Control over which pages appear where must be a concern of the designer, not just the printing company, because the page sequence determines which pages can contain which colors, both for spot and for process color.

For instance, a catalog publisher can print one side of a 16-page signature in four-color process, while the other side is black plus a single spot color. When the pages are printed, folded, and bound, the reader may never notice that only some pages contain full-color graphics and images, while the publisher has realized a significant saving in printing costs. That isn't possible, of course, if the designer has inadvertently placed a full-color photograph on a spot-color page.

In order to maintain precise alignment between the different pieces of film, pin register systems are commonly used, in conjunction with the registration marks in the original art. These consist of devices for punching various shapes of holes in each piece of film or copy, then lining them up on pins built into the various prepress devices.

Figure 2-21
Page sequence in a
typical press signature

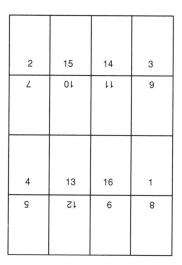

Film stripping is time-consuming and labor-intensive. It is also one of the last aspects of graphic arts production to be automated. For the most part, this job continues to be done manually, although software products that electronically strip the complete signature form are becoming available.

From film to printing plates

In any printing process, the role of the image carrier—the plate or cylinder—is crucial, because the image carrier is the center around which all other printing apparatus revolves. Plate-making has been largely automated, so that it proceeds more or less directly from the final film.

A number of manufacturers have introduced systems that eliminate this step entirely, placing the digital separation data directly onto plates, but the resolution is still too crude for high-quality work. Others are working on ways to write the digital information directly to the plate cylinder, although this may be impractical at present, it could represent the long-term direction of prepress technology.

Printing paper and ink

Printing is the crucial step in the reproduction process: errors at that stage obliterate the quality controls exercised at every previous step.

Both major kinds of printing presses, sheet-fed and web, have advanced significantly during the past few years, but are fundamentally mechanical technology. Therefore, if quality is to be assured, they will always require close control of physical processes such as the balance between ink and water.

One of the first factors you can control is the paper, which accounts for between a third and a half of the cost of most printing jobs, but is often given little attention. The paper's physical characteristics will determine both its overall appearance and the ability of the printer to print on it.

Among the factors important to quality are:

- whiteness: the absence of a color cast, or the paper's ability to reflect equal amounts of red, green, and blue;

- brightness: the total of all light reflected from a paper, which must be very high for reproducing with good contrast and sharpness;

- gloss: high gloss improves the reproduction of photographs and color tints, but is not appropriate for most drawings and watercolors;

- opacity: the more opaque the paper, the less visible the images on the other side and on subsequent pages;

- smoothness: the smoother the paper, the higher the line frequency at which color halftones can be reproduced;

- absorbency: low absorbency is necessary for good color quality, but ink transfer and drying are better with higher absorbency.

Recycled paper

These days, people and companies are increasingly sensitive to environmental issues, including the question of whether a given piece was printed on recycled paper and whether it is, in turn, recyclable.

What actually constitutes recycled paper? Most grades contain a mix of virgin fiber, post-commercial fiber, and post-consumer fiber. Post-commercial fiber comes from scraps produced by printing companies, binderies, and envelope makers. Post-consumer fiber is collected from offices, stores, and homes to be reused. Most of the recycled coated papers available today contain one-half virgin fiber and one-half post-commercial fiber, with little or no post-consumer fiber. Uncoated stocks may come entirely from post-commercial fiber, or may contain up to 20% post-consumer fiber. The use of the word "recycled," applied to these papers, is a bit misleading, because post-commercial and post-consumer paper has been recovered for decades. Truly recycled paper made completely from post-consumer fiber is new, and not yet widely used.

Recycled paper stocks are still somewhat more expensive than paper created with virgin pulp, but the price gap has narrowed in recent years and, with continued public support for the recycling concept, there might soon be little or no price difference.

Ink

Finally, there is ink. Often taken for granted, ink consumes just 3 percent of the printing budget, but has a significant effect on the overall quality of the printed piece.

Theoretically, the most important characteristic of ink is its color strength or range, the objective being to use inks that give the widest possible color gamut, which allows more accurate reproduction of original colors.

In practice, other concerns must be considered as well: the pigment's resistance to light, moisture, and chemicals; fineness of pigment particles; ability to flow well; its low toxicity and minimal environmental damage.

For the designer with stringent production requirements or a generous budget, there are specialty inks formulated for a variety of purposes. They include fluorescents, metallics, matte or dull inks, fade-resistant or ultraviolet (UV)-resistant, scuff-resistant, moisture-resistant, scented, magnetic, heat-transfer, invisible, and luminescent inks, and inks that change color when water, heat, or chemicals are applied to them.

Back to the future

As we saw at the beginning of this chapter, there are crucial differences between the technologies used for creating documents and those used for reproducing them.

Offset litho and the other major printing technologies are not about to fade away like yesterday's newspaper. The desktop publishing revolution has already transformed the way most kinds of documents are created. In the next few years, color printers and photocopiers are almost certain to have a similar effect on the document reproduction business, especially for short-run color publishing.

Since it began almost 500 years ago, the purpose of printing has been to place ink, with precision, on paper. If anything at all has changed, it is that the ink has become tiny particles of toner.

Quality Color— The Eternal Quest

*"Colors seen by candlelight
Will not look the same by day."*
ELIZABETH BARRETT BROWNING

There's an old saying among graphic designers: the work looks great—until it comes off the press.

Color printing is a perilous process, rife with opportunities for error, and when it goes wrong, people look to someone else to bear the blame—and the expense. At one time or other, every printing company has had to eat at least one big print job that didn't meet the client's standards, and disputes about color quality are legendary in the industry.

Despite the best intentions on all sides, it is simply too easy for a color printing job to go seriously, critically, expensively wrong. Among the disasters witnessed recently by one print shop owner:

- the brochure that was printed with PANTONE 223 spot color (bright pink), when the client company thought it was ordering PANTONE 323 (dark green);

- the glossy sports-car brochure in which the fire-engine red looks distinctly orange;

- the annual report cover with grotesque moiré patterns crawling all over corporate headquarters.

67

As more and more color production shifts from professional systems to the desktop, it becomes increasingly important to have a way of confirming—"proofing"—color accuracy. At least some disasters can be avoided by producing an appropriate color proof and interpreting it properly. The whole issue of quality is especially important for desktop color, not only because less expensive equipment is being used, but also because many of the new users have little or no experience in color production.

This chapter focuses on how to attain and maintain quality throughout the color reproduction process. The purpose is to identify each point in the production process at which quality is threatened, then identify and discuss each factor contributing to quality. Different methods of proofing a color job before it goes on press will be examined, to minimize the chances of unpleasant surprises when a job comes off the press.

Quality is important throughout the entire process—from original artwork or photograph, to scanning, processing, displaying, proofing, filming, and going to press.

Let's begin by taking a closer look at color quality in order to become more astute observers, able to detect warning signs of poor quality before the job has been reproduced a few hundred thousand times.

Why good color can be so elusive

There's a rule of thumb in the printing industry: color jobs are ten times more difficult than those in black-and-white. (Of course, the printing company that has to pick up the tab for a make-good probably finds it a thousand times more difficult.) Color reproduction raises many interesting questions:

- Why can so many things go wrong?
- What are the crucial factors in determining the quality of color printing and how can they be isolated?

- How can colors be defined so that they remain consistent from the screen to the proof, and from the proof to the printed piece?

Answering those questions begins with a definition of optimal color reproduction, and how it is different from merely good color reproduction.

Optimal color reproduction

There was little concern about the characteristics of optimal color reproduction until very recently. In the past, the problems associated with obtaining even half-decent color printing were so great that everyone settled gratefully for a reasonable quality rather than attempting to achieve an optimal one.

But improvements in color reproduction technology have been so pervasive, especially during the 1970s and 1980s, that many problems of consistency and control have been effectively solved, making optimal quality a valid goal. For all kinds of publications, optimal color reproduction requires proper trapping (chokes and spreads), minimal moiré and banding, and the absence of objectionable color shifts, topics we'll discuss in more detail later in this chapter.

For continuous tone images, optimal reproduction also means:

- a tone reproduction curve that favors the interest area in the photograph;
- color balance that includes good neutrals;
- preferred skin and sky colors that are often deliberately distorted from the original scene;
- correct saturation of important color areas;
- high resolution;
- a low level of graininess;

- appropriate sharpness;
- high gloss and perfect smoothness.

To generate a high-quality halftone, always begin with a high-quality photograph. Of the various technical factors in the photograph, tone plays the most important role because it visually defines details, textures, depth, and dimension.

Photographs should be inspected for scratches, dust, cracks, or other damage. Keep in mind that, throughout the reproduction process, quality will degrade in each generation. Therefore, always start with an image that is the original art, or as close to it as possible.

Characterization and calibration

To be reasonable certain of attaining good—let alone optimal—quality when working with desktop color, it is essential that scanners, screen displays, output devices, and printing presses be calibrated with one another. In reality, of course, that remains the impossible dream: because humans have different perceptions of radiant light and reflected light, it will never be possible to perfectly map the colors of a screen onto a printed page. Some colors can be printed but not displayed, and others can be displayed but not printed. This is vividly shown by the TekColor Picker shown in Color Page 4.

The RGB model used in scanners and displays is also of little use when working with the printed page, because different monitor manufacturers use different conversion schemes to change RGB values to CMYK. These variations become even more pronounced over time, as the phosphors within each display tube fade. More importantly, a monitor must be viewed under controlled dim lighting conditions, not everyday office lighting, for effective calibration. Also, many of the monitors used for color prepress tend to have a slight blue cast. The hard fact of the matter, though, is that you must rely on RGB data when editing natural images, until you create a proof.

Figure 3-1
The difference between the Video Leaf and the Printer Leaf in the TekColor Picker shows there are colors you can display but not print, and vice versa.

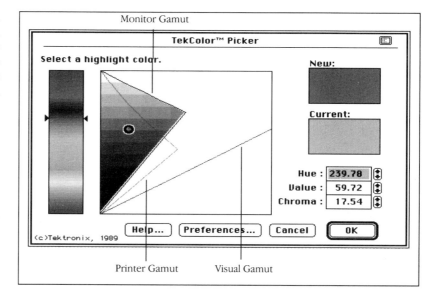

Another problem is color correspondence—making sure the colors displayed on screen and on proofs are similar to, or the same as, those coming off the press. Color correspondence is important throughout the production process—for the screen, color printer, color proofs from film, and the printed piece.

As we have seen, color matching systems such as the PAN-TONE MATCHING SYSTEM offer some relief from this, by providing the designer and print shop with identical printed swatches, which are automatically "calibrated" without regard to the RGB values used by the display monitor. Thus, for optimal color fidelity, specify colors from a swatch book, such as PAN-TONE, wherever possible. (Note that the swatch colors will change considerably as they age, making it prudent to purchase a new swatch book every year or so.)

Better still, create your own swatch book, using the same combination of display, output device, and printing press as for your final output; tape it next to the monitor for comparison so that the screen rendition is a reminder of which colors are where, and gives a general impression of how the colors look together.

Unfortunately, the PMS and similar color matching systems are based on specified ink colors and therefore are limited to use in spot-color printing, in which a specific ink is formulated to create each color, rather than the full-color printing done with the cyan, magenta, yellow, and black process inks. This renders them useless for working with process-color images, except in special cases.

In response to this limitation, PANTONE and its competitors (such as Trumatch and Focoltone) have moved recently to establish new standards based on CMYK definitions of colors. All three companies now market color specification charts and swatches that represent colors only in terms of their CMYK values.

For example, the charts in the Focoltone system on Color Page 5 show not only the specified color, but all the other colors that make it up. Each line on the chart starts with a four-color process color and continues by showing the 14 colors that can be created from it. There are four single colors, six combinations of two colors, and four combinations of three colors. This is a simple but unambiguous way in which the designer and the press operator are guaranteed that they're talking about the same color, and that it can actually be printed.

Focoltone specifications refer to colors printed on single-sheet rotary presses with industry average dot gain and ink density levels. From these conditions the standard specification will allow a quick match to the reference color by normal press adjustments. When you change printing conditions, such as changing to offset web, the shift in specified dot gain causes Focoltone to recalculate each of the color percentages so that the color remains the same.

Device-independent color

The solution to the problem of color correspondence—to the extent that one currently exists—is to use a color model based on how human beings perceive color, rather than on RGB or CMYK values. Fortunately, such a model was developed in 1931 by the Commission Internationale de l'Eclairage, or CIE. Today, there are almost a dozen variations on CIE, all based on the notion of a "standard observer" whose color vision has been carefully measured.

The value of CIE and its derivatives is that they provide a device-independent color model, one that is defined without reference to a particular display or output technology. Until recently, the question of which color models would become central to desktop color production has remained unanswered, as various emerging technologies and companies have vied for position. But the dust is beginning to settle, and the consensus seems to be that both CIE and RGB types of models will remain important in the foreseeable future.

Most computer users will want to work with the colors on the monitor, and have the software take care of problems in printing those colors. Therefore, RGB or one of its derivatives will continue to be important as a device-dependent way of dealing with different display monitors. At the same time, the systems software and applications programs will exchange color information using one of the CIE color models.

In PostScript Level 2, Adobe uses the original 1931 CIEXYZ model as its internal representation of color information, but provides extensive support for a wide variety of other color models. Until recently, one problem for Adobe was that potentially crucial patents governing the portability of colors between different hardware platforms were held by Electronics For Imaging, a start-up firm with big ambitions in color publishing. In early 1991, this barrier was eliminated, as Adobe licensed EFI's color portability technology, and the two companies agreed to work together on building advanced color information exchange into future versions of PostScript.

The goal remains to develop a single device-independent color model with rapid access to color lookup tables for every available hardware device. The typical desktop publisher will find that, in the next two years, virtually all graphics and page layout programs will begin to offer the ability to calibrate using a standard color model supported by leading scanner, monitor, and printer vendors—whether that is offered as an option or as standard equipment.

To be truly useful, the standard color model must:

- be based on international standards, such as CIE, and be convertible to many other standard color systems;

- be based on human perception, so that both color novices and professional graphic artists can select colors with ease;

- be device independent, so that colors on different devices will appear to match;

- translate easily to and from the device-dependent color models used by each display and output device.

Color calibration devices

There are a variety of hardware devices available for calibrating a monitor's display, starting with the high-end Barco devices that establish and modify a constant feedback loop between the display card and the monitor, dynamically changing colors in order to maintain calibration. Those on more modest budgets tend to purchase calibrators from RasterOps, Radius, SuperMac, and others, which correct individual display biases and calibrate the display to achieve accurate color simulations on screen.

They are all based on a small optical sensor that can be placed on the screen, accompanied by software that measures the light output from the display and lets you adjust the color temperature and gamma settings to achieve specific design objectives, or to calibrate with monitors in another location. The color temperature controls allow you to compensate for lighting conditions, while gamma control permits improvements in the display of scanned images so that shadows and details appear more accurately on screen.

Figure 3-2
Radius ColorCalibrator is typical of the optical sensors which can be used to calibrate your color display. Photo courtesy of Radius, Inc.; © 1991 Radius Inc.

There are roughly 1,000 colors in the normal PANTONE Color set, specified as a subset of the CIE color space. Radius bases its PANTONE Color calculations on these CIE values because they provide an accurate, objective color definition.

When a PANTONE Color is specified in an application, the computer refers to a table to find out what the corresponding CIE coordinates are. CIE is specified in x, y, Y coordinates, where x and y define the color and Y represents its brightness or luminance. Radius stores the x, y, Y values for each PANTONE Color in a lookup table for each luminant supported, and uses a complex calculation to convert the CIE coordinates of a desired color to RGB.

Because RGB is not standardized (each monitor has its own RGB space), it is necessary to translate the PANTONE Color into a specific RGB for a specific type of monitor. This is achieved through the lookup table, to which each monitor manufacturer contributes the required conversion data.

In 1989, Tektronix Inc. introduced TekColor for the Macintosh, a color specification that supports color devices such as scanners, video displays, printers, and film recorders, by working within a color model that is independent of the output device. TekColor is used in the color thermal printers and phase-change printers made by Tektronix, and is based on the company's patented TekHVC (hue, value, chroma) color model, which, in turn, is based on the CIE international standard. The TekColor specification is also used by SuperMac in the SuperMatch color calibration system.

But calibrating the monitor to printed color samples is only part of the overall task of maintaining color fidelity and quality, because it does not yet take into account the characterization and calibration of the imagesetter used to create the film for reproduction. Also, before the presses begin to roll, you'll need "proof" that the printed piece will look the way it's supposed to.

Halftone quality issues

In any print production method, the size of the halftone dot is a decisive factor in determining the printing quality. As we have seen, the dot size is determined by the halftone values for each specific area of the image, with highlight image areas being broken down into smaller dots, while dark image areas consist of larger dots. When a dot is transferred first from the film to the printing plate, then to the blanket, and finally to the printing stock, the dot size, and thus the halftone value, can be altered by a variety of factors.

Dot gain and other variations

These variations must always be anticipated and compensated for during the prepress process, or they will cause problems later for the press operator. One such factor that must always be taken into account is *dot gain*, which occurs when dots spread out as they are placed on paper. Dot gain always makes the printed piece appear darker than the film, usually by 10 to 20 percent. (For example, a 50 percent dot will appear as a 60 or 65 percent dot.)

Dot gain varies from press to press, from web to sheet-fed, and with different kinds of paper and ink. It affects the midtones much more than the highlights or shadows: the tiny dots in the highlights are too small to show much increase in size, while the dots in the shadow areas already overlap. The solution is to deliberately make the negative films slightly lighter (less dense) than desired, especially in the midtones, knowing that dot gain will darken the printed piece.

Another kind of dot gain takes place as the film is exposed, due to reflections within the film itself that create a small halo around each dot. Many kinds of film now contain an *anti-halation* backing that minimizes this effect. Dot gain is inevitable, so the goal is not to eliminate it but to ensure that it is compensated for consistently.

Some of the other dot variations that can reduce printing quality include:

- filling in, the reduction of nonprinting areas in the shadows until they disappear completely;

- sharpening, a decrease in the size of halftone dots;

- slurring, a distortion in the shape of halftone dots from circles into ovals, caused by relative motions between the printing plate and rubber blanket, or between the blanket and the press sheet;

- doubling, the appearance of a shadow halftone dot, adjacent to the regular printed dot, resulting from the ink on the dot being transferred by the rubber blanket.

Such variability can be controlled only by checking the press during the make-ready process, and taking densitometry readings for each process color. As the run continues, the press operators are responsible for monitoring densitometer readings to ensure that there are no dot gain, slur, doubling, or other significant distortions.

Many of these problems can be minimized or eliminated by a skilled press operator, though there are some quality problems that can't be solved, even after many adjustments and proofs. Given exactly the same CMYK data, for example, every printing company will produce slightly different results because of variations in paper, inks, temperature, and humidity, among other factors. The best way to minimize these variations is by constant reference to an approved proof.

PostScript halftone dot errors

To obtain screen percentages from 0 to 100 percent, each halftone dot can be created with the appropriate number of pixels, and PostScript does its best to arrange the machine pixels in a pattern that resembles a halftone dot. But because of limitations in the digital halftoning process, the pixels that make up each digital halftone dot are not always in precisely the right place, and round or elliptical dots are not shaped correctly, especially with smaller grids. In order to achieve the appropriate screen angles in a digital halftone, it is often necessary to vary the screen frequencies, which can lead to moiré patterns unless the new accurate screen algorithms are used.

PostScript halftones are also awkward at the 50 percent range of a gradient blend, the point at which the black dots on a white background become white dots on a black background. The eye will often see an artifact in which the dots appear to take on a square shape, causing an obvious dividing line. This problem is less noticeable at higher screen frequencies, and when using an elliptical rather than a round or square halftone spot. It is also minimized by proprietary halftone routines, such as those used on high-end color prepress systems.

Hard versus soft halftone dots

In the PostScript halftone, unlike a conventional photographic halftone, the appearance of dots depends on the quality of the machine spot. A hard dot provides a more precisely defined area—a sharper image—than a soft one, at least in theory.

The concept of hard versus soft dots was intensely debated twenty years ago, when many people proposed a hard dot because they felt it was essential to any attempt to calibrate different devices. However, the soft dot proponents won the battle because of technical limitations in the imaging hardware, and because the soft dot acts to soften the edge of lines and curves found in type, and can be more easily adjusted through dot etching. In other words, the fuzzy logic of the soft dot made type look better than the precise logic of the hard dot.

But the technology has advanced significantly in twenty years, and, with continuing innovations in the PostScript language and in imagesetter film and laser technologies, the quality of PostScript spots—and, therefore, in PostScript halftones—continues to improve. For example, most PostScript imagesetters create a dot about 20 microns in diameter, while the newest hard dot machines create a dot less than 8 microns across.

Banding, and how to avoid it

Another important issue concerns the problem of *banding* in graduated fills, a distracting effect in which there are distinctly visible steps rather than a smooth progression of shades.

We have already seen the relationship between the *dpi* (the dots per inch, or number of distinct pixels that can be created on each linear inch of output), and the *lpi* (the lines per inch, a measure of screen frequency). And we know that PostScript can produce only 256 shades of each of the process colors, but that the number of shades produced in a specific image can be much less, depending on the dpi of the output device and the lpi of the halftone screen.

Figure 3-3
Banding can be minimized by raising the output resolution or lowering the screen frequency.

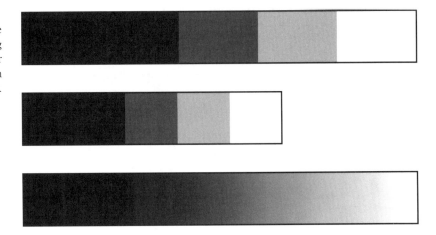

At any given output resolution, the lower the screen frequency, the greater the number of gray shades available.

To create smooth color blends or gradations (when using manual rather than automatic blends), you need to calculate the number of shades, using the following formula:

$$(^{dpi}/_{lpi})^2 = \textit{Total number of shades.}$$

For example, a 300 dpi laser printer generating a 75 lpi screen will produce 16 shades of gray (300/75, or 4, squared), while a 2,400 dpi imagesetter generating a 150 lpi screen will produce 256 shades (2,400/150, or 16, squared).

It is possible to measure the distance between the extremes of the blend (in points), and calculate the size of each step in points by dividing the distance by the number of gray levels. If the result is greater than 1, you will probably have problems with banding. There are a variety of adjustments that can be made to minimize the effect, including decreasing the distance or increasing the percentage of gradation; raising the output resolution, or lowering the screen frequency. Alternately, you can use an imaging program to blend in a small amount of background noise, thus minimizing the banding effect.

Screen frequency

There have been a few major improvements to the PostScript language recently, especially in controlling screen frequency and screen angles, although it still supports only 256 levels of gray. The screen frequency of a digital halftone (in lines per inch) is crucial to its quality. However, selecting the screen frequency for a laser printer or imagesetter involves certain trade-offs between output resolution, screen frequency, and the number of gray levels available:

- to get fine screen frequency, it is necessary to sacrifice the number of gray levels available, though usually to no less than 256;
- obtaining many gray levels (necessary for bringing out detail, for instance) means losing screen frequency;
- increasing the resolution of an output device diminishes the negative effects of screen frequency and gray levels.

However, these problems can be minimized or eliminated by using an output device with sufficiently high resolution. One way is by using a handy formula: divide the output resolution by 16 to get the maximum line screen you can use without forcing gray levels to go below 256. For instance, an imagesetter with a maximum resolution of 2,400 pixels per inch can be used to create digital halftones with screen frequencies of up to 150 lines per inch, because 2,400 divided by 16 is 150.

Screen angles

In traditional separations a halftone screen is created from each of the four colors. The screens are rotated to precise angles so that the dots that comprise the halftone overlap to form small colored circles called rosettes. Looking at printed color graphics and images using a magnifier shows the dots and rosettes of which they are composed. The screen angles are an essential component in constructing the rosettes, and it is this careful construction that creates the illusion of color on the page. If the angles are wrong, the dot patterns interfere, creating moiré patterns.

Figure 3-4
The traditional angles—
cyan 15°, magenta 75°,
yellow 0°, black 45°.
Photo courtesy of Agfa
Corporation.

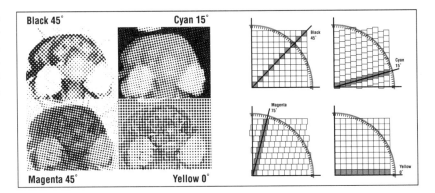

Moiré patterns cause the eye to see the printing itself, rather than the images being printed, thus destroying the illusion of realistic color. The effect is most common when three or more colors are printed together.

As discussed in the previous chapter, moiré can now be virtually eliminated from desktop color through the use of improved screening algorithms.

The emergence of PostScript Level 2 has improved the quality of PostScript halftones, because it provides more precise control of screen angles and frequencies via the new Adobe accurate screen algorithms. Meanwhile, other competitors including Linotype, Scitex, and Optronics have developed their own screening algorithms to minimize moiré.

PostScript Level 2

PostScript Level 2 provides a number of other enhancements of importance to color publishers, including:

- data compression, which improves performance by reducing transmission times and conserving disk space;

- new color models, including both those that incorporate industry-standard color spaces for device-independent color, such as CIEXYZ standard, CIE Y, CIELAB, and CIE L, and those that are calculated from lookup tables, such as indexed color, device gray, device RGB, device CMYK, and device separation;

- color extensions, including CMYK-model support, black generation and undercolor removal functions, screen and transfer functions for four separate color components, and a *colorimage* operator for rendering colored sample images.

All programs that print to conventional PostScript printers (which we can now think of as Level 1 printers), will print to Level 2 printers. In other words, PostScript Level 2 is upward-compatible with existing PostScript language programs and print drivers.

Trapping—essential for quality color

Despite their sophistication, modern printing presses often have trouble maintaining exact registration between the different colors, which causes problems on the printed page wherever colors adjoin.

The time-tested solution to registration difficulties is a technique known as *trapping*, in which one color is expanded, or spread, while another is contracted, or choked. Examples of good and bad registration, and the improvement made by trapping, are shown on Color Page 12.

Consider, for example, a solid blue square on a solid red background. If the blue ink is allowed to overprint the red, the result is a purple square on a red background. To prevent that from happening, the software knocks out the shape of the square from its background, leaving a blank for the blue ink.

Figure 3-5
The object is "knocked out" of its background, leaving an empty space for the other ink.

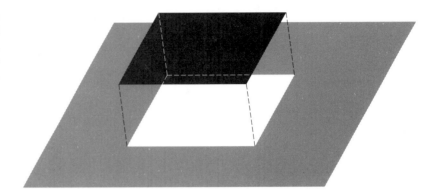

Although the knockout has prevented an unwanted color shift, it has created a situation that makes press registration crucial. Even small shifts or stretches in the paper can cause noticeable problems, such as obvious white gaps between an item and its colored background.

Trapping is now the designer's concern

Until very recently, trapping was the printer or color house's concern. But as designers have taken more command of the production process, it has become their responsibility as well, whether they like it or not. Among the programs providing varying degrees of control over trapping type and objects are Aldus PageMaker and FreeHand, QuarkXPress, and Adobe Illustrator.

Trapping is done somewhat differently on the desktop than in a traditional prepress shop. It is done after the separations have been made, by a camera operator who makes a series of exposures of each separation, purposely under- or overexposing each piece of film so that areas in which different colors adjoin will slightly overlap one another.

Traps are constructed from chokes and spreads: enlarging the foreground object is called spreading, and shrinking the hole beneath the object is called choking. A skilled operator is able to adjust the extent of the chokes and spreads to accommodate different printing presses, papers, and inks. Typical values for chokes and spreads would be .003 of an inch, or about .25 point.

Figure 3-6
Trapping minimizes the white gaps caused by poor registration on press.

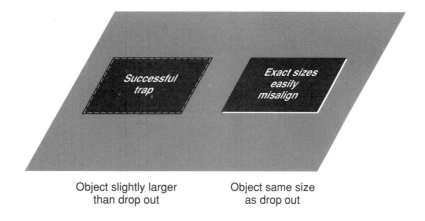

Object slightly larger
than drop out

Object same size
as drop out

In the desktop method, new elements (usually lines) must be created that will overprint the color under them, forming a trap. (If you're not experienced with a desktop draw program such as Adobe Illustrator, Aldus FreeHand, Corel Draw, or Micrografx Designer, you may want to detour to the first part of Chapter 6, which covers the tools and features common to these programs.)

Essential software features for trapping

The most essential skill in trapping on the desktop is being able to adjust the stroke (external outline) of an object with precision. In PostScript, the width of the printed stroke is centered on the path, as shown in Figure 3-7, with half the specified width printing inside the path and half printing outside it. The stroke (which can be of a different color than the object) is often specified to overprint, which means that the adjoining color will print under the outside half of the stroke, thereby creating the trap.

Another essential concept is ink mixing. The trap should share the color characteristics of both the object and its background. Mixing the inks properly can be challenging, especially where fills adjoin other *gradient* or *radial* fills, in which one color blends seamlessly into another.

Graphics and type must be placed by the program with absolute precision, because errors in the accuracy of the overall positioning will be emphasized in trapping. The ability to work with graphic elements on multiple levels is an important feature, because it allows isolation of traps for easy access and manipulation. You need to be able to specify that a given color will overprint all others.

Figure 3-7
In PostScript, the width
of the printed stroke is
centered on the path.

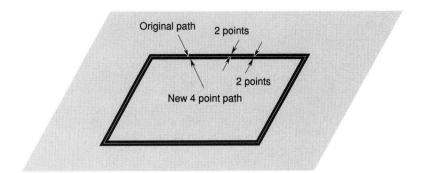

Note that overprinting is an important control, even when you're not trapping. For instance, black ink will normally overprint all others, even though this can cause a color shift where it crosses colored areas. One common solution is to add 30 percent cyan to the black, which minimizes the effect. But overprinting must be used judiciously, because it can result in too much ink in a given area.

**Solutions for
common trapping
problems**

Although the only way to become really conversant with trapping is to try it a few times and observe the results, there are a few guidelines worth following:

- The goal behind any trap is to maintain the integrity of the edges being trapped. For the purposes of trapping, the darker color defines the edge of an object.

- In general, use a .25 point area of overlap. Otherwise, the appropriate amount of overlap will depend on the printing press, paper type, and total ink coverage, so be sure to consult the printing company when deciding on the optimal amount of trapping.

- Solid black elements such as type or rules should always overprint; don't produce traps for these. Trapping small serif type is difficult because there has to be enough of a trap to avoid gaps, but without destroying the shapes of the characters. Because registration is a real problem with thin lines, always use plain overprinting black (no other colors) for them.

- In imaging programs, type is often improved by using *anti-aliasing* to soften the edges where a dark foreground object (such as a character) abuts a lighter background.

- When working with spot color inks (either spot-on-spot or spot-on-process), make the trap outline the same color as one of the objects it touches. When working with process color inks only, give the trap a third color that combines the two colors of the touching objects.

The examples following show the general procedures for effective trapping, whether performed in PageMaker, FreeHand, QuarkXPress, Adobe Illustrator, or other programs. They cover the main categories of trapping, including how to trap rules, trapping type against process colors, and trapping multiple objects.

Figure 3-8
Structure of a typical trap, showing different layers and objects

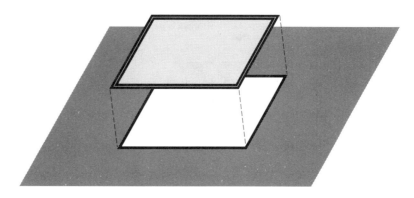

Trap line overlaps both objects.
It is drawn in black with a heavy
rule for clarity.

Trapping is handled differently in draw programs (most of which support object-level overprinting), imaging programs (which work with pixels rather than objects), and page layout programs (which don't have overprinting built in, but some of which honor the overprinting information within EPS files imported from draw programs). Let's begin with trapping situations common in page layout programs.

Trapping a graphic

In the example shown on Color Page 12, the triangle should knock out from the rose background, but trap around its edges. To make this trap, a smaller triangle is placed behind the blue one, which knocks out the triangle beneath it. The box is colored "paper" (the color of the background), and is slightly smaller than the blue one, thus trapping the box.

Figure 3-9
Trapping a spot color
graphic

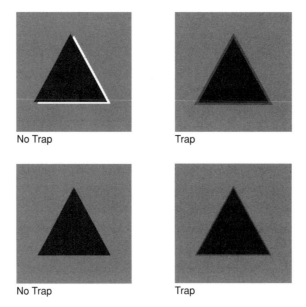

No Trap   Trap

No Trap   Trap

Trapping a TIFF image

To trap a gray-scale TIFF image against a background spot color, the image should knock out the background spot color, but trap around its edges. This is achieved by drawing a box .25 point smaller than the image on all sides, then placing the box behind the image. The edges of the TIFF image overlap the spot-color rectangle behind it, and thus trap correctly. The only problem with this method is that you have to turn knockouts off to make it work, and do all your knockouts manually.

Figure 3-10
Trapping a TIFF image
with a spot color box

Trapping a rule

You have even more control over trapping in a draw program than in a page layout program. When a spot-color rule is printed on top of a process color, the rule must knock out the process colors beneath it, yet still overprint slightly at the edges, as shown on Color Page 13.

Figure 3-11
Trapping a spot color
rule on a process color
background

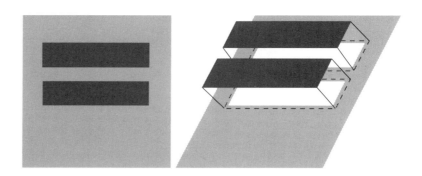

Simply set the original rule to overprint, clone it, then move the clone to a higher layer to isolate it. Reduce the cloned line by .25 point all around (reduce its weight by .5 point and shorten each end by .25 point). Finally, make the clone knockout by setting it to not overprint.

The original rule acts as a .25 point outline around a slightly thinner, shorter rule that will punch out a hole in the background. Overprinting therefore occurs only around the edge of the rule, and no gaps appear.

Trapping process color type

Printing advertising matter frequently requires careful trapping because colored type is often used on top of tints or other color images. Color Page 13 shows an example in which both a letter and its background are process colors. When printed, the yellow type should knock out the purple color behind it, but be trapped by a thin outline of a third color.

This kind of trap can be performed easily in any major draw program, using text strokes and the appropriate CMYK values to produce the trap's color.

Figure 3-12
Trapping process color
type

First give the type a .25 point stroke that overprints. Then create a new color for the stroke. For large or heavy text, take the highest values of CMYK for each of the text and background colors, and use these to create the third color to apply to the stroke.

For fine or small type, the trapping stroke must have a color that helps the letter retain its integrity. To achieve this, create a new process color that includes only the CMYK values that are higher in the lighter than in the darker area.

In this example, the letter is lighter and the background is darker. The lighter color is made of 0% cyan, 10% magenta, 70% yellow, and 0% black. The darker color is made of 40% cyan, 80% magenta, 20% yellow, and 0% black. Because only the yellow is higher in the lighter area than the darker area, the new color for the stroke would be 0% cyan, 0% magenta, 70% yellow, and 0% black. This works visually because the new color will blend in seamlessly with the darker background without destroying the fine detail in the type itself.

Let someone else worry about it

Finally, there's always one other way to handle trapping, if you couldn't be bothered doing it yourself: pay a commercial printer to set the traps conventionally, starting with your regular graphics or page layout files. Because you will have turned knockouts off, be sure to provide the printer with a color composite, or *comp*, to show what the colors are supposed to look like.

Without in any way minimizing the value of desktop publishing, it is true to say that—at least for the time being—trapping is one area in which it may be both cheaper and easier to contract out than to do it yourself. Further information about trapping can be found in the product discussions in Chapters 6, 7, and 8.

Proofing—"the chrome is the contract"

In the printing industry, where million-dollar print runs proceed on the basis of the client's signed approval of a Cromalin or other prepress proof, there's an old saying, "the chrome is the contract."

In other words, if the printed piece looks pretty much like the proof you approved, you have very few grounds for complaint.

Indeed, the standard printing trade customs that govern most commercial printing in North America do not require that the printed piece exactly match the original or the proof. According to the Graphic Arts Council, "Because of differences in equipment, processing, proofing substrates, paper, inks, pigments, and other conditions between color proofing and production pressroom operations, a reasonable variation in color between color proofs and the completed job shall constitute acceptable delivery." The question remains as to what a "reasonable" variation might be.

To be precise, one should distinguish between an actual proof, from which the client is expected to evaluate and approve colors, and a comprehensive or *comp*, used only for layout and design approval.

Leading proofing methods and materials

Color proofing provides excellent examples of the perennial trade-offs between time, money, and quality. If you can wait and aren't particularly fussy about matching colors, a proof can be obtained for a few dollars, which is about all that kind of proof is worth. But even if the client hasn't requested a proof, most printers will create one for their own use, rather than take a job on press without some kind of proof.

There are six main kinds of proofs in commercial use today, each with its own relative advantages and deficiencies. Ranked from cheapest to most expensive, they are: thermal, overlay, integral, digital, electronic, and press.

(There is also the so-called "soft proof," which is a fancy name for staring at the colors on the screen and guessing about how they will look when printed.)

Thermal proofs, such as those from QMS, Tektronix, Seiko, Calcomp, Océ Graphics, and Howtek, are relatively quick and cheap, but will not match the results from the print shop. Moreover, their 300 dpi resolution is far too low to reveal detail in a color photograph. However, such color comprehensives give an approximation of the assigned colors, and permit you to correct any obvious mistakes before you incur the expense of color printing. Basically, these should be considered as comps rather than as proofs.

Overlay proofs, such as 3M Color Key and DuPont Chromacheck, combine four pieces of colored film (cyan, magenta, yellow, and black) in register over a single white sheet. This makes it easy to check details on each separation negative, but produces a proof in which the density of the overlays adds a yellowish-gray tone.

Integral proofs, such as DuPont Cromalin, 3M MatchPrint, Polaroid Spectra, and Fuji Color-Art, are photographic prints created by exposing each of the four separations to a primary-colored, thin-pigmented emulsion layer, which is laminated in register to a sheet of white paper. Integral proofs, though more expensive than most overlays, provide a much better indication of how the four separation halftones will print.

Digital proofs, such as the 3M Digital MatchPrint, work directly from digital data. The Kodak XL7700 outputs continuous-tone hard-copy proofs on color photographic paper directly from color-separated digital data, without the creation of separation negatives. The prints are excellent, and have the look, feel, and stability of conventional photographs. The Iris color ink-jet printer, which uses CMYK pigments and can produce 256 distinct dot sizes, also works directly from digital separation data. Although still in their infancy, digital proofs are expected to become a dominant force during the next few years, despite the fact that they are not made from separation films.

Electronic proofs, such as the new Kodak Signature technology, work with proprietary electrically charged liquid toners that contain pigments almost identical to printing inks. The separation negatives adhere electrostatically to virtually any stock, providing a proof that closely mimics the actual printing conditions and colors. Unlike overlay proofs, these have no intermediate layers to degrade optical appearance. Electronic proofs are like digital proofs in that they are made directly from the original CMYK data, although through a different process.

Press proofs, using the separation negatives, press, paper, and inks intended for the actual job, offer the highest possible quality. The cost, however, is very high, because of the time and expense of the press make-ready process. In fact, there are special little presses that some printers use exclusively for making proofs.

Proper tools for evaluating color

To evaluate a color proof, you need to look at it closely. Start by purchasing a good magnifying glass with a minimum 8-power magnification, and preferably 12-power or higher. A magnifier may also be called a loupe, glass, or linen tester. Most professionals prefer a swivel-arm design, because it can rotate to any position and is relatively free of distortion. If you often carry a magnifier to the color house or printers, invest in the more expensive fold-up models, because once the lens is scratched it is useless.

For optimal color correspondence between the original, the proof, and the printed piece, the major variable is the illumination of the viewing area, which by convention is set to a color temperature of 5,000 degrees Kelvin. Even within this standard, there is plenty of room for variation. The correct color temperature must prevail throughout the viewing area, which is why many printing companies will have viewing booths scattered throughout various parts of the plant. Indeed, some film houses are lit throughout by 5,000 K fluorescent tubes, something you may not notice unless it's pointed out.

Assessing proofs and reproductions

When looking for quality, whether in a proof or a reproduction, let your eyes be the judge. In some market segments, such as merchandising catalogs and advertising, if you can tell the difference between the original and the printed piece, the quality isn't acceptable. The growing exception to this rule is the emergence of "good-enough" color produced on the desktop, where the lack of quality is more than compensated for (in the opinion of the observer) by the reduced cost and turnaround time.

Here are some important factors to look for, especially with continuous tone images:

- Do the images match the original?
- Do food, fabric, metallics, and flesh tones look natural?
- Are images clean, sharp, and bright?
- Are there details in the highlights or are they blown out?
- Are the neutral tones neutral?
- Are there undesirable color casts?
- Are there moiré patterns, streaking, or banding?

Prepress proofs—a checklist

You don't have to work with color for long before you're able to recognize that the brilliant colors displayed in a proof can be difficult or impossible to accomplish on press. Many factors can contribute to unsatisfactory results, from subjective color perception to paper and ink densities. Color proofs can help you avoid unpleasant surprises, but only if you know what to look for. Here, too, some factors apply to synthetic color graphics, while others are relevant only to natural photographic images.

Sharpness	Use a strong magnifier to ensure that detail areas are crisp and clean.
Color accuracy	Compare the proof to the original under a standard 5,000 K color-correct light source.
Neutral areas	Make sure they are completely free of green or blue casts, all the way from white to gray to black.
Registration	Confirm that all elements are properly registered to eliminate fuzziness, shadows, and color changes.
Size	All photos, art, type, and pages must be precisely the correct size.

Borders	These should be correct size, color, position.
Captions	Check for correct content, size, position.
Pagination	All pages and folios must be placed correctly, with crop marks and scores indicated where necessary.
Spots and scratches	Along with pinholes and dust, these must be removed from film and plates.
Broken type	There should be no white specks on type, no sections partially or completely covered.

To identify potential press problems, many printers use color control bars, such as those sold by the Graphic Arts Technical Foundation. A typical GATF color bar is shown on Color Page 8. The entire control bar series is usually printed on progressive proofs, with various specific elements included on the production run, depending on available trim space.

A carpenter friend of mine once said that the first rule of woodworking is to measure twice and cut once. The same general principle applies to color publishing: before giving the go-ahead for a color printing job, forget intuition, and don't depend on a two-dollar thermal print. The few dollars extra spent on proofing are the best insurance against the horrendous cost of reprinting a botched job.

Plato explains color

Before leaving the quality of color, consider the problem of defining "quality." As we observe the relative quality of different goods and services, we make assessments, express opinions. But there are no scientifically "correct" colors, only those that please the ever-changing whims and preferences of individuals and entire cultures. This leaves us little guidance when it comes to adjudicating color disputes, and such disputes are certain to become more common as novices produce complex color work and send it to be printed.

As the Greek philosopher Plato said, there's no accounting for taste.

Computer Hardware Essentials

*"The technicalities matter a lot,
but the unifying vision matters more."*
TED NELSON, INVENTOR OF HYPERTEXT

After countless references to the metaphorical desktop on which all this color activity is taking place, let's now look at exactly what equipment is sitting on, under, next to, and inside the desk.

Although each user's specific needs and budget will govern the mix of hardware and software selected, there are some components that are essential in any computer system: a central processor, memory, and mass storage. Other components have particular relevance for color publishing—high-resolution graphics boards, color printers, and slide film recorders.

This chapter explores in detail each of the hardware components necessary for desktop color publishing with the exception of scanners, which are discussed in Chapter 5. A thorough understanding of the hardware issues is necessary even for users fortunate enough to delegate to others the responsibility for selecting, buying, installing, integrating, and maintaining equipment.

Macs, PCs, Windows, and Unix

Until quite recently, the specialized computers used for graphics applications were often built around proprietary architectures that locked the user into a specific vendor's total hardware and software "solution."

However, the inexorable trend in color publishing is toward systems that have, at least as their front ends, industry-standard microcomputers, whether IBM compatibles, Macintoshes, or Unix-based machines.

Figure 4-1
A typical color publishing system includes a systems unit with keyboard and mouse, a monitor (shown here), as well as a scanner, and black-and-white and color printers. Photo courtesy of Radius, Inc.; © 1991 Radius Inc.

A variety of factors have constrained the use of microcomputers for producing high-quality graphics. Foremost among the problems has been the speed of the central processing chip, which calculates the values of all the pixels that make up the graphic. Access to large memory spaces has also been a problem, although less so with the success of Microsoft Windows 3 in the PC world and the arrival of Apple System 7 for the

Macintosh. Other problems have included hard disk storage, data exchange between systems, display of color, and the lack of calibration between various components.

A spreadsheet program may need high-speed processor chips to rapidly recalculate the value of every number in a five-year financial forecast, and a database program may require a very large, high-speed hard disk to quickly gain access to immense data files. But a color layout or image processing program needs *both*—it must have high-speed processing to constantly redraw the screen, and it must continuously load and save massive graphics files.

Therefore, before worrying about specific color graphics, imaging, and page layout applications, it is essential to have sufficiently powerful hardware to run these heavy-duty programs. A slow processor will make you spend plenty of time waiting for your software to redraw the screen every time an object is changed.

Some popular computer applications, such as character-based word processing programs, run quite comfortably on first-generation machines from the nether ages of microcomputing (some ten years ago), or at least on second-generation machines dating from the mid-1980s. Not so with electronic publishing and imaging programs, which are typically so powerful and so feature-laden that they tax the resources of all but the most high-powered microcomputer systems.

Operating systems

The *operating system* directs the flow of information between the various resources and devices comprising your computer environment. The operating system is a necessary evil, a complex but essential element in making your computer work.

In order to decide on a central processor, you need to know which of the three main computer operating systems you will run, a decision that is usually determined by your choice of hardware platform:

- most IBM compatibles run MS-DOS, many with the Microsoft Windows graphical environment;
- all Macintoshes use either System 6 (with Finder or MultiFinder) or the newer System 7;
- most minicomputers run one version or another of Unix.

In addition, some of the high-end and mid-range prepress systems use proprietary operating systems, although this use is diminishing as users continue to shift to open computing systems of all kinds.

To a limited extent, the hardware platforms and operating systems are interchangeable, with PCs routinely running DOS, OS/2, or some variation of Unix, and Macs running AU/X, another Unix derivative. Meanwhile, most of the major Macintosh software developers have rushed to produce Windows versions of their programs.

Regardless of the operating system being used, you should follow guidelines to ensure you make choices appropriate to your requirements and budget.

Apple Macintosh

The Macintosh operating system, called System, has an intuitive interface known as Finder. There are a number of features that have distinguished the Macintosh System since its inception, such as the use of pull-down menus and the mouse, plus the representation of programs and data files as pictures, or *icons*, stored in *folders*. To copy a Macintosh file, you simply point at its icon with the mouse and drag it to its destination, such as another folder.

Another advantage of the Macintosh System is that it supports 24-bit color at the operating system level, a feature currently missing from its IBM-compatible competitors. For instance, to get 24-bit color on a Windows-based PC, you need a hardware-specific driver for your particular display, which is usually provided by the display manufacturer. By comparison, every Mac is now shipped with 32-bit QuickDraw (with the extra eight bits reserved for additional information) as part of the operating system. This makes it easier and cheaper for users who want to display "true" colors.

In 1991 Apple released System 7, an upgraded version of its operating system that features improved support for multi-tasking and easier communications with other systems. Another improvement is the capability to intelligently link diverse applications programs. For example, a photo retoucher can now retouch a picture in an imaging program, knowing that a page layout in which the picture appears will automatically be updated, regardless of the page layout program being used and where it is on the network.

For color publishers, the key benefits of System 7 include:

- multi-tasking (without the need for MultiFinder), which allows you to keep your imaging program busy calculating a color correction in the background while you digitize your next image in a scanning program;

- *Publish and Subscribe*, which allows you to "publish" onto the network any variable information (such as the contents of a job ticket for a particular image file), so that everyone concerned can tell their applications programs to "subscribe" to it, and be automatically updated when the information changes;

- *Inter-Application Communications* (IAC), which lets you write a script, or macro, that transfers information between diverse applications programs, such as between an imaging program and a picture database application. More important, it also allows your script to instruct other applications programs to take specific actions with the data.

- Access to up to 128Mb of main memory, plus support for gigabytes (billions of bytes) of *virtual memory* (hard disk storage that appears as main memory to the processor).

Apple gained a further advantage in color publishing when it released QuickTime, an extension to the System that enables any color Macintosh to automatically compress, decompress, and display play video, animation, and sound as part of *multimedia* presentations.

DOS/Windows

When the IBM PC was released in 1981, it was accompanied by a rather crude operating system known as Personal Computer Disk Operating System (PC-DOS), or its variant from Microsoft, MS-DOS. By the end of the 1980s, computer hardware was improving by leaps and bounds, but PC users were still chained to DOS anachronisms, such as a 640 Kb memory limit.

Figure 4-2
The icons, menus, and graphic user interface of Windows 3 have brought a Macintosh-like feel to many PCs.

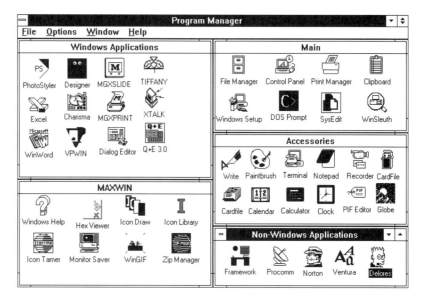

A better solution appeared in mid-1990 when version 3 of Microsoft Windows was released. Since its introduction in 1985, Windows has offered many of the same easy-to-use features that made the Mac so popular—icons, pull-down menus, and support for a mouse. Windows 3, however, has finally demolished the 640 Kb barrier by permitting applications to address as much as 16 megabytes of contiguous memory (provided there are sufficient memory chips in your computer).

Windows version 3 also added a feature of great significance to many publishers—multi-tasking, the ability to run more than one application at a time. You can have multiple windows open on screen at the same time, so that an illustration created in a drawing package in one window can be seamlessly integrated into a page layout package running in another. Moreover, you can continue working in an application in a foreground window while processing continues in other applications in one or more background windows.

It's important to note that Windows is not a true operating system—it is a graphical environment that operates on top of DOS. This presents some problems—DOS was originally designed as a single-tasking operating system—but millions of people have bought Windows, and virtually all publishing and graphics programs running on IBM compatibles do so under Windows.

DOS has recently been upgraded to version 5, which provides more flexible memory management, especially when used with 80386- and 80486-based computers.

OS/2

Having recognized the inherent limitations of DOS, in 1987 IBM announced a "second-generation" operating system, known as OS/2. At that time it seemed natural that PC users, especially those with intensive computing requirements, would eventually grow weary of the memory and single-tasking limitations of DOS, and would migrate to OS/2.

From the outset, it was designed to meet the heavy-duty computing needs of today's large corporations and government departments, with the emphasis on links between desktop microcomputers and mainframe and minicomputers.

In fact, OS/2 dovetails perfectly with a systems-wide strategy announced by IBM in late 1987, known as Systems Applications Architecture (SAA). Under the SAA model, applications look and act the same while running under any one of four supported operating systems—OS/2, OS/400 (for minicomputers), VM, or MVS (for mainframes).

Until mid-1990, it looked as though many large corporate and government users—especially those with IBM mainframes and minicomputers—would automatically move from DOS to OS/2. However, the success of Windows 3 has made many information systems managers decide to stay with the DOS/Windows combination for the foreseeable future.

In the meantime, Microsoft ceded responsibility for OS/2 version 2.0 (a true 32-bit version) to IBM, while announcing that in 1992 or 1993 it will release a totally new OS/2 version 3.0, compatible with 32-bit Windows. This New Technology (NT) operating system would be OS/2 in name only: it would consist of entirely new code, fashioned after mainframe and minicomputer operating systems.

In the long term, those using either DOS/Windows or OS/2 will probably find their applications programs supported under future versions of either operating system. These include color publishing applications currently running under OS/2: PageMaker, Ventura Publisher, Corel Draw, and Micrografx Designer. Starting with version 2, OS/2 can also run Windows as a task.

Unix

The Unix operating system was invented at Bell Labs in the 1960s, and has been widely used in minicomputers made by numerous manufacturers. Until the late 1980s, there were two primary obstacles in the way of Unix becoming an important operating system for microcomputers: its unwieldy interface and the fact that it had at least 17 different "standard" versions. This was acceptable for semi-proprietary high-end prepress systems, but is not well suited to off-the-shelf commercial software applications.

Within the past few years, graphical shells have been added to Unix to make it resemble the Macintosh interface, and most of the competing dialects have united, leaving just two "standard" versions of Unix—and there are signs that even they may converge. In combination with recent increases in the speed and power of microcomputers, there is at least a possibility that Unix could become an important operating system for color publishers.

This is especially apparent when considering the NeXTdimension and NeXTstation color systems from NeXT Computer, Inc. NeXTdimension is a high-end 32-bit color board that gives the NeXTcube advanced color capabilities suitable for color graphics and imaging applications. The NeXTcube computer is based on the Motorola 88100 processor with up to 64Mb of main memory.

The board contains a true-color display function (16.7 million colors), a 64-bit RISC-based dedicated graphics coprocessor, and video capture and display. Its Intel i860 RISC-based microprocessor operates at 33MHz, enabling PostScript color imaging applications to process pictures in near real time. The board also lets you connect to a video cassette recorder, camcorder, laserdisc player, or still-video camera without additional hardware.

NeXT also offers the NeXTstation 16-bit color system, with 8Mb of main memory supplemented by 1.5Mb of dedicated video memory, which helps display 4,096 colors simultaneously at a resolution of 1,120-by-832 pixels.

Both NeXT color systems work with the NeXT MegaPixel color displays, which are available in 17" and 21" sizes. Like the rest of the NeXT product line, the color systems have both thin and twisted-pair Ethernet built in, which allows quick connection to a network. Some of the leading desktop color applications, such as Adobe Illustrator, have now been ported to the NeXT, and others are on the way.

From the outset, NeXT computers have used Display PostScript to control the fidelity of images between the screen and printed output. Software applications written for a black-and-white NeXT computer will also run on a color NeXT computer, and vice versa.

Which operating system should you choose?

The best place to begin evaluating which operating system is most appropriate for you is with your application. In this regard, it is sometimes helpful to distinguish between different domains of desktop color, such as photographic imaging, graphics drawing, page layout, and process color separations.

In the early days of color on computers, Macintosh imaging software remained clearly ahead of IBM-compatible programs, with little or nothing to compare with programs like Adobe Photoshop and Letraset ColorStudio. With the release of Aldus PhotoStyler and other imaging programs running under Windows, that is beginning to change.

When it comes to illustration software, PC-based illustration packages such as Corel Draw and Micrografx Designer provide every bit as much power and flexibility as their Macintosh counterparts, Adobe Illustrator and Aldus FreeHand.

In terms of page layout, two of the three major contenders, PageMaker and Ventura Publisher, are currently shipping versions for both platforms, and the third, QuarkXPress, was expected to ship its Windows version in early 1992. The color capabilities of PageMaker are virtually identical regardless of whether you are running it on a Macintosh or on a PC under Windows or OS/2, except that PrePrint is not currently available on PCs.

Central Processing Unit

The Central Processing Unit (CPU), the essential chip in any computer, is a few square centimeters of silicon that have been hard-wired to add zeros and ones together and pass the results to other chips.

Graphics and desktop publishing are among the more challenging applications demanded of a computer. Generating the ever-changing screens so that What You See (on the screen) Is What You Get (WYSIWYG) from your printer puts enormous demands on the CPU chip. It must constantly compute the intensity and color of every pixel making up the screen (unless your system contains a specialized graphics coprocessor chip).

Adding full-color photography (that is, images) makes matters even more complex, which is why image processing tasks are best performed on workstations that use the fastest CPU chips available. One good way to put this in context is to distinguish the four generations of CPU chips that have marked the evolution of the IBM-compatible and Macintosh computers.

Four generations of micros

Since they were introduced in 1983, Macintosh computers have gone through four generations of central processing chips, the Motorola 68000, 68020, 68030, and 68040 series of microprocessors. Since their inception in 1981, IBM-compatible personal computers have gone through a similar evolution, based on a series of Intel microprocessors: the 8088, 80286, 80386, and 80486.

The processing speed of each generation has been at least twice that of its predecessor, meaning that today's fastest desktop computers are at least 16 times as fast as the original Macs and PCs. The third-generation computers (68030-based Macs and 80386-based PCs) have become the *de facto* standards for many publishing applications, although most professional color publishers will prefer machines based on fourth-generation chips. Even these will ultimately be superseded by newer, faster processing chips.

In a production environment, or when working with color image files, it is usually most cost-effective to buy the fastest processor available, even though it's the most expensive. In other words, for color publishing, buy as much CPU power as you can afford. Math coprocessors add to the cost but can significantly boost performance.

From time to time, there are complaints that the industry is pushing new-generation hardware at the expense of the existing user base. But this ignores the speed with which current systems perform when compared with earlier models. If the electronic publishing industry seriously heeded such sentiments, we'd still be publishing documents with WordStar 3.0 on a PC with 64 Kb RAM. The price of keeping up with new technology may be high, but so are the rewards.

Memory

The crucial truth about memory is that you can never have too much. In general, any publishing application requires at least 2Mb to 4Mb, and a black-and-white imaging application needs at least twice that.

For color imaging, 16Mb or more is appropriate. One good rule of thumb is to ensure your system has three times as much main memory as the largest image file you will want to manipulate. This enables memory to hold the original image, the current filter or image variation, and the resultant image, all at the same time, thus improving performance by reducing the necessity of retrieving data from the hard disk.

Another important factor is the speed of the memory chips. During the past five years, the speed of RAM chips has dropped from 200 milliseconds (ms) to 60 ms or less.

In Chapter 7, Desktop Color Imaging, we discuss the way most heavy-duty image enhancement programs rely on disk caching, in which the computer acts as if a large area of disk storage is actually main memory. By *caching* large files to disk in this manner, your application program can manipulate an image in its entirety, even one that is far too large to fit within the actual memory available

Storage

Because graphics and images play such an important role in desktop publishing, it's wise to understand the storage requirements associated with visual information before you invest in a system. There's no trade-in market for used hard disks, so you should purchase as much storage as you are likely to need in the foreseeable future.

Color Models

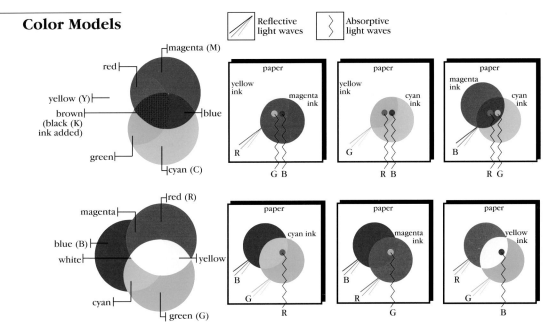

☑ Reflective light waves   ☒ Absorptive light waves

RGB (top) Red, green, and blue are *additive* primaries; they add up to white.

CMYK (bottom) Cyan, magenta, and yellow are *subtractive* primaries; they add up to black, or more precisely to muddy gray, to which solid black is added.

HLS Hue, lightness, and saturation can be represented in three dimensions, with the hues arranged around the circumference of a disk, saturation increasing toward the central axis, and brightness varying vertically with distance from the plane of the disk.

The TRUMATCH 3-D Model (right), based on HLS, employs digital technology to create even saturation steps of 4-color hues. The system was developed for desktop design and electronic output.

©TRUMATCH, Inc., 331 Madison Avenue, New York, NY 10017

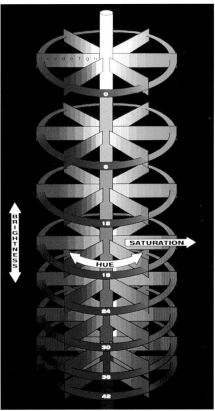

Visible Energy

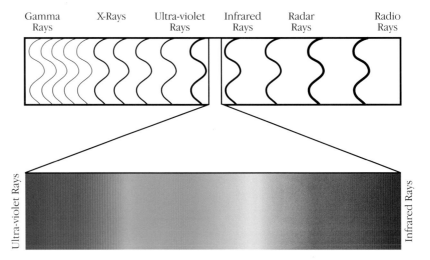

Gamma Rays   X-Rays   Ultra-violet Rays   Infrared Rays   Radar Rays   Radio Rays

Ultra-violet Rays   Infrared Rays

Visible light is one small part of the electro-magnetic spectrum of energy, extending from infrared to ultra-violet through an unchanging rainbow of red, orange, yellow, green, blue, indigo, violet.

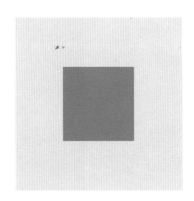
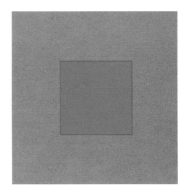

Color illusions result from changing background colors: a green square looks quite different to the eye when seen against light gray and dark gray backgrounds.

CIE Color Model

The CIE color model goes beyond RGB and CMYK by creating three imaginary points that together define a space of colors. All the colors humans can perceive fall within the horseshoe-shaped CIE space.

Because of physical differences in how various devices produce colors, each display and printer will have a different gamut, or range of colors. In this example, you can see that the gamut of a specific display is different from that of a specific color copier. In other words, there are some colors you can see but not print, and other colors you can print but not see.

The CIE model is based on human perception, rather than on a specific hardware device. it is a crucial element in developing systems software that allows calibration throughout the entire color production process, from scanner to display to proofer to printing press.

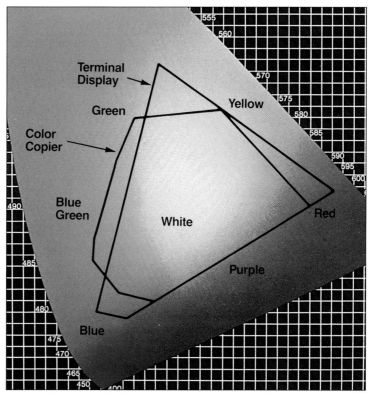

Courtesy of Tektronix.

Hue-Value-Chroma Color Wheel

For any color on the hue wheel, the Tektronix Hue Value Chroma system maps out a leaf of possible colors. The black "video leaf" triangle shape in the TekColor Picker screen contains all the shades that can be displayed, while the red "printer leaf" shows only those that can be printed.

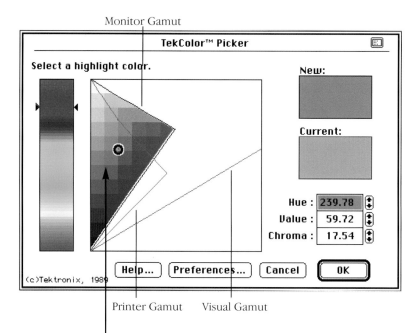

Monitor Gamut

Printer Gamut   Visual Gamut

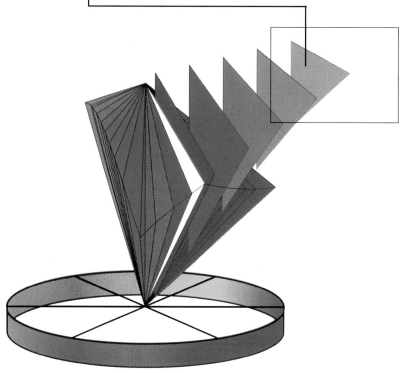

Color Swatch Systems

The Focoltone color range consists of 763 four-color combinations which contain single tints of all four process inks from five to 85 percent.

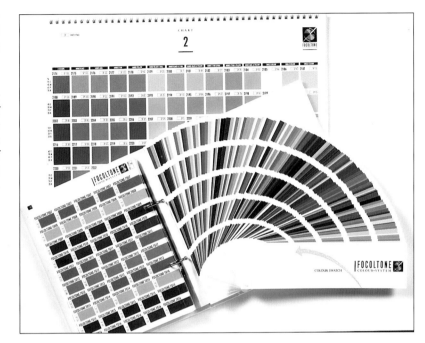

Each of these colors was specified as Pantone 294 in an application program, but variations in how each program converts from Pantone to CMYK percentages can lead to visible color shifts.

Aldus PageMaker and FreeHand
C: 100   M: 91   Y: 57   K: 0

Quark XPress
C: 100   M: 56   Y: 0   K: 18.5

Adobe Illustrator and Photoshop
C: 100   M: 52.5 Y: 0   K: 12.5

Letraset ColorStudio
C: 88   M: 89   Y: 74   K: 0

Micrografx Designer
C: 100   M: 66   Y: 13   K: 0

Moiré

Moiré can occur when two repeating patterns, such as those in halftone screens, are overlaid. The screen frequency, screen angle, and the overlap of colors all contribute to the visibility of moiré.

Shown here are three examples of the same illustration, all output on a Linotronic 330 imagesetter, with different screen frequencies. The top example uses the original RT Screening, which can only approximate the traditional color separation screen angle and frequency values. As a result, significant moiré can occur in some types of images, particularly those containing significant amounts of black or neutral colors. The middle example also uses RT Screening, but with screen angles and frequencies recommended by Adobe Systems in 1989. This tends to minimize the moiré problem. The bottom example uses the new HQS Screening, which allows more accurate production of the traditional screen angle and frequency values. With HQS Screening, moiré has been virtually eliminated from desktop color separations.

© 1991 Linotype-Hell and/or its subsidiaries. The artwork for this illustration was created by Network Graphics of Hauppauge, New York, and appeared in a Linotype-Hell technical information bulletin on moiré. It is reproduced here courtesy of Linotype-Hell Company and Network Graphics.

Drawing and Painting

Drawing

Andre Oberc used Upfront™, a 3D drawing program from Alias Research, to create this design proposal for a staircase.
© Upfront is a trademark of Alias Research, Inc.

Painting

Mark Smart chose the OASIS program from Time Arts, plus a pressure sensitive stylus, to create "Van," his homage to a painter from the past.

Seamless Blends

Visible steps in gradient fills (banding) can be reduced or eliminated by changing the number of steps in the fill (determined by the formula $[\frac{DPI}{LPI}]^2$) distance over which the fill occurs, or the resolution of the output device.

300 dpi output at 150 LPI shows only 5 shades.

By shortening the fill distance, less banding occurs.

2,470 dpi output at 150 lpi yields no banding.

Quality control bars, such as the GATF Color Offset Control Panel, help the press operator compensate for color variations during make-ready and as the run progresses.

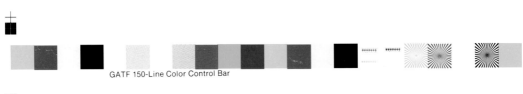

GATF 150-Line Color Control Bar

First, it should be noted that modern applications programs often require 5Mb or more themselves, plus additional storage space for sample files, tutorials, driver libraries, fonts, and utilities. A typical user may have half a dozen such applications, consuming 30Mb or more of hard disk space.

Then there's the problem of file size, which is an important concern when working with draw-type graphics and page layouts, and is a crucial factor when working with photographic images. Simply put, desktop publishing in color results in huge files.

It is easy to calculate the size of any file for bit-mapped graphics, such as scanned images or pictures created in a "paint" program. For example, a 2"-by-3" color photograph scanned at 300 pixels per inch will result in a file of almost 2Mb:

- the area of the photo is 6 square inches;
- each square inch contain 90,000 pixels (300 x 300);
- each pixel contains 24 bits (8 bits for each of three colors);
- 90,000 x 24 x 6 = 12,960,000 bits = 1,620,000 bytes.

Graphics created in a draw program usually require much smaller files than is required for images, typically only one-fifth the size or smaller. However, you will still require a substantial hard disk to store the many iterations of a complex graphic, not to mention an ever-expanding library of clip art. It's hard to generalize about mass storage because it is so dependent on your particular application requirements and budget, but at an absolute minimum, you should purchase 150Mb of hard disk storage, and possibly much more.

For any application involving color photographic images, you will probably need at least 500Mb of on-line storage, and may well find it cost-effective to have many gigabytes (Gb, or billions of bytes) of off-line archival storage on tape or optical disks.

Backup storage

Most people don't drive without auto insurance because the risks of an accident are too great if you get caught without it.

The same goes for backup systems. A number of companies have failed financially because of an untimely collision between a high-speed read/write head and a disk's delicate coating of magnetic material.

The system administrator of a local area network is responsible for ensuring that all data files get copied to off-line storage on a regular basis (preferably at least once a day). But just because someone is responsible for it doesn't mean it actually happens, so be sure to confirm that a prudent network backup strategy is in place.

Those on stand-alone systems should consider including a tape or cartridge backup drive with time-sensitive software that, at four o'clock every morning, automatically copies all new or modified files from the hard disk. This means you leave your hard disk on all the time, which many experts recommend you do anyway, to reduce mechanical stress from power-up.

Most backup tapes store from 40Mb to 150Mb of data, while the removable hard disk cartridges made by SyQuest can store 44Mb or 88Mb. The SyQuest cartridges are also popular as a means of exchanging page and image data with a color house or service bureau.

One final note—even tape or cartridge backup isn't infallible, especially if you don't keep multiple backups and cycle them from time to time. You don't want to arrive at work one morning to discover that your entire computer system has been stolen—including the cartridge on which you've been making your only daily backups for the past month. Which leads us to optical storage.

Optical storage

There are a variety of optical storage methods that have relevance for color publishing. For distribution of fonts and clip art, nothing beats the cost and convenience of CD-ROM (compact disk, read-only memory) storage, which uses the same optical compact disks popular in home stereos. Instead of music, each disk holds up to 600Mb of data, about 500 times the capacity of a typical floppy disk.

As its name implies, CD-ROM is a read-only medium, which means it cannot be used to save data. However, CD-ROM is a very cost-effective distribution medium for large volumes of data, such as fonts, clip art, and image databases. The cost of a CD-ROM player has dropped to less than $500, complete with interface to your Macintosh or PC.

Although almost all users of CD-ROMs consider them only as a source of fonts or picture data, it is getting easier to become a CD-ROM publisher, even if you want to "print" fewer than 1,000 disks. Three years ago, it cost more than $100,000 to create a "master" disk from which CDs could be duplicated; today the same master costs less than $3,000, excluding the cost of any retrieval software required. This makes it feasible to create specialized collections of data or images for distribution on CD-ROMs.

A second optical storage method, the potential of which has dimmed recently, is the Write Once Read Multiple (WORM) drive—prior to the development of erasable optical drives the only way for users to store information optically.

The big advantage of WORM drives was especially apparent to the financial, insurance, and security industries—once a file is written it can never be erased. On the other hand, this is also the disadvantage of WORM drives, because it means they quickly fill up with extraneous versions of files you no longer need.

For a while, WORM cartridges were popular for color publishing, because they allowed you to store up to 800Mb of data on a single disk, which could be easily transported to another computer, another user, or a service bureau. For most color applications, however, WORM drives have been superseded by erasable optical drives.

For most color publishers, the optical medium that offers the greatest potential is the *erasable optical* drive, which includes magnetic and optical components. These *magneto-optical* devices combine a laser beam with an electromagnet to achieve very high storage densities.

On a high-intensity setting, the laser writes to the disk by producing a set of heated spots that the electromagnet then magnetizes, converting them into the equivalent of zero and one bits on a standard magnetic disk.

On a low-intensity setting, the laser reads the disk by using a variation in the way polarized light reflects from the magnetized spots. Because lasers focus light so tightly, they can store huge amounts of data in a small space.

In general, optical drives offer higher capacities than magnetic drives, typically more than 600Mb, but tend to be somewhat slower, with average access speeds of more than 50 milliseconds, as compared with hard disk access times of less than 10 ms. However, with the recent trend toward lasers of ever shorter wavelengths, the data density of optical disks is expected to increase by a further factor of four in the next few years.

DAT's the one

Of all the storage media you're likely to encounter, digital audio tape (DAT) will probably be among the most impressive. As a computer user, you're no longer surprised by the fact that a single floppy can store an entire megabyte of data—more than 500 pages of text. But it takes a while to get used to the idea that a single DAT cartridge, which is not much bigger than a floppy, can store more than 2,000Mb of data, or about 1,000,000 pages of text—especially when each 2-gigabyte (2Gb) tape costs less than $10.

DAT is a serial medium: the tape must be mechanically wound to a specific location to access data, as compared with the random-access mechanism of a magnetic disk drive. This means DAT drives are not appropriate as a primary storage device, although they are ideal for backup of large volumes of data, such as color image files.

As long as your color house or service bureau has standardized on the same kind of DAT drives, these little tapes provide a very effective way of passing back and forth thousands of megabytes of image data.

Display systems

There are a number of concepts in screen display that apply to IBM compatibles, Apple Macintoshes, and Unix-based workstations, but there are also factors that are specific to each.

Figure 4-3
Most color publishers will want to equip their computer with a large-screen color display monitor.
Photo courtesy of Radius, Inc.; © 1991 Radius Inc.

Virtually all color displays are raster devices: they employ a scanning beam that selectively excites different picture elements to make them emit light. (A new generation of flat-panel color displays are beginning to appear, that use direct addressing rather than a scanning beam.)

In either case, the resolution or *addressability* of the matrix being scanned is crucial to the quality of the resultant image: the higher the resolution, the better the image quality. This is especially important for color displays, in which there are separate beams for red, green, and blue.

Screen size is an important factor for anyone whose job involves substantial computer graphics or publishing work. A standard 13" or 14" monitor (measured corner to corner) will suffice for most word processing applications, but is too small for serious publishing tasks. A 19" monitor is required to display a standard 8.5"-by-11" page *size-as*, at its original size. Large screens improve productivity by allowing multiple windows and applications to be open and visible at the same time.

Similarly, when working on an intricate graphic, it helps immensely to be able to zoom in on a tiny detail while retaining a wide-angle view of how it fits into the overall picture. Although a large monitor might seem cumbersome, and can eat up most of the real estate on your desk (and most of the money in your budget), it is an essential component of any professional publishing system.

The bits-per-pixel conundrum

The number of colors a monitor can display is a direct function of the number of bits available for each pixel in the image. A monochrome monitor is limited to one bit per pixel, and therefore displays two (2^1) possible colors—black and white. A monitor that displays four bits per pixel can produce $2^4 = 16$ colors or shades of gray—black, white, and 14 intermediate shades.

An eight-bit-per-pixel monitor can display $2^8 = 256$ colors or shades of gray. To achieve so-called "true color" requires eight bits per pixel in each of three channels—red, green, and blue. This is what is referred to as 24-bit color, and the number of colors possible is 2^{24}, or 16,777,216 colors.

Most 24-bit color display boards support a screen resolution of 72 dpi, which works out to a resolution of 1,024-by-768 on a 19" monitor, 800-by-600 on a 16" monitor, and 640-by-480 on a 13" monitor.

There are a number of other variables to be considered when choosing a color monitor. Among these are the cost, the number of colors that can be displayed at once, the resolution, and the refresh rate.

Given that the number of colors that can be displayed at once is determined by the number of bits per pixel, if you simply want to see pretty colors on screen, eight-bit color is all you really need. However, if you are serious about matching colors to an original image, 24-bit color is a must.

As for resolution, the higher the numbers, the better. Different manufacturers of large-screen color displays have settled on a variety of resolution levels, most in the 1,000-by-800 range. By comparison, a Hell Chromacom is 19" at 1,024-by-1,024. Although increased resolution is an advantage, never buy a monitor by the spec sheet unless you've actually seen it perform, preferably in comparison with competing models.

Macintosh color display options

The original Macs, with their built-in monochrome screens, were obviously unsuitable for color work. With the advent of the Mac II, however, came a flood of color display boards and monitors from manufacturers such as E-Machines, Radius, RasterOps, and SuperMac.

First generation color displays refreshed the screen 60 times per second (60 Hz), which created a noticeable image flicker for many users. By raising the refresh rate of a monitor to 72 Hz, flicker virtually disappears, enabling users to work for longer periods without undue eye strain.

Some monitor manufacturers include software utilities with each display. Radius, for instance, bundles a set of utility programs for tear-off menus (allowing menus to be detached from the menu bar and placed anywhere on screen), a screen saver, a screen capture routine (to save any portion of the screen as a PICT file), and an enlarged menu font for easier viewing.

If you're using a Macintosh, another important factor is whether your display board supports Block Mode Transfer, the Apple standard for transferring large amounts of data rapidly across the bus. Many vendors sell video cards with built-in accelerators that improve the speed of QuickDraw, especially for

24-bit graphics-intensive applications. These typically increase overall performance by intercepting QuickDraw graphics functions and simplifying them for rapid transfer to the screen. Most such boards accept up to 16Mb of memory chips: the key to speed is the use of a memory buffer for off-screen to on-screen data transfer.

VGA, XGA, and beyond

For the past few years, professional illustrators working with IBM compatibles and willing to pay for high resolution and speed have used display systems based on TrueVision Targa boards. Although these provided eye-popping color, they were relatively expensive, and their significance is diminishing as other graphics standards emerge.

In the IBM-compatible world, the original PCs used a Color Graphics Adapter (CGA) and, later, an Enhanced Graphics Adapter (EGA), both of which lacked sufficient resolution for use in graphics or publishing. With the arrival in 1987 of the Visual Graphics Array (VGA), resolution was boosted to 640-by-480 pixels, which was just enough to display type on screen with reasonable fidelity. This was soon increased to 800-by-600 in SuperVGA displays, which for a few years were the standard for graphics display on IBM compatibles.

In recent years, SuperVGA has been superseded by an Ultra VGA standard with 1,024-by-768 resolution, capable of displaying 256 colors at once from a palette of 262,144 colors. For many PC color publishers, an Ultra VGA compatible video card and monitor is probably the most economical choice. This is especially true for those running Windows applications exclusively, as virtually all Extended VGA cards come with a Windows 3 driver, and support for less popular applications programs is spotty.

At the high end of the marketplace, in 1987 IBM introduced a high-resolution (1,024-by-768 pixel) display standard, the 8514. But the product was criticized for flicker caused by use of *interlacing*, a technique in which the display beam scans down the face of the tube twice for each image frame it displays, tracing out every other scan line each time.

In 1990, IBM introduced new models of its PS/2 computers with an Extended Graphics Adapter (XGA) built in. Both 8514 and the XGA standard will display 256 colors in resolutions up to 1,024-by-768, as well as being downward compatible with VGA applications. But XGA doesn't interlace and offers better color resolution (8-bit rather than 4-bit color at its highest resolution), and XGA display boards are likely to cost significantly less than 8514 boards.

One problem remains for those wanting to work with high-quality color images on PCs: Windows does not yet provide direct support for 24-bit color. The latest generation of PC video cards are able to generate 24-bit "true color," but they require custom Windows display drivers. Nonetheless, a growing number of video card manufacturers have recently released or announced boards capable of running Windows imaging applications with full 24-bit color.

Color output choices

Once you've selected the appropriate hardware for capturing an image (a scanner), for processing the image (a computer), and for displaying the image (a graphics board and monitor), the problem of generating hard-copy output remains.

For color output, you have a number of choices:

- a low-cost ink-jet printer costing a few hundred dollars, used primarily for creating business charts;
- a color thermal printer, which produces medium-quality hard-copy color output at moderate cost;
- a color copier, for producing short-run color jobs;
- a digital proofer, which costs at least five times as much as a thermal printer, but offers distinctly higher quality;
- a slide film recorder, for generating 35mm color slides;

- an imagesetter, which produces black-and-white film separations that your commercial printer will use to create color reproductions of your original image.

Color thermal printers and slide film recorders are described below, while imagesetters and high-end proofers are discussed in Chapter 10 on Output Service Bureaus.

Color thermal printers

Figure 4-4
PostScript thermal printers provide vivid colors at relatively low cost. Photo courtesy of Tektronix.

The color thermal printer has been a crucial element in the popularization of color desktop publishing, because it provides a relatively quick and inexpensive way to generate hard copy from your color graphics and publications.

Many color thermal printer vendors have received certification from Pantone, Inc., which will be important if you have specified colors in a software program according to PANTONE numbers.

There are a few other factors to consider when evaluating color thermal printers. Although most use letter-sized (8.5"-by-11") paper, few can print anywhere close to this size, with most limited to printing in an area about 7" by 10". And if you work on a local area network, be sure the printer you're considering can be shared by users working in noncompatible systems, such as IBM compatibles and Macintoshes.

Another factor to watch for is the cost of consumables. Most PostScript color thermal printers require the use of special paper, which can be quite costly. Finally, before signing on the dotted line, check out the size and weight of the machines, as well as the operating noise level. Among the leading vendors of PostScript color thermal printers are QMS, Tektronix, Seiko, Calcomp, Mitsubishi, and Océ Graphics.

Dye sublimation printers

The output from thermal-transfer printers is enormously useful for color publishers, but its quality leaves a lot to be desired. To produce color prints of substantially higher quality, Kodak, Nikon, Mitsubishi, and others have developed *dye sublimation* printers.

Dye sublimation transfer is similar to thermal transfer, in that both use a heated printhead to liquefy ink or dye and apply it to the paper. They differ, however, in the method of application and in the paper they use.

Dye sublimation printers use three-color ribbons—cyan, magenta, and yellow—coated with dye. Instead of being merely on or off, the pins in the printhead can generate up to 256 distinct levels of heat. Consequently, these printers can control the amount of dye released, thus producing more than 16 million shades as the three dye colors mix.

Figure 4-5
KODAK XL7700 contin-
uous-tone color printer.
Photo courtesy of
Kodak Canada Inc.

The KODAK XL7700 color printer uses dye sublimation to produce excellent color prints up to 11" by 11". Although the
resolution is just 200 pixels per inch, the prints look like photographs, because they are continuous-tone, meaning the colors
have a range of intensities, rather than just on-or-off.

By comparison, dithering printers can simulate only ranges of
hues and intensities by using patterns of color dots. Because the
KODAK XL7700 doesn't dither, it doesn't lose resolution to create
its colors. It currently interfaces to the desktop through a GPIB
NuBus card on a Macintosh; PostScript support is through
third-party PostScript-compatible drivers, such as the SuperPrint
driver for Windows from Zenographics. Other drivers and interfaces will be supported in future versions.

Nikon Electronic Imaging makes a dye sublimation printer, the CP-3000, which prints at a resolution of 1,280-by-1,024 dpi on paper or overhead transparency material up to 5" by 6". The CP-3000 prints cyan, magenta, and yellow in 256 gradations each to produce 16.7 million colors. It connects to any Mac or PC through GPIB, SCSI, and Centronics parallel interfaces.

Mitsubishi also makes a series of dye sublimation printers, ranging from small 3"-by-4" size (the CP-100U) to 8"-by-9" size (the S340-10U).

Slide film recorders

One of the most popular ways of displaying color graphics and publications is with a slide show. A slide film recorder is a device that connects to your computer to produce color output, usually on conventional 35 mm color slide film, although as larger sizes become cost-effective, they may be a significant format for color publishers.

A word about terminology is appropriate here. Although these machines are usually known as "slide film recorders," the term is often abbreviated to "film recorders." Don't mistake them for the film recorders described in Chapter 9, which provide film output from high-end color electronic prepress systems.

How film recorders work

A film recorder is basically a black-and-white television cathode-ray tube (CRT) attached to a conventional 35 mm camera. The larger the CRT and the smaller the spot size (the size of each pixel on the face of the CRT), the better the quality of the resulting image. Most film recorders now include automatic exposure calibration, which frees the operator from having to adjust the brightness controls to accommodate the content of each slide.

Figure 4-6
Schematic view of a
typical slide film
recorder.

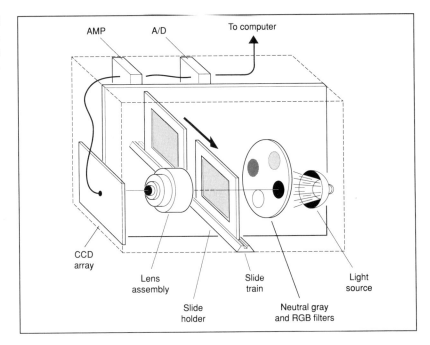

In addition to the standard 35 mm, some recorders offer alternate camera backs including a bulk-load 35 mm back for high-volume producers, Polaroid backs for use with instant-print film, and 4"-by-5" and 8"-by-10" backs for large format transparencies.

Leading vendors of slide film recorders include Agfa, Lasergraphics, Mirus, and GCC Technologies. It may come as a shock to color publishers for whom access to PostScript and its fonts and graphics is a given, but most film recorders are designed only to interpret and convert QuickDraw (the graphics engine that runs a Macintosh display) into a format that they can image onto film. On the PC side, most film recorders use CGM or SCODL files, and a variety of Windows drivers are available.

Because a film recorder is reading QuickDraw, it can't process the PostScript in an EPS graphic, and must instead image the low-resolution screen version of the image, which is pretty coarse. In addition, most film recorders are limited to the same 35 fonts found in virtually all PostScript laser printers.

This situation is changing, however, with the Agfa ChromaScript and other film recorders that use Adobe PostScript interpreters, plus the use by service bureaus and others of third-party PostScript-compatible interpreters such as Freedom of Press.

Resolving the meaning of resolution

Before buying a film recorder, you will need to clarify the meaning of the resolution figures that vendors use on their spec sheets.

The image produced by any film recorder is composed of individually colored pixels. The *addressable resolution* is the actual number of pixels which make up the image. Thus, a film recorder with an addressable resolution of 8 K (8,192-by-5,460 pixels) or 4 K (4,096-by-2,730 pixels) will generate smoother shapes than one with 2 K (2,048-by-1,365) resolution.

Although higher resolution is generally a good thing, there is little advantage to using resolutions higher than 4 K, because they exceed the resolution of commonly used slide films such as Ektachrome. In addition, the time required to generate very high-resolution images (8 K or higher) quickly gets out of hand (up to an hour per slide).

The pixels created by a film recorder are not perfect little squares, but rather blobs that sometimes overlap their neighbors. The amount of this overlap is specified by the *optical resolution* of the recorder, and the higher this number, the better.

Finally, there is the *color resolution* of the device, which is usually expressed in terms of bits per pixel or bits per color. A film recorder that works with 8 bits per pixel per color can specify 256 distinct levels for each of red, green, and blue, resulting in 16.7 million possible colors. Unfortunately, because of the physical properties of the film and CRT, these 256 levels are not evenly spaced. The result is that graduated blends from one color to another are often spoiled by sharp transitions, known as *banding*.

The solution to this problem is to increase the color resolution. Some vendors have introduced film recorders that provide 11 bits per color (33 bits per pixel), which provides up to 2,048 levels of each color, thereby producing perfectly smooth transitions between colors.

In the final analysis, the only way to judge the quality of a film recorder is by looking at the output. If possible, provide prospective vendors with a sample file from your application, preferably one typical of your everyday output requirements. The two key variables (other than cost) are the quality of the resulting image and the length of time needed to generate it.

Why hardware is hard

Ever wonder why they call it hardware? As you may have concluded from reading the ads, all currently available computer hardware represents a vast improvement over what preceded it: the awe-inspiring breakthrough purchased last year looks like this year's dusty antique—which leaves you wondering how long it will be before today's purchases seem just as obsolete. The answer in most cases: soon.

And if you've ever tried to sell used computer equipment, you know that you have to practically pay somebody to haul it away if it's more than six months old. The hard truth about computer hardware is that it's hard to know when to buy it, because there will always be even better equipment available in the future.

Desktop Color Scanning

*"To imagine that which is to be embodied in light, and shadow,
and color—that which is strictly pictorial—
is an accumulative work of the mind."*
THOMAS COLE, ROMANTIC PAINTER

Nature's infinite variety is expressible in painting, in poetry, in dance, but not in zeros and ones. Because computers work in an abstract digital space, to make sense of the real world, they need a connection to it—the scanner.

Scanners bridge the distance between analog and digital, mapping the imprecise yet real world into the cool synthetic precision of the machine. We leave to philosophers the debate about whether something essential is inevitably left out in transforming from analog to digital.

Scanners come in every imaginable shape and size, from hand-held models costing a few hundred dollars, to desk-sized rotary drum scanners costing hundreds of thousands of dollars. Even a home video camera can be used as a scanner, when it is equipped with the appropriate interface and software.

Desktop color scanners are useful input tools for many applications, including graphic design, desktop publishing, and multimedia presentations.

Because different people have different color production requirements, there is no single scanner that will fit the needs and budgets of all users. Indeed, the scanning market is a continuum of quality and expense that stretches from the "bright and pleasing" color used in daily newspapers to "critical color match" advertising photography.

This chapter explores desktop scanners, with an emphasis on how to use them to capture high-quality color images in your computer, where they can be enhanced, modified, and printed or color-separated.

Traditionally, commercial color separation companies, also known as trade shops or color houses, have used massive rotary drum scanners about the size of a large upright piano. The piano metaphor is apt, because the quality of the separations produced is often a direct result of the skill of the person at the keyboard, regardless of the type of scanner or software used. (The high-end scanners, and the prepress systems they commonly work with, are discussed in Chapter 9 on Color Electronic Prepress Systems.)

You don't need to own a scanner to find this chapter valuable:

- Some people use scanners to capture low-resolution "position only" images, or *view files,* for use in the design and layout process. The originals are rescanned at high resolution by the color house and the view files are used to show the cropping and scaling of each image.

- Others hire a color house to scan the originals at high resolution and provide them as color TIFF (tag image file format) files, often on 45Mb or 88Mb removable cartridges. These images are manipulated and enhanced on the desktop, integrated into page layouts, and separated to film on a PostScript imagesetter.

- Some people get the color house to scan the originals at high resolution but provide a low-resolution color TIFF view file for design and approval purposes. The low-res file is replaced by its high-res counterpart during page assembly on the high-end system, either manually or through a semiautomatic link such as the Open Prepress Interface (OPI) or Desktop Color Separations (DCS).

Even if you won't be operating the scanner hands-on, you really need to understand the basics of scanning before you commit your precious transparencies or reflective art (prints or original artwork) to the scanning process. In fact, scanning is such an essential concept that it is relevant even for publishers who will be operating exclusively with synthetic color graphics rather than natural photographic color.

Scanning on the desktop

Most of the problems in producing high-quality color on the desktop are associated with scanning, processing, and outputting color images. Although the essential scanning skills take practice to develop, scanning software has also gotten a little "smarter" and can automatically set parameters to improve the chances for a good scan. However, less is understood about selecting the correct settings for the color separation parameters, such as tone, cast, selective color correction, unsharp masking, and black generation.

The most essential element to a good color separation is a good scan with a proper tone curve. An analogy might be to think about the photography of Ansel Adams. One rarely looks at his photographs and wishes they were in color. This is because Adams understood how to work with tone. Certainly his pictures do not lack definition or impact due to lack of color. The same is true with color scans. If a proper tone range is set, the color version will not lack detail or definition when separated.

It has generally made a lot more sense to perform all design and page layout tasks using desktop publishing and graphics tools, and then have color images stripped in by professionals using traditional scanners. For instance, a company using desktop publishing for a large color catalog will often hire a color house to scan the original transparencies on a high-end scanner, such as one made by Hell, Scitex, Screen, or Crosfield. The scans are stored as two identical files, differing only in the scan resolution and the number of colors. The high-resolution file is retained by the color house, to be integrated into the page layout at the final prepress stage. The low-resolution file is returned to the client as a position-only image for use in composing the page.

When page layout is complete, the high-resolution scanned images are integrated into the page at the color house, either manually or through semiautomatic software and hardware "links" sold by most of the high-end prepress vendors. Many professional color publishers continue to insist on starting with high-end scans, even if they have moved all their other page layout and production tasks from traditional to desktop methods.

Many users find that it is convenient to use a low-cost color scanner to make low-resolution position-only images. The high-end scanning doesn't begin until the page design is complete, with all the text, graphics, and keylines in place. These low-res images take much less time to scan, and consume far less disk storage, then their high-res counterparts, and are more than adequate for showing the page assembler at the color house what you want done.

What this means is that as a color publisher you have a number of choices:

- you can forego color scanning entirely, and pay a color house to scan, process, and separate the images, and to provide the low-resolution images they will later replace with high-resolution images;
- you can pay the color house to scan the images and give you actual high-resolution image files, which you process and separate on the desktop;
- you can do everything on the desktop, including scanning and separating the images.

It helps to keep a historical perspective on scanning. To the chagrin of color prepress houses that have invested heavily in high-end color scanners, the emergence of high-quality desktop scanners represents the second radical shift in scanning technology during the past 20 years.

First, in the 1970s, after decades of experience with camera-based color separations, the prepress industry had to adjust to the arrival of digital color scanners and film recorders. Then, in the early 1990s, just as the high-end digital prepress systems are maturing, the same technologies are beginning to show up on desktop scanners costing half as much as their expensive equipment: the rotary drum scanner technology used in million-dollar color prepress systems is now becoming available on the desktop—albeit a rather large desktop.

Main types of color scanners

There are five main configurations for color scanners—flatbed, slide, multi-format transparency, video, and rotary drum scanners. (There are also black-and-white scanner designs, such as overhead scanners and hand-held scanners, but these are not well suited for working with color.)

- *Flatbed* scanners resemble a photocopier: the lid is lifted, the original image placed, face down, on the glass, and the scan begins. Beneath the glass, a motorized scan head travels the length of the page on tiny rails, illuminating the original and measuring the intensity of the reflected light. Many flatbed scanners accept an optional transparency adapter, for scanning slides and transparencies.

- *Slide* scanners shine a high-intensity light through 35 mm positive film. The light then passes through a series of color filters and a lens onto a light detector, where electronics convert the analog image information to digital. Slide scanners are typically higher resolution and have better detail and focus than flatbed scanners.

Figure 5-1
The CIS-4520 multi-film format transparency scanner is ideal for transparencies from 35mm to 4 × 5 inches. Photo courtesy of Barneyscan® Corporation Color Imaging Systems™; © Mark Johann, San Francisco, CA.

- *Video* scanners use the same technology as ordinary television and video recorders to get color into the computer. Although their impact so far has been slight, they are rapidly opening up the market for low-cost low-resolution color publishing.

- *Rotary drum* scanners have long been the mainstay of the professional color house, costing hundreds of thousands to millions of dollars and requiring highly trained operating technicians. Drum scanners are rapidly being adapted to color desktop publishing.

- *Multiple-format transparency* scanners, which have a dynamic range that rivals that of drum scanners, are the newest format, and could represent the biggest threat to drum scanners. They operate similarly to slide scanners, but accept a variety of film formats commonly used in professional photography, such as 35 mm, 2.25-by-2.25 in., 6-by-7 cm, and 4-by-5 in.

There are a variety of ways of connecting a scanner to your computer. The most common is through a SCSI (Small Computer System Interface) connection to your Mac or PC, either directly or with a converter box. Another popular scanner interface is a GPIB (General-Purpose Interface Bus) card that fits in a NuBus slot on a Macintosh. Alternatively, you can connect a scanner through a serial port, although this is slower than the other two methods.

The scanning process

Every scan you make is another opportunity for proving the old computer adage about "garbage in, garbage out." This is true both in terms of the original photograph and in terms of the quality of the scan. Dust, dirt, smudges, fingerprints, or other garbage present on the original slide, transparency, or print will be difficult or impossible to remove later. On the other hand, the whole point of desktop color is to give you the tools to fix such problems yourself, so that marginal input is transformed into vibrant output.

More important, if the parameters used in scanning the original do not capture all the color information it contains, fixing the image in the computer later will be difficult or impossible. Every brand of slide film, for instance, has a distinct reaction to different colors, a unique *spectral response* curve, which must be compensated for during the color separation process.

The scanner operator normally receives the original with an attached form specifying what the customer wants. This is a crucial communications tool, and it must provide information that is clear, concise, and free from ambiguity. Such information should include details on:

- the degree of enlargement or reduction required, and any cropping required;
- whether the original is a negative or positive;

- the desired line screen (100, 125, 133, etc.);

- the emulsion of the original (Kodachrome, Ektachrome, Fujichrome, etc.), and the emulsion speed;

- whether sharpness should be increased, decreased, or left unadjusted;

- whether local or overall color casts should be partially or completely removed;

- the main area of interest in the original, and whether particular tonal ranges in the original should be emphasized, or "opened up";

- any specific colors that must be matched;

- the intended press, paper, ink, and standard dot gain.

Setting scan parameters

Traditional scanners have dozens of knobs and switches, few of which are present on desktop color scanners. Instead, the software that determines their power and ease of use comes in a variety of forms: as desk accessories on the Mac, as Windows drivers on the PC, as plug-in drivers, or as separate application programs.

Plug-in drivers tell popular image-editing programs such as Photoshop, ColorStudio, Digital Darkroom, and PhotoStyler how to access the features of a particular brand of scanner. This allows you to scan and edit images within the same application.

Software for all the major desktop scanners lets you perform a quick low-resolution preview scan that can be used as a basis for cropping the image and adjusting the exposure controls. You can not only control the *brightness* (the intensity of light) and *contrast* (the variation between lightest and darkest), but also change the *gamma* of the image by adjusting the midtone levels in an image without changing the highlights and shadows.

How scanners work

The most common basis for comparing scanners is *resolution*, the number of pixels (picture elements) a scanner can see in a given area. Resolution is expressed as dots per inch (dpi), although a more precise description is pixels per inch (ppi), which avoids confusion with digital halftone dots.

The best way to reproduce good color is to capture it fully and accurately on the input scan. However, this is more than a matter of resolution, as it requires you to detect accurately the complete range of colors present, as well as the shades of gray and the detail of lines.

The quality of a color scanner is a function of its *dynamic range*, or ability to capture detail in both highlights and shadows. A typical slide or color photograph with a good range of brightness values would have to be scanned at about 15 bits per pixel per color to capture all the intermediate shadings of color in the original. Most desktop scanners capture only 8 bits per pixel, although some scan 12 bits per pixel, then compress the information into eight bits before transmitting it to the computer.

The result is that either the dark areas in the original go black or the light areas go white: it's especially hard to pick up shadow details in dark slides. This problem increases when you correct an image after scanning, because you've already lost information from the high and low ends, so that boosting the brightness forces you to lose even more detail in the light areas.

Some scanners use *interpolation*, or super-sampling, a technique that gives resolutions higher than their stated maximum. The interpolation routines average an image's bilevel or grayscale values and place new pixels between the existing ones.

Interpolation doesn't add detail to a scan, but smooths it, providing better transitions between grays and reducing the jaggies. For this reason, the technical literature for some manufacturers shows both the "true resolution" and the "theoretical resolution" of their scanners.

Inside a scanning mechanism

Regardless of the scanner's mechanical configuration, the fundamentals of image recording remain essentially the same.

As shown in Figure 5-2, each pixel in the detector array consists of a charge-coupled device (CCD), a tiny segment of a computer chip that converts a bundle of light energy (a photon) into a bundle of electrical energy (an electron). Alternatively, some scanners use a photomultiplier tube (PMT) rather than a CCD.

Figure 5-2
The charge-coupled device (CCD) array inside a scanner converts light energy into electrical energy.

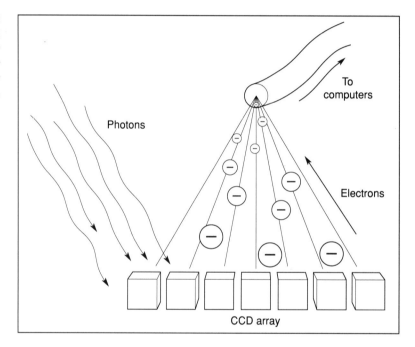

In the simplest case of a bilevel black-and-white scanner, each pixel measures every incoming photon to determine whether it is greater than or less than a preset threshold level. If it's greater, the pixel emits an electron.

The electrons from each activated pixel are lined up in a row, one after another, and the rows are sequenced together into a file, which is most commonly stored as a TIFF (tag image file format) file.

In the case of a grayscale scanner, each pixel is capable of storing more than one bit. Just as in the case of the display monitors, storing two bits per pixel allows four colors or shades of gray (white, black, dark gray, and light gray) to be created. With eight bits per pixel, 256 shades of gray can be stored, which is generally recognized as the minimum needed to render photographic detail with reasonable accuracy. It also happens to be the maximum number of gray scales supported in PostScript.

Figure 5-3
In a grayscale scanner, each pixel stores multiple bits; the greater the pixel depth, the more shades of gray can be detected.

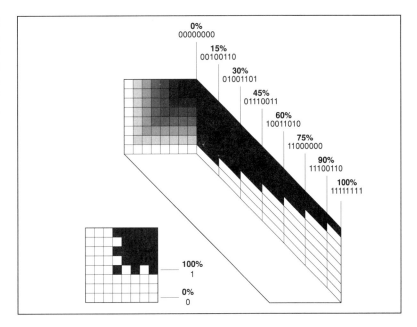

For color scanning, we must measure with 256 gray shades for each of three additive primaries (red, green, and blue), which requires 24 bits per pixel (three times eight). There are two different approaches used by color scanners to achieve this.

Some scanners feature a three-pass system in which the detectors move past the original three times (once each for red, green, and blue), with the values from each pass creating one channel in the color image. Unfortunately, tiny tracking errors in the scanning mechanism can lead to misalignment of data acquired during successive passes, resulting in small but potentially noticeable color shifts. This problem can be minimized with good scanning software and motor transport control mechanisms.

Figure 5-4
In a color scanner, each
pixel must record the
intensity of the original
image in each of three
colors—red, green, and
blue.

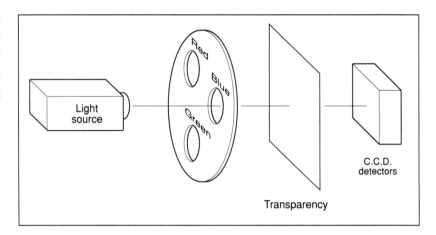

Another way of doing it is to sequentially illuminate each row with red, green, and blue lights during the scanning process, so that only one scan of the original is required. Vendors who use this method, known as strobing, claim that it minimizes color shifts caused by tracking errors. Proponents of the three-pass system point out that even small discrepancies in the intensity of the bulbs as they are strobed on and off can also cause noticeable color shifts. Other vendors apply RGB filters to three separate light sources at the same time.

Irrespective of what numbers and charts of scanner performance tell us, nothing competes with the final arbiter, the viewers' eyes.

Pixel depth

In the simplest case of a black-and-white bilevel scan, each pixel generates a single bit, either a zero or a one, depending on whether the incident light striking that pixel had sufficient energy to go over the detector's threshold level.

The problem with bilevel scanning is that it provides no way of representing shades of gray, and hence no way of creating color.

However, consider a scan array that has been modified so that each pixel has "depth": instead of generating a single bit, it can transfer to the processor two or more bits per pixel.

A detector that can sense and transmit multiple bits per pixel can be used to gather grayscale information, and increasing the number of bits greatly increases the number of shades of gray. Remember, a single bit only represents black or white, whereas two bits per pixel gives you pure white, basic black, light gray, and dark gray. Increasing the depth to eight bits per pixel gives you 2^8 or 256 shades of gray.

Number of bits per pixel	Number of shades of gray
1	$2^1 = 2$
2	$2^2 = 4$
3	$2^3 = 8$
4	$2^4 = 16$
5	$2^5 = 32$
6	$2^6 = 64$
7	$2^7 = 128$
8	$2^8 = 256$

Once again, color scanning requires eight bits per pixel times three to create 24-bit color, which uses 256 shades of gray within each of the three colors to produce some 16 million colors (256 x 256 x 256 = 16,777,216).

File sizes

One of the biggest issues in color imaging is the size of the files. This is inevitable, considering that each file must store the value of every pixel, in multiple colors, in many shades of gray, at relatively high resolution.

With a little practice, you can quickly predict the size of any image file based on its size, resolution, and number of shades of gray.

Take, for example, a 4-by-5-inch color photograph that has been scanned at 300 dpi with 256 shades of gray. To create a sufficient number of shades of gray, you must store eight bits per pixel.

Figure 5-5

Each square inch of a 300-dpi image contains more than 10Kb of data for a bilevel black-and-white scan, 90Kb for a 256-grayscale scan, and 270Kb for a 24-bit color scan.

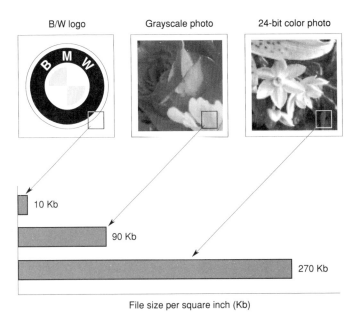

To calculate the number of bits in each square inch, multiply the resolution by itself (300 x 300 = 90,000 bits), and by the number of bits per pixel (90,000 x 8 = 720,000 bits). Finally, multiply by three for the red, green, and blue channels in the image (720,000 x 3 = 2,160,000 bits), and divide by eight to convert from bits to bytes (2,160,000 / 8 = 270,000 bytes = 270 Kb).

The area of a 4-by-5-inch photo is 20 square inches, so the file size is calculated by multiplying the area times the number of bits per square inch, as determined above (20 x 270 Kb = 5.4Mb).

This example shows that even a relatively small photograph can require a multi-megabyte file. Because most scanning software now shows the size of the proposed image file, you can change settings such as cropping, scaling, and resolution to modify the file size until it comes within acceptable limits.

Color and grayscale files grow in proportion to the size of the image and the *pixel depth* (the number of bits assigned to each pixel to define its color or gray level).

Using a 300 dpi image saved as an uncompressed TIFF file as an example, the following table shows how the size of the file varies with the pixel depth of the image:

Bits per pixel	1	4	8	24
Image type	line art	grayscale	grayscale or color	color
Shades of gray or colors	1	16	256	16,777,216
4"-by-5" image (Mb)	0.2	0.9	1.8	5.3
8.5"-by-11" image (Mb)	1.0	4.1	8.2	24.7

Fortunately, most scanners save files to disk as they scan, so you can scan any file that will fit on your hard disk. However, this does little to solve the problem of image file sizes. Until recently, nothing could be done about the massive size of image files—the user had to compute around them.

But recent developments in file compression programs mean that soon it will be possible to save compressed files on disk while working with decompressed images on screen. Many adjacent pixels in an image contain the same information, or change gradually in predictable ways. This redundant data can be compressed without sacrificing image quality.

The first standard compression products for microcomputers are based on the Joint Photographic Experts Group (JPEG) specification, and are discussed in detail in Chapter 7 on Desktop Color Imaging.

Selecting the optimal scanning resolution

Some color publishing novices scan all their images at the highest resolution available on their scanner. The result is huge files that take forever to save, load, separate, and print.

At the other extreme, if the scanning resolution is too low, there will not be enough color information to form correct digital halftone dots, and the color image quality will also be adversely affected.

As a rule of thumb, your scanning resolution for color imaging should be 1.2 to 2.0 times your line screen frequency. In other words, scan at a resolution between 160 to 266 dpi to create a 133 lpi screen.

The scanning hardware and software you use may be optimized for a particular multiplier, but if it is not, start with 2.0 times the desired lpi. Produce a few test images while reducing the resolution—say, to 1.8, 1.6, 1.4, and 1.2 times. Compare the quality of the resulting images, and use the lowest setting at which there is no reduction in picture quality.

Scanning resolutions lower than the lpi of the desired line screen will have a noticeable negative impact on image quality, while resolutions higher than twice the lpi will have a beneficial impact, but will result in substantially larger files.

The size of the file is also affected by any required change of scale between the original and the output image file. Ideally, the original would be exactly the same size as the image to be output: you would start with a 4-by-5-inch transparency to produce a 4-by-5-inch picture. In reality, of course, the image usually must be scaled.

If you increase the scale of a scanned image for output, more scan data is needed than if you output the image at its original scan size. This additional scan data is needed by the output software to correctly interpolate additional pixels, and results in increased file size.

Figure 5-6
Scanning resolution (in
dpi) should be 1.2 to
2.0 × output line
frequency (in *lpi*).

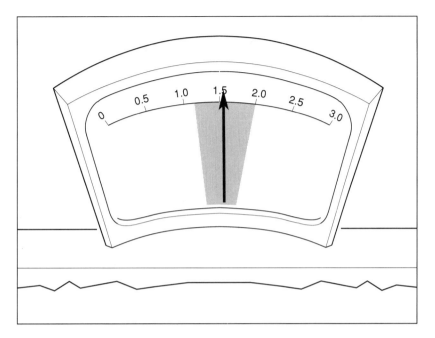

Conversely, if you scale down an image for output, the software will consolidate pixels and discard excess scan data. This means that when you plan to output an image at reduced scale, you can start with less scan data, and a correspondingly smaller scan file. By computing output scale before you scan, you can optimize the scan file size to include just the data you need.

The sampling ratio allows you to reduce the size of the image file by pixels in a consistent pattern. For instance, with a 3:1 sampling ratio only every fourth pixel is captured, resulting in a file that is 75% smaller (and that contains correspondingly less color information).

There is a formula you can use to integrate these variables. For a given set of values for the desired sampling ratio, output line screen frequency, and output size, it will help you quickly estimate the optimal scanning resolution.

The first step is to calculate the number of pixels you need to reproduce the longest dimension of the image:

- Number of pixels needed = longest output dimension × line screen frequency × sampling ratio

Then divide by the longest input dimension to get the scanning resolution:

- Scanning resolution = number of pixels needed / longest input dimension

In calculating the longest input dimension, you may find it helpful to know the longest full-frame dimensions for the two most popular transparency formats: 1.42" (36.4 mm) for 35 mm and 4.75" (121.8 mm) for 4-by-5 inches.

For a 35 mm transparency being scanned to create an image 5-by-8 inches with a 133 lpi line screen frequency, the number of pixels needed (8 x 133 lpi x 2 pixels per halftone dot = 2,128) is computed, and then the scan resolution (2,128/1.42 = 1,499) is calculated. In other words, the optimal scan resolution for this example is 1,499 dpi (usually rounded off to 1,500 dpi). Some scanners allow you to set the scan resolution independently, in which case you can use the value derived above. In other cases, you must use the available scan resolution that is closest to the optimal value.

Desktop scanners take over

As color scanners become part of everyday desktop publishing, they are appearing in a variety of sizes, shapes, and prices. Although the specific models are certain to change rapidly during the next few years, they will most likely fit into the existing scanner categories, such as flatbed, slide, multi-format transparency, video, and rotary drum.

Flatbed scanners

The main advantages of flatbed scanners are their relatively low cost and their flexibility for scanning small and large reflective (and optionally transmissive) originals.

Sharp JX series scanners

Sharp Electronics Corporation makes a series of three color desktop scanners that have use in desktop imaging—JX-300, JX-450, and JX-600. All employ the same basic technology: a single high-resolution CCD sensor combined with red, green, and blue fluorescent lamps. Unlike many scanners that require three passes of the original, the Sharp scanners need just one pass, during which sequential strobing of the red, green, and blue lamps allows it to gather all the necessary image information.

Software included with the Sharp scanners allows you to adjust white balance and edge emphasis for sharpness control, download gamma tables for fine-tuning scans, and adjust zooming to specified sizes.

The JX-300 offers 300 dpi resolution with eight bits per pixel (256 gradations per color), and a GPIB (IEEE-488) bus is standard. The JX-450 accepts originals up to 11-by-17 inches, and can be combined with an optional mirror unit to scan from 35mm or overhead projection film. The JX-600 provides 600 dpi resolution, with 1,024 gradations per color, at sizes up to 11-by-17 inches. It samples 10 bits per pixel, which is processed to produce an eight-bit color output file with optimal dynamic range.

Imapro scanners

Imapro Corporation has taken the scanning engine in the Sharp JX-600 and added a variety of enhancements to capture more color and picture detail. The Imapro QCS-1260 is a flatbed scanner with switchable resolution of 600 and 1,200 dpi, able to scan reflective art and transparencies up to 11-by-17 inches. It includes an optical feedback system that maintains a constant intensity from each lamp during the scan process, allowing accurate calibration.

The QCS-1260 has other enhancements added to the original Sharp scanning engine, including the use of 12-bit internal correction rather than the 10 bits used by Sharp, preventing streaking at higher densities. It sells for under $30,000, which is twice the cost of the simpler Sharp unit.

Epson ES-300C scanner

The Epson ES-300C is one of a new breed of low-end flatbed color scanners that cost less than $2,000 and provide moderate quality, sufficient for many color publishing applications. Unlike most desktop scanners, which capture eight bits of data in each of three passes (one each for red, green, and blue), the ES-300C can scan a full-color image in a single pass.

At each scan line, the scan carriage flashes a green light and reads the result, flashes a red light and reads the result, and flashes a blue light and reads the result. This single-pass design provides for fast, accurate scans. The ES-300C will scan reflective originals up to 8.5-by-11 inches, and comes bundled with the ScanDo desk accessory.

Howtek scanners

Howtek Inc. currently offers three models of scanners. The Scanmaster D-2000 is their professional-level product, a high-speed rotating drum scanner for digitizing color or black-and-white transparencies or reflective material up to 10-by-10 inches. The scanner consists of two parts—the actual scanner mechanism is table-top, and the electronics unit sits on the floor.

The Scanmaster D-2000 captures a full 12 bits of color data in a single pass (up to 4,096 levels of gray), from transparent and reflective originals 35 mm to 10-by-10 inches in size, at resolutions up to 2,032 dpi. By using three precision matched photo-multiplier tube (PMT) sensors to collect the RGB data, the machine achieves a dynamic range of 3.80.

Using Howtek's Colorscan software, you can select a specific area to be scanned and make any necessary adjustments to enhance the detail, increase the contrast, compensate for over- or underexposure, and enhance the edge detail. These modifications are applied to the image data during the scan, and further enhancements can be made once the data are saved to disk.

The Howtek Scanmaster 3 is a more economical flatbed scanner that handles reflective art and transparencies up to 11-by-17 inches, scanning at resolutions up to 400 dots per inch. It handles color and black-and-white continuous tone images, pre-screened images, and line work, producing RGB files of varying density depending on the input size of the image. It supports full 24-bit color, or 256-level black-and-white.

The Scanmaster 3 uses a multi-element charged-coupled device (CCD), and a single fluorescent bulb light source with dichroic filters. It incorporates a digital signal processor (DSP), which increases the speed and quality of the images produced. Images can be saved as TIFF, PICT, PICT2, TGA, RIFF, Artisan, and Sun Raster formats.

The Scanmaster 3+ is a 1,200 dpi flatbed scanner capable of scanning an 11.7-by-17 inches area as well as transparencies. The Scanmaster 3+ scans 400 dpi native, and then up to 1,200 dpi through interpolation. Available for both Mac and PC platforms, the Scanmaster 3+ is excellent for prepress work as well as standard scanning applications.

The Personal Color Scanner is a 300 dpi flatbed, 8.5-by-14 inches scanner capable of scanning in 24-bit color or 256 levels of grayscale. The Personal Color Scanner is a three-pass scanner capable of scanning continuous tone, halftone, line art, and reflective images. Images can be saved in a variety of standard formats for both Mac and PC platforms.

Agfa color scanners

The Agfa ACS 100 is a flatbed color scanner that offers variable resolution scanning from 300 dpi to 2,400 dpi for professional color prepress applications. It uses separate scanning modes for color and black-and-white, and images can be scanned as continuous tone (6, 8, or 10 bits per pixel) or line art originals.

The camera module of the ACS 100 contains a single linear array of 3,648 CCD elements, mounted on a rail system and precisely moved back and forth with a stepping motor. By minutely changing the optical distance, the scanner can vary the resolution to best accommodate the size of the original. Agfa also claims that flatbed CCD scanners offer better throughput than traditional drum scanners (a suggestion with which most drum scanner manufacturers would take exception).

A 35 mm transparency can be scanned with a maximum resolution of 2,400 pixels per inch, and in the highest quality mode (10 bits per pixel per color) scanning takes about 90 seconds. Maximum size is 12-by-16.5 inches for reflective originals, and 8.5-by-16.5 inches for transmissive originals. For reflective art, the resolution ranges from 1,200 dpi for a 3-inch original, down to 300 dpi for a 12-inch-wide original. For line art, the ACS 100 can scan at 1,200 dpi over the entire 12-by-16 inches copyplate.

Agfa also makes the Focus Color Scanner, a flatbed that provides resolution of up to 800 dpi, with eight-bit 256 gray levels per RGB color, providing 24-bit scanning of up to 16.7 million colors. An optional transparency module is now available, enabling you to scan 35 mm to 4-by-5 inches transparencies, using a halogen lamp for superior clarity.

The Focus comes with Agfa's View Color software, which takes a series of density readings from various parts of the original during the pre-scan, then automatically determines the optimal exposure parameters. The software, which is available for the Mac or PC, also features automated white balance correction, which enables compensation for color casts associated with different types of paper. Unsharp masking (to sharpen a "soft" original) and descreening (for scanning something already printed as halftones) are built in, and can be applied during the scan or after the data are stored.

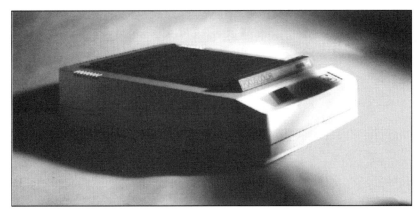

The Focus color scanner also comes with Calibrator software for calibrating the scanner input with your printer or image-setter output. A gray wedge is produced on the output device, then scanned on the Focus to measure and compensate for any deviations.

If the images need further adjustment, the ColorMap feature lets you change the image densities, to compensate for an image that's too dark, for instance. The program also produces a color histogram that allows you to verify whether the scan result covers the density range selected before scanning. You can also scan to disk an image larger than your computer's RAM.

**Multi-format
transparency
scanners**

Barneyscan has introduced the CIS-4520 scanner that will handle transparencies up to 4-by-5 inches with a maximum resolution of 2,000-by-3,000 pixels. Images are scanned at 12 bits per color and processed by a digital signal processor (DSP) chip for optimal reproduction of highlight and shadow detail.

The CIS-4520 costs under $30,000 and comes with an Intel 80386 processor, 8Mb of RAM, and a 40Mb hard disk to allow background scanning without tying up the workstation processor. It comes with QuickScan software that lets you select the highlight and shadow dot during the pre-scan, thus setting an optimum tone curve for color reproduction. It also comes with ColorAccess software for producing color separations with professional-level prepress controls that emulate those from the drum scanner environment. QuickScan and ColorAccess are tuned for the CIS scanners, and are also available for the Sharp JX-series scanners.

CIS-ColorAccess provides a full set of tuning controls for characterizing a separation in terms of specific inks, paper, imagesetter, and press conditions. Barneyscan in conjunction with GATF (the Graphic Arts Technical Foundation) is developing PostScript versions of the print quality control targets now widely used by printers in film form. The concept is that test targets, once integrated into an electronic page and output on film, can be used to burn plates which will be run through the press. The output from the press can be read with a densitometer and readings can be fed back into CIS-Color Access lookup tables which will allow the separation engine in the software to compensate for the actual density range, dot gain, and other measurable characterisics of a specific printing press. This concept supports the reality that the customer is ultimately buying ink on paper and that the job is not complete until the customer accepts their job in print. Such a system provides printers with far greater control over final print quality and will ultimately save them part of the usual 25 percent waste factor associated with "make-ready."

Barneyscan also sells the CIS-Gallery relational image database program, which helps you locate and track images, even if you have tens of thousands of them (presumably stored on optical disks or digital audio tape). The program stores 24-bit color images as 8-bit thumbnails for easy search, sort, and viewing. You can enter information on what each image is called, how it was scanned, who owns the rights to it, and so forth.

CIS-Gallery comes with a master program for creating the image database. A simple double click of the mouse on any 8-bit thumbnail provides immediate access to the full 24-bit color scan. CIS-Gallery also provides lender/borrower tracking of image files, plus image searches based on multiple criteria.

Figure 5-8
Barneyscan Color
Access software
provides complete
control of all scanning
parameters, including
unsharp masking (left)
and screen angles
(right).

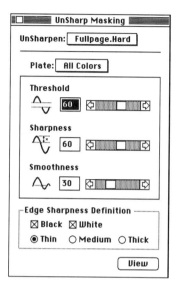
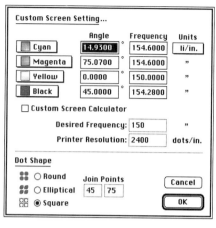

Slide scanners

Slide scanners, which scan 35 mm photographic transparencies, are an excellent way of capturing 24-bit color images for desktop publishing. As a source for scanned images, the major advantage of transparencies is that they are capable of a much wider range of brightness, contrast, and color saturation than is possible on reflective materials such as color prints. A secondary benefit of slides is that they are easier than prints to handle, store, and transport. One limitation of 35 mm slides is their relatively small size, as compared with 4-by-5 inch transparencies and other larger originals: any enlargement of the image will more easily reveal the underlying grain structure of the photographic emulsion.

Nikon LS-3500 scanner

Among the more popular desktop color scanners is the Nikon LS-3500. To use the scanner, you simply place a color slide or black-and-white negative in the holder. It takes densitometry readings throughout the image area, establishes color table data, scans the image (at variable resolutions up to 6,144-by-4,096 pixels), and sends the data to your computer.

The Nikon scanner's ease of use stems from its self-calibrating and automatic focus features. The first time you choose the Color Preview function, the scanner performs a task called pre-scan sensitometry, which examines the range of light to dark tones in the image. It scans, and then displays the result, which you can use as a basis for adjustments to the exposure and gamma controls.

Other features of the LS-3500 include RGB gain setting for individual analog control over each primary color, and lookup table-based gamma control for precise gradation corrections. Nikon recommends a Mac or PC with a minimum of 8Mb of RAM and 300Mb of hard disk storage.

In addition to basic color controls, such as brightness and contrast, the Colorflex software that comes with the LS-3500 provides three other sets of controls. The Analog Exposure controls let you assign numeric values for red, green, and blue gain that effectively change the *f*-stop of the exposure. The Black Level Threshold control allows you to lighten or darken the blackest black in an image without affecting the midtones or highlights. The Gamma Curve controls permits you to set a gamma value for each channel (red, green, and blue) and set values for the highlights and shadows in each one. In effect, the gamma value sets the slope of the gamma curve, while the highlight and shadow controls set the curve's end points.

The LS-3500 supports a variety of file formats including TIFF, PICT2, PostScript, Targa, Vista, and 9-track tape output in Scitex and Crosfield formats. It uses a specially designed lens to provide the best aperture for sharpness and optical registration across the limits of the CCD.

Eikonix 1435 slide scanner

The Eikonix 1435 is a desktop scanner for 35 mm slides; it features resolution up to 2,800 dpi, with a dynamic range of up to 12 bits per pixel per color. It has a patented scanning mechanism that moves the camera's sensor array rather than the object film, which the manufacturer claims ensures better positional accuracy in multiple RGB scans.

The 1435 has a flexible film-holding mechanism, a fixed-focus 75mm lens, a color filter wheel, and a high-intensity diffused light source. It supports a variety of file formats, including TIFF, PICT2, Targa, and IOPIC.

The software that comes with the Eikonix 1435 lets you control a variety of scanner functions, including dynamic range; automatic bias and gain calibration; automatic exposure and color balance adjustment; gamma correction; output to display or disk; image enhancement and editing; crop, zoom, and rotate; and data compression.

Howtek Scanmaster 35

The Howtek Scanmaster 35 scanner handles 35 mm color negatives or color transparencies, or black-and-white negatives. Film can be mounted or unmounted, and scanned in either direction. Cropping and scaling of the image are performed during a preview scan. In the final scan, the high density of these files allows a 35 mm image to be enlarged up to 1,500 percent (poster size), although this will always entail some reduction in image quality.

Scanning is accomplished with a 2,048-element CCD array, a fluorescent lamp, and a color filter wheel. A 6,000-step motor moves the film horizontally between the lamp and the CCD, making the motion extremely accurate over the entire scan. Both the basic Scanmaster 35 and the enhanced Scanmaster 35/II scan 12 bits per color, with a total accuracy of 24 bits per pixel (4,096 gray levels). The user can choose to read the raw 12-bit CCD data, or 12- or 8-bit values that have been color corrected.

The Scanmaster 35 has a scanning resolution of 2,000-by-2,000 dpi, yielding an effective resolution of 1,333-by-2,000 dpi, and features full 180-degree image rotation. Scanmaster 35/II has a scanning resolution of 2,000 by 3,000 dpi, but does not support image rotation.

Figure 5-9
Barneyscan 3515 color
slide scanner.
Photo courtesy of
Barneyscan®
Corporation, Color
Imaging Systems™; ©
Mark Johann, San
Francisco, CA.

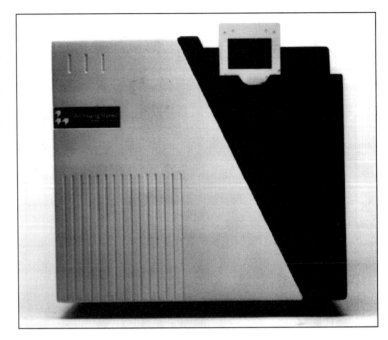

Barneyscan CIS-3515

The CIS-3515 is the follow-on product to the Barneyscanner, which, back in 1986, was the first desktop 35 mm scanner on the market. It scans at 1,000 dpi and comes with Photoshop LE (a limited edition of Photoshop without separation capabilities).

Scitex SmarTwo PS scanner

The Scitex SmarTwo PS scanner attaches to a Macintosh, and scans 35 mm slides, as well as 2.25-by-2.25-inch and 6-by-7-cm formats. At a 300 dpi output resolution, the image can be scaled from 20 to 1,700 percent for 35 mm transparencies, and 20 to 850 percent for the other sizes.

Images can be saved in a variety of formats, including EPS, TIFF, DCS, PICT2, and Scitex PS Image and Handshake CT. To operate the SmarTwo, you first mount a transparency in a special cassette, and load it in the scanner. You can pre-scan the transparency at low resolution and display it on your Mac screen, where it can be cropped, scaled, and rotated. SmarTwo then scans the final image exactly to these specifications.

The scanner automatically analyzes the transparency and adjusts the general tone and the highlight and shadow points, and accepts user instructions for corrections such as color cast removal. The SmarTwo also supports image sharpening, under-color removal, and gray component replacement. It scans 32 bits of color information, and saves it either as RGB or CMYK data at 256 gray levels per color.

The SmarTwo PS comes with an interactive training program, designed for those with little or no experience in either prepress or computer operations.

Video digitizers

The image files used for publishing are, in principle, no different than those recorded with a video camera. Although scanners are fine for capturing images from a flat photograph or slide, they can't capture the image of a real-world three-dimensional scene. But a video digitizer can, accepting input from standard video sources such as camcorders, videocassette recorders (VCRs), still-video cameras, and laserdisc players.

Although video digitizers are a very inexpensive means of gathering visual information into the computer, they do so at the expense of resolution. Most capture an entire video frame in 1/30th of a second, at a resolution of 640-by-480 pixels. In addition to the North American video standard NTSC (Not The Same Twice), some also accept the European standard PAL (Purely Arbitrary Luminance).

The MacVision from Koala Technologies is a popular low-cost video digitizer, creating 8-bit color images at up to 640-by-480 pixels. ComputerEyes Color is a Mac NuBus card that captures a 24-bit color image from a static source. In addition to NTSC (National Television Standards Committee), it has a 4-pin mini-DIN connector for S-video devices such as SuperVHS and Hi-Band video recorders.

The Array Technologies AS-1 scanner makes use of innovative technology to improve the resolution of video digitizing. The

AS-1 uses a 256-by-256 pixel color television matrix sensor, and is described as an *integrating camera* because it samples the image continuously and then sums and averages the results. To increase resolution, the AS-1 uses a tiny piezoelectric crystal to jiggle the pixels around a bit (move the matrix subpixel distances) and resample the image.

The advantage of this approach is that by increasing the integration time, the operator can get better and better color fidelity—simple scans can be done in two minutes, while very high-resolution scans will take two hours. The camera head is detachable from the unit that holds and illuminates the slide, and you can buy extras such as copy stands and tripods that allow you to scan not only 35 mm slides but also large-format transparencies, hard-copy originals, and three-dimensional objects.

The Eikonix 1412 Digital Imaging Camera is an advanced linear CCD array camera offering a resolution of 4,096-by-4,096 pixels, with a dynamic range of 12 bits per pixel per color. The originals may be black-and-white or color, transmissive or reflective, or even three-dimensional. When mounted on a column, the 1412 allows scanning of a broad range of formats.

The Eikonix 1412 also features a data normalizer that corrects for any differences in bias and gain between array elements, thereby reducing streaking, and an integral optical viewer for rapid setup and focusing.

Rotary drum scanners

For many professional color publishers, drum scanners are considered the only way to obtain a high-quality scan. A scanner based on a rotating drum will tend to provide better shadow detail and possibly more accurate color than one based on any kind of flatbed or linear track, in part because the high speed of rotation ensures that horizontal misalignment is kept to an absolute minimum.

Optronics ColorGetter

The Optronics ColorGetter was the first rotating drum-based color scanner to appear on the desktop, and although $68,000 might seem pricey for a computer peripheral, it's downright cheap compared to the $200,000 cost of the high-end scanners from Hell, Crosfield, and Screen. (The high-end scanners, which provide additional scanning control features, are described in Chapter 9.)

The ColorGetter Plus, introduced in mid-1990, is a higher resolution model of the scanner, aimed at applications requiring high resolution or substantial enlargements of small format originals. The original ColorGetter scans originals up to 10-by-14 inches in a single pass at resolutions up to 2,000 scan lines per linear inch, while the Plus model scans at up to 4,000 lines per inch. Both models include an intelligent controller that contains the control software, plus hardware interfaces to a host unit such as a Macintosh, IBM-compatible, or Unix-based system.

Unlike most desktop scanners, the ColorGetters use three photomultiplier tubes (PMTs), rather than the newer CCD technology. According to Optronics, the PMTs support a broader dynamic range (0.0 to 3.8 D_{max}), or maximum density, in order to capture both bright highlights and deep shadows.

The PMTs simultaneously gather red, green, and blue data from the original, providing precise registration off the RGB information. Color information is captured up to a full 12 bits (4,096 gray levels) per color, to provide excellent detail and colors. Color images are output as TIFF 5.0 files, either as 12 or eight bits per color through the use of lookup tables. The ColorRight software that comes with it allows you to define the type of original, scan area, sampling interval, color selection, and color correction curves.

The ColorGetter scanners feature interchangeable removable drums. One can be loaded with new originals while another is being scanned, and they can be pre-loaded with multiple "ganged" images to handle high-throughput scanning.

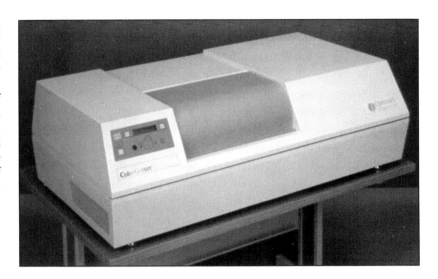

Figure 5-10
Optronics™
ColorGetter® brings
rotary drum technology
to the desktop.
Photo courtesy of
Optronics™, an
Intergraph Division.
Intergraph® and
ColorGetter® are
registered trademarks of
Intergraph Corporation.

Scanner calibration

Calibration is an essential part of operating a slide scanner. The process establishes the proper values for absolute white and absolute black, then compensates for minute variations in the lighting and in the response to each element in the CCD array.

There are a variety of techniques for calibrating a scanner, most based on a test sample of known color values inside the scanner itself. These typically operate whenever the scanner is turned on or as requested by the user. The test patch is scanned, and the resulting values are compared with standard values stored in the scanner. Whenever they differ, the output signal is adjusted to compensate for the error.

Specialized scanning software

Many serious color users find the scan acquisition software that comes bundled with the scanner insufficient to the task, in which case a specialized scanning program such as SpectreScan from Pre-Press Technologies should be considered. It is available in versions for most desktop color scanners, such as those from Sharp, Howtek, Imapro, and Eikonix.

SpectreScan

The program begins with a quick pre-sampling of the original to determine values for the brightest and darkest areas. It then performs a full pre-scan, measuring 4,000 to 6,000 pixels on the slide for highlights and shadows, color balance, and saturation levels.

You can enter values for film type (Ektachrome, Fujichrome, and so on) and light source (daylight, fluorescent, electronic flash), if those are known. The program contains lookup tables for most scanners, so that these factors can be accounted for at the moment the scan is acquired.

Many experienced users add a bit of both brightness and contrast during the initial scans, and make further adjustments based on the results. You can set the exposure times independently for the neutrals, red, green, and blue.

SpectreScan users have emphasized the importance, for trouble-free performance, of removing all extraneous start-up files (INITS) from the system folder, and ensuring that all system files are the same version number.

In technical notes, Pre-Press Technologies says that its scanner produces optimal results when the ratio of dpi resolution to lpi screen frequency is 1.25:1, rather than the conventional 2:1. In other words, if you're creating a 133 lpi screen, you only need to scan at 166 dpi, rather than 266 dpi.

The difference is significant, because scanning at the lower resolution means the file for a given color image would be about 17Mb, instead of 27Mb. Once the desired resolution and line screen have been specified, the program performs the detailed scan, a process which takes about five minutes for a typical 35 mm slide.

The future of desktop scanning

There are still some major problems to be solved before desktop scans are routinely as good as those produced on high-end scanners. But these problems—resolution, dynamic range, file size, and processing speed—are capable of being solved, and an enormous amount of research is currently directed toward doing just that.

The arrival of the first desktop rotary drum scanners gives a good indication of where desktop color scanning is going—up in quality and convenience, and down in cost.

Desktop Color Graphics

"Color, once reduced to certain definite rules,
can be taught like music."
GEORGES SEURAT, IMPRESSIONIST PAINTER

Computers work with visual information in two distinct ways. In *paint* programs, images are created, manipulated, and stored as individual dots. In *draw* programs, graphics are constructed from mathematical descriptions of lines and curves.

There are some kinds of visual effects that can only be created in paint programs such as Adobe Photoshop or Letraset ColorStudio. They provide the artist with an electronic palette of pens, brushes, airbrushes, and other tools for creating original images and for modifying scanned photographs. These paint programs are described in detail in Chapter 7, Desktop Color Imaging.

However, for line art graphics, illustrations, technical drawings, logotypes, and fancy typographic effects, you need a draw-type graphics package such as Adobe Illustrator, Aldus FreeHand, Corel Draw, Micrografx Designer, or Arts & Letters.

The lines and curves used in these draw programs provide tremendous flexibility and control in creating complex illustrations that can be modified or reshaped quickly. And the objects you draw can quickly be filled with a color, pattern, or graduated blend of colors.

People use such draw programs to create everything from postage stamps to billboards. They include:

- the graphic artist who uses a blend tool to create elegantly fluid logotypes in which type and other graphic elements seem to be in motion relative to one another;

- the medical illustrator who creates precise anatomical color graphics, separated onto different layers according to function;

- the advertising typography expert who creates unique variations on hundreds of typefaces, then fine-tunes them for use as headlines;

- the fabric designer who draws a tiny motif, then uses an array command to automatically generate a perfectly tiled full-width fabric pattern, with infinite color changes a further few clicks away;

- the woodworker who drafts the plans for a cedar blanket box, then uses the parts list feature to print out a detailed description to take to the lumber yard.

Why not bitmap?

All paint programs allow the user to create and edit pictures, each one of which consists of a large number of pixels. Because paint programs construct images by mapping out the location of each individual pixel with bits, they are known as *bitmapped* programs. Their major limitations involve working with line graphics (as opposed to grayscale images). Most paint programs are limited to a resolution of approximately 300 dots per inch (dpi), which mean that images look jagged when printed on a typical 300 dpi laser printer, and positively crude when positioned next to typeset text at 1,000 dpi.

Figure 6-1
Bitmap images appear
jagged close up
(left). They cannot be
scaled (right) without a
loss in quality.

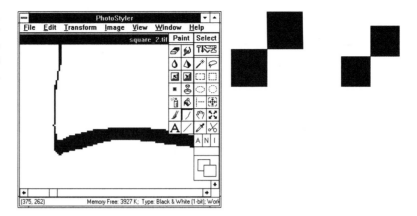

Moreover, the fact that each graphic has been formed from discrete bits means there is no simple way to scale or resize a bitmapped image. In a graphic that is being enlarged 25 percent, a thin line that is one bit thick must either double in size to two bits, or remain a single bit thick. Either option distorts the true shape of the graphic, which can result in the staircase effect known as *aliasing*, or the jaggies.

PostScript-based draw programs, on the other hand, construct graphics from lines and curves. This means they can be resized quickly without any loss of detail. Line segments are represented not by a series of dots, but by mathematical formulas, so they can always be printed at the ultimate resolution of the output device—whether it's a 300 dpi desktop laser printer or a 3,000 dpi imagesetter.

Drawing on the desktop

Since its emergence in 1985, the unifying factor in desktop computer illustration has been the PostScript language. Graphics programs built around PostScript let the artist achieve (and sometimes surpass) the quality of artwork created by hand. Curves are rounder, tints can be applied easily and evenly, and continuous-tone gradients are smooth as silk.

Figure 6-2
In a typical draw program, graphics are created from the lines and curves joining the many nodes.

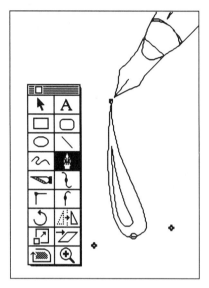 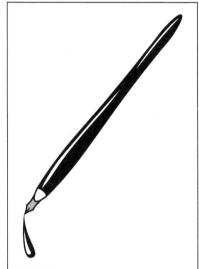

But these programs are much more than replacements for existing drawing and painting tools. They are a whole new medium. They have inspired a new breed of designers and artists of all ages and from all backgrounds who have learned this new language and are creating innovative art with graphics programs.

PostScript drawing programs enable the user to:

- manipulate type to create outline, shadow, skewed, distorted, and other effects;

- print type and graphics at the highest resolution possible on any PostScript output device;

- draw fluid curves, smooth arcs, and perfectly straight lines, even if the user can't draw a straight line;

- trace around bitmapped images to create a graphic that can be further edited or enhanced;

- select and cut masks to allow editing of specific parts of a graphic;

- color a drawing using hues specified in any of the major color models; and

- maintain palettes of colors to be used repeatedly.

All this creative freedom is available because the pictures are drawn as paths (lines and curves), not dots. Indeed, if it is true that color can be reduced to certain definite rules, an entire new generation of computer artists calls those rules PostScript.

The history of PostScript

PostScript is a computer language for describing pages, a *page description* language devised by John Warnock and Charles Geschke of Adobe Systems in the early 1980s. Fortunately for the graphics world, Warnock and Geschke hooked up with Steve Jobs of Apple Computer, who in 1984 was looking for a printer language for the Apple LaserWriter; it became the first laser printer to come equipped with a PostScript *interpreter*, which translated images from QuickDraw (Macintosh's graphics programming language) into vector descriptions that took full advantage of the printer's 300 dpi resolution.

With the release of PageMaker for the Macintosh in July 1985, three elements essential for desktop publishing were in place:

- a page layout program able to integrate all text, illustrations, and images into a single graphic;

- a page description language able to translate the graphic for optimal printing on any device;

- an output device able to interpret the language and re-create all the detail in the original page layout.

For the first year or so thereafter, this combination dominated desktop publishing. Ventura Publisher and other page layout programs appeared in late 1986, but there was still no easy way to create high-quality graphics on the screen.

All that changed in March 1987, when Adobe Systems released Adobe Illustrator: suddenly an entirely new set of powerful tools was readily at hand. Software such as Aldus FreeHand, Corel Draw, and Micrografx Designer soon followed. By mid-1991, these programs were still dominating the market for micro-based drawing software; this chapter focuses on their capabilities, as well as their interaction with other software.

Figure 6-3
A PostScript graphic such as this took but a minute to create, but would have been impossible by hand.

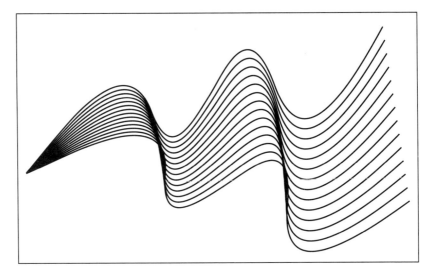

Page layout programs provide line, box, and ellipse drawing tools, but typically little more. A draw program, on the other hand, quickly turns a sketch into a logotype, can give a vivid picture of rearranged floor plans without anyone moving the furniture, or create eye-catching headline type. It is essential for most desktop publishers to have at least one graphics program in their repertoire.

Draw programs also provide immediate access to libraries of clip art, the quality of which has continued to improve. Most such graphics are provided in black-and-white, but objects can be colorized individually.

How PostScript draws a picture

A PostScript-based drawing package will describe a design as a set of lines and curves drawn on the page: "start one inch over and one inch down from the top left corner of the page, and draw a rectangle eight inches wide and ten inches long." It defines the length and direction of lines and the formulas for curves until all the outline shapes are complete, and then fills the outlines with patterns constructed from other PostScript commands, after which it will apply the desired fill colors.

Figure 6-4
In PostScript, even a simple graphic (left) can result in a few pages of PostScript code, a sample of which is shown at right.

%!PS-Adobe-3.0 %%Creator: Adobe Illustrator(TM) 3.0 %%For: (Karl Barndt) (Electric Ink, Ltd.) %%Title: (Fig 6-4.ps) %%CreationDate: (8/26/91) (3:10 PM) %%DocumentProcessColors: Black %%DocumentNeededResources: procset Adobe_packedarray 2.0 0 %%+ procset Adobe_cmykcolor 1.1 0 %%+ procset Adobe_cshow 1.1 0 %%+ procset Adobe_customcolor 1.0 0 %%+ procset Adobe_IllustratorA_AI3 1.0 0 %%BoundingBox: 180 482 268 555 %AI3_ColorUsage: Black&White %AI3_TemplateBox: 306 396 306 396 %AI3_TileBox: 30 31 582 761 %AI3_DocumentPreview: None %%EndComments %%BeginProlog %%IncludeResource: procset Adobe_packedarray 2.0 0 Adobe_packedarray /initialize get exec %%IncludeResource: procset Adobe_cmykcolor 1.1 0 %%IncludeResource: procset Adobe_cshow 1.1 0 %%IncludeResource: procset Adobe_customcolor 1.0 0 %%IncludeResource: procset Adobe_IllustratorA_AI3 1.0 0 %%EndProlog %%BeginSetup Adobe_cmykcolor /initialize get exec Adobe_cshow /initialize get exec Adobe_customcolor /initialize get exec Adobe_IllustratorA_AI3 /initialize get exec %%EndSetup 0 A *u 0 O 0 g 0 i 0 J 0 j 1 w 4 M []0 d %AI3_Note: 0 D 257.9745 485.4903 m 266.9393 485.4903 L 266.9393 482.25 L 230.9722 482.25 L 230.9722 485.4903 L 240.585 485.4903 L 240.585 550.6199 L 240.369 550.6199 L 219.3072 482.25 L 215.4189 482.25 L 194.7891 550.8359 L 194.5731 550.8359 L 194.5731 491.9708 L 194.5731 484.8422 198.4614 485.4903 204.7259 485.4903 c 204.7259 482.25 L 181.72 482.25 L 181.72 485.4903 L 187.6605 485.4903 191.3328 484.8422 191.3328 491.9708 c 191.3328 551.16 L 181.72 551.16 L 181.72 554.4002 L 212.0706 554.4002 L 224.5997 510.8725 L 237.6688 554.4002 L 266.9393 554.4002 L 266.9393 551.16 L 257.9745 551.16 L 257.9745 485.4903 l f *U %%PageTrailer gsave annotatepage grestore showpage %%Trailer Adobe_IllustratorA_AI3 /terminate get exec Adobe_customcolor /terminate get exec Adobe_cshow /terminate get exec Adobe_cmykcolor /terminate get exec Adobe_packedarray /terminate get exec %%EOF

The PostScript language makes it possible to construct very complex shapes with just a few command lines, as shown in the figure above. It offers tremendous flexibility and power to those who like to write computer programs. Indeed, by reading the

PostScript code created within the draw programs, a programmer can pick up useful tips and tricks about writing PostScript code.

For example, try using your draw program to construct a page that contains nothing but a large Helvetica "A." Print the graphic to disk as a PostScript file, then print out the PostScript code, using your word processor or editor. You'll find that it consists of three or four pages of descriptions of various PostScript parameters, ending with a few lines of text that refer to Helvetica and "A".

Go back into the graphic with your draw program and add some more text or change a few fonts, then print the graphic to disk again. When you compare the resulting PostScript code with that of your first try, you will find the code modified to reflect the changes in the graphic. Repeat the process while adding some lines and curves, modifying rotation, scaling, gradient fills, blends, arrays, and many other effects. After each modification, print out the resulting PostScript code, making note of how your draw program has rendered each graphic in terms of PostScript.

Most people, of course, don't want to actually write a program—they just want to draw on the screen. Even if you can't draw a straight line, simply by holding down a command key you can direct the software to keep a line perfectly straight. Curve-shaping tools make it just as easy to re-create complex shapes or patterns without the plastic French curves used in traditional drafting. Those experienced with desktop publishing will find many of the new concepts familiar, although there will be a number of new distinctions to master.

Among the issues that must be considered are:

- creating your own colors and saving them as custom palettes;
- specifying colors in a graphic that will ultimately be printed in a page layout program;
- copying graphic files back and forth between programs, such as Illustrator to FreeHand and back;

- exchanging color graphics between Macintoshes and IBM compatibles;
- controlling the production of color separations.

Working with graphics programs

Artists who were accustomed to traditional pencils and brushes were initially taken aback by the new electronic toolbox, which is based on such concepts as outline fonts, layers, paths, and fills. It didn't take most long to discover the incredible flexibility and power of the new technology. Heavy-duty illustration packages provide complete control over all the tools needed by a professional artist or designer, while being easily accessible to people without formal training in graphic arts.

It's useful to see what characteristics these programs have in common, and then examine each of the leading packages individually, concentrating on how capable each is at creating and separating color graphics.

Graphic file formats

To fulfill their role as software integrators, page layout programs must be able to import and export text, graphics, and images from many different sources. Among the file formats supported by the leading page layout programs, the main text formats include:

.TXT	ASCII text;
.WP	WordPerfect;
.DOC	Microsoft Word;
.DCA	Document Content Architecture.

The advantage of ASCII text is that it is universal, making it ideal for passing text between different computer platforms, such as from a mainframe to a microcomputer, or from a Macintosh to a PC. Unfortunately, it retains no formatting information, not even boldface and italic selections.

The various word processing formats offer greater control over formatting, including the use of many different typefaces, sizes, and attributes. This trend toward desktop publishing features in word processing programs has been accentuated by the arrival of Word for Windows, WordPerfect for Windows, and other graphically based word processors.

Unless the word processing program is being used for final page layout, the use of fonts and other design features should be kept to a minimum, with all formatting applied in the page layout program. Wherever possible, any tagging instructions used to format the text should be inserted from within the word processing package, often with the use of keyboard macros, which automate repetitive tasks by recording and playing back sequences of keystrokes.

For graphics and imaging programs the major formats include:

.PS	PostScript;
.EPS	Encapsulated PostScript;
.PICT	Macintosh picture;
.PICT2	Macintosh color picture;
.TIFF	Tag Image File Format;
.CGM	Computer Graphics Metafile;
.WMF	Windows Metafile;
.TGA	Targa;
.BMP	Windows Bitmap.

For transferring drawings and images within the Macintosh environment, the PICT2 format works well and is widely supported. For photographic images, the TIFF format now dominates, and is widely used both with desktop scanners and for image files created with high-end scanners.

For transporting illustrations between programs, the encapsulated PostScript (EPS) format is often the most effective, and is supported by most of the drawing packages.

**A note on
PostScript and
EPS**

Virtually all graphics programs allow you to import and export files in the Encapsulated PostScript (EPS) format. Alternately you can direct the output from any application to a disk file rather than a communications port, a procedure known as *printing to disk*. An illustration exported as an EPS file includes much of the same code as the illustration printed to disk, but with a few important differences:

- A PostScript file printed to disk contains all the information needed by any PostScript printer to produce the desired graphic or page, including page size information, fonts and TIFF image files, a header used by the printer, and, in some PostScript files created on the Mac, a copy of the Apple LaserPrep file.

- By contrast, EPS files are used primarily to transfer graphics between different software programs. They cannot be printed directly because they do not contain page setup information or fonts, may or may not have the necessary TIFF files, and do not contain headers. Also, unlike PostScript files printed to disk, EPS files may or may not contain a PICT (for Mac) or TIFF (for MS-DOS or OS/2) screen image of the illustration.

**Transforming
dots into lines**

All scanned graphics are stored as bitmaps. One problem that has proven costly and time-consuming for catalog publishers and others whose documents contain many images is of converting these bitmaps to line-art files, a job that can be extremely tedious and time-consuming, but that must be done to produce graphics that can be modified or enhanced, or that will print smoothly at high resolutions.

One way to do this is to load the scanned image into the draw package and manually trace over each line in the image. Although some designers prefer the handcrafted approach, most take advantage of the auto-trace function built into all major graphics programs that automates this otherwise Herculean task. Auto-trace routines compare the values of adjacent pixels in a bitmap image, then connect pixels with similar of equivalent values into discrete line and curve elements.

For the most part, images are traced in black-and-white or grayscale only. The resulting graphics can be quickly filled with any color, tint, or pattern. Color TIFF files can be imported and auto-traced to create colored line-art graphics. For those with more advanced auto-tracing requirements, Corel Trace (PC only) and Adobe Streamline 2 (Mac and PC) provide refinements such as batch image conversion and the ability to compensate for slightly skewed lines.

Layers

When working with oil paints, watercolors, or many of the other traditional media, an artist can make subtle changes based on an understanding of how underlying colors will be affected when new colors are placed on top. But PostScript illustration works in opaque layers, from back to front.

Figure 6-5
By breaking a drawing into multiple layers, you can more easily isolate and control the individual elements.

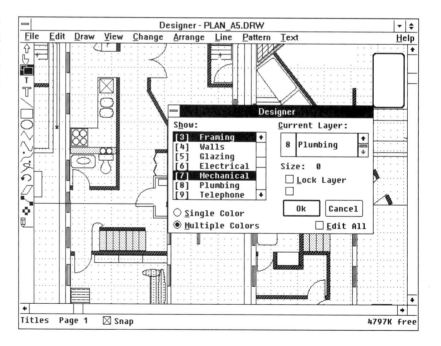

Each object is displayed and printed as if it's on a separate layer, in front of or behind all other objects in the drawing. In other words, an object on top (unless it's transparent) completely obscures whatever lies beneath it; therefore, as an artist you must think in terms of opaque paint, rather than transparent watercolors.

Paths

PostScript paths are collections of lines and curves. They can be open (having two end points) or closed (completing themselves, with no endpoints). A PostScript path can be *stroked* (drawn) and filled with a color or pattern, or can be used to mask other graphic elements.

In most draw programs, paths are created with a freehand brush tool, with a polyline tool, or with any tool that operates like a paintbrush or pencil. Individual anchor points can be selected and joined by straight lines or curves.

Paths are defined according to *Bézier curves*, named for the French mathematician who worked out the original calculations for drawing complex shapes (as an exercise in theoretical sheet-metal construction for his employer, the French car manufacturer Renault).

As shown in Figure 6-6, a Bézier curve can be modified after it's drawn by relocating individual anchor points, or by dragging the handles attached to each anchor point. Moving the handles changes the angle at which the line approaches the anchor point. Bézier curves are an important tool for the artist, because the shapes look much more fluid than in previous kinds of computer drawings.

Figure 6-6
Bézier curves allow you to create and modify all kinds of shapes.

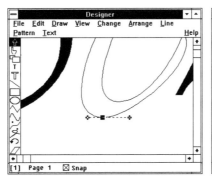 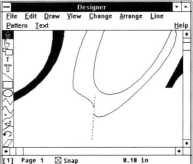

Printing complex illustrations

The number of segments that PostScript needs to represent a path depends on the complexity of the path, the size, number, and sharpness of curves, and the resolution of your printer. A path that requires more line segments than PostScript can handle (with available memory) will produce a "limitcheck" error that prevents your graphic from printing. To overcome a limitcheck error, or to speed up printing, change the settings to increase the *flatness* of complex elements in illustrations, or add more memory to your system.

Flatness controls the number of segments that make up the path of an object. By increasing flatness, you are reducing the quality of the curve. Flatness applies only to graphic elements, not to imported EPS files. The flatness required to print a complex path with acceptable quality depends on the resolution of your printer. For a specific graphic at a given flatness setting, printing to a high-resolution imagesetter produces a much smoother image than printing to a desktop laser printer.

In some programs, such as Corel Draw, you can set the flatness default in a Print dialog box, while in FreeHand or Illustrator you specify the default flatness by opening or creating the UserPrep file and appending "/df n def" to the end of the file, where *n* is the default flatness setting.

Chokes and spreads

Because draw programs permit you to control a path and its stroke and fill with such precision, they are excellent for creating "color traps" between adjacent areas of different colors.

Chapter 3, on Color Quality, discussed the necessity of trapping color objects to compensate for mis-registration on the printing press. One can understand why colors don't always align perfectly when they're being printed at speeds often in excess of 10,000 sheets per hour. The ability to create custom colors of specific CMYK values is essential to building good traps, as is the ability to modify the color and thickness of the stroke around any object.

The best trap value varies with a number of factors, so it is always best to check with your printing company. Indeed, some printers rarely use trapping and ask their customers not to add it. The following table shows the usual range of trap thickness required for a number of common printing situations.

Type of paper	Minimum	Maximum
Sheet-fed offset of stable coated stock	.1 pt	.3 pt
Sheet-fed offset of large uncoated stock	.5 pt	.8 pt
Offset web on newsprint	.4 pt	.7 pt
Quickprint, Multi	.3 pt	1.0 pt
Flexographic Web	.7 pt	5.0 pt
Screen-printed t-shirt	1.0 pt	5.0 pt

These values must be doubled when specifying line weights, because PostScript-language graphics programs draw lines that straddle the paths of objects. To achieve a 0.25-point choke on either side of a line, you must specify a 0.5-point line. This ensures that half the width of the line will be inside the object, and half will be outside.

Figure 6-7
You can construct a trap in a draw program by changing the thickness of a stroke.

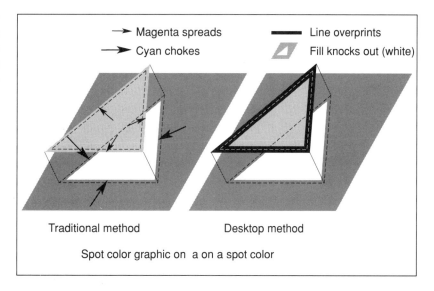

When trapping four-color type on top of four-color art, the way you achieve the trap depends on the overall size of the type. For large or heavy text, take the *highest* values of CMYK of each of the text and background colors, and use them to create a third color to apply to the stroke.

For small or finely detailed type, the color of the trap must be selected to help the characters retain their shape. To do this, create a new process color that includes only the CMYK values that are higher in the lighter area than in the darker area.

Take the example of a light-colored letter against a dark-colored background, as shown in Figure 6-8. The lighter color is made of 0% cyan, 10% magenta, 70% yellow, and 0% black. The darker color is made of 40% cyan, 80% magenta, 20% yellow, and 0% black. Because only the yellow is higher in the lighter area than the darker area, the new color for this stroke would be 0% cyan, 0% magenta, 70% yellow, and 0% black.

Figure 6-8
Trapping four-color text against a four-color background

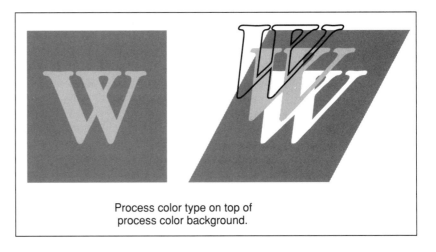

Process color type on top of
process color background.

Note that because a computer monitor can't replicate the transparency of printing inks, trapping effects will not be visible on screen. (Future graphics software may simulate this effect, so the designer can preview the trapping without making a proof.) There is further information on trapping in the sections of this chapter devoted to individual graphics packages.

Spot color and process color

You can assign color values to objects as you draw them or after you have finished the linework, using either the process color system or spot colors. When working with process colors, you assign percentages of cyan, magenta, yellow, and black to objects in the illustration, often with the help of color tint books available from graphic arts supply stores.

If you are debating whether to use spot or process color when both are available, keep in mind that the overall objective is to produce as few negatives as possible. Thus if your document contains only two colors, it will be slightly cheaper to produce with spot color, but if you have defined 37 different colors it makes more sense to use the four-color process so that you have four negatives rather than 37.

All the major draw programs now support the PANTONE MATCHING SYSTEM, and some have begun to support other color specification systems including Trumatch and Focoltone.

To use the color matching feature, determine the ink color you want in a swatch book, such as the PANTONE Color Formula Guide 747XR (available from graphic arts supply stores). When you specify a PANTONE Color on screen, your monitor will attempt to display the closest match based on lookup tables for each kind of display. If you are printing spot color overlays, your printing company will mix the appropriate ink, based on the labels you assign each layer (such as "Dark green PMS 343").

When working with process color, you can create custom colors, either by specifying their CMYK values or by fiddling with the color controls in any of the other color models your software supports, then converting back to CMYK. If you use certain colors regularly, create a document that contains all these colors. As long as that document is open, you can use the colors in other documents.

Color blends and fills

To maximize the quality and reduce banding in blends and fills, there are five main factors that can be adjusted. For the best possible results, especially when blends and fills are an important part of an illustration:

- use a high-resolution output device, preferably one of 2,000 dpi or better;
- reduce the screen frequency to produce 256 shades of gray;
- increase the change in tint values between the beginning and ending tints in a fill;
- reduce the distance over which the blend extends;
- use the highest available resolution settings when printing your files, to take advantage of the maximum number of shades permitted by the available screen ruling and printer resolution.

With blend functions that allow you to control the number of steps, there are two equations for finding the optimal number for producing smooth gradations. First, calculated the number of tints available for a 0-100% color change by dividing the printer resolution (in dpi) by the screen frequency (in lpi). Second, multiply this number by the desired percentage change in color to determine the optimal number of steps to use in the blend.

From these equations, you can conclude that:

- to take maximum advantage of the number of tints available, you must use a step for each tint;
- using more steps than there are tints available doesn't improve the look of the blend, but does increase the file size and therefore the print time;
- using a printer with higher resolution increases the number of tints available and, therefore, increases the potential smoothness of the blend;

- if you have control of screen frequency, increasing the frequency always decreases the number of tints available, thereby decreasing the potential smoothness of the blend;

- decreasing the screen frequency increases the number of tints available; however, it also increases the coarseness of the printed artwork;

- increasing the percentage change in a color always increases the optimal number of steps in the blend, and therefore improves the likelihood it will print smoothly.

To sum up: at 2,400 dpi, you have access to 256 shades with a 150 lpi screen, which is fine for most color work.

Halftone screen rulings

All the major graphics packages provide control over the screen ruling of the halftone pattern that will be used to print the separations. The default settings and available choices will depend on the output device and PostScript printer device file you are currently using.

When using a desktop laser printer with 300 dpi resolution, there will always be a trade-off between the screen ruling and the number of gray shades available. A screen ruling of 60 lpi (less than the 75 lpi used in most newspapers) gives you a halftone dot with a 5-pixel-by-5-pixel matrix, for a total of 26 possible shades of gray (including white, or no pixels). If the screen ruling is increased to 100 lpi to improve detail, the dot matrix is reduced to 3 pixels by 3 pixels, for a total of 10 possible gray shades.

Crop and registration marks

All major graphics (and page layout) programs allow you to place crop marks defining the trimmed page boundaries when you print your graphics, with registration marks to maintain precise alignment between each separation. Most also allow you to select options that print the name of each color, and in some cases the time and date, on each separation.

Adobe Illustrator

Adobe Illustrator is one of the leading drawing programs on the Macintosh. Version 3 of Illustrator lets you create color illustrations using the four process colors, the PANTONE MATCHING SYSTEM, or other ink colors that you create. Using the built-in Adobe Separator utility, you can print these as negatives that a commercial printer can use to print color reproductions of your work.

You can preview color illustrations (in up to 24-bit color), work with Adobe Photoshop files, and import Encapsulated PostScript (EPS) language files.

Adobe Illustrator and most other draw programs work noticeably faster when color display is turned off and the monitor is set for two levels of gray. Colors can still be assigned to objects, and you can turn on color display again when you are ready to preview your work.

Before beginning work with Adobe Illustrator, calibrate your monitor and output devices as shown in Figure 6-9. For best results, make sure the Control Panel is set for 256 colors (rather than 16), and wait at least 20 minutes after turning on the display monitor before calibrating.

Figure 6-9
Progressive colors show the appearance of progressive combinations of ink.

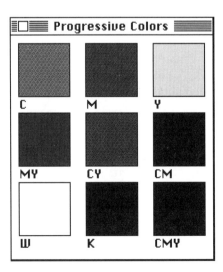

By selecting Change Progressive Colors from the Edit Preferences dialog box, you can view and modify color values for the cyan, magenta, and yellow primaries, and for their combinations—MY, CY, CM, and CMY. You can also edit the white value in order to match the color of the paper stock being used.

For each color and combination, compare the on-screen color chart to the printed color bar or other color samples. If the colors displayed on the monitor closely match the colors on the print sample, no adjustment is necessary. If the colors do not match, click on the box containing the color or color combination that needs adjusting.

The color can be adjusted in three ways:

- by dragging the white color-adjustment dot that appears inside the color wheel, which changes the hue and saturation but does not affect the selected color's brightness;

- by clicking on the arrows or dragging the box in the scroll bar that appears to the right of the color wheel, which changes the selected color's brightness but does not affect hue or saturation;

- by clicking on the arrows next to the Hue, Saturation, and Brightness fields or the Red, Green, and Blue color fields, or entering specific values between 0 and 65,535 in these fields.

As discussed in Chapter 1 on experiencing color, there are inevitable differences between the screen and the printed page, but the calibration process gives a better idea of how colors will look.

As shown in Figure 6-10 custom colors appear in the Paint dialog box when they have been created, listed alphabetically with the other custom colors, and can be used just like any other color.

Colors are saved with the documents in which they were created and become part of the list of colors available in that document. As long as the document in which you created the custom color is open, you can assign the color to objects in other documents.

Figure 6-10
You create custom
colors in Illustrator's
Paint dialog box, and
save them with
documents.

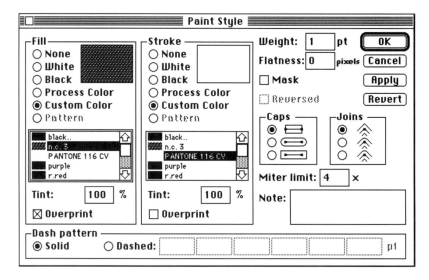

Although custom colors are made by specifying their process color components, there is only one negative, not four, when the separation for that color is printed. (Your commercial printer will mix the inks to your specifications before printing the document.) To convert a custom color back to its process color components, use the convert-to-process feature in Adobe Separator.

Illustrator was one of the first programs to provide overprint and trap control, to compensate for registration errors created on press. If any areas of the image touch, you may need to add trap—overprint them slightly to prevent tiny gaps from appearing when the document is printed.

Trap control

In PostScript, objects that overlap one another are automatically masked ("knocked out"), so that the object on the bottom does not print where another object overlaps it. This is usually the way you want your artwork to appear.

Adobe Illustrator allows you to control overprinting—printing one color on top of another. To create special effects, you may want to overprint a specific color, which can be selected from the Style menu Paint dialog box.

The overprint feature is especially useful for adding traps. In the print shop, traps are normally created with photographic chokes and spreads, but because you are printing your files directly to film, traps (if desired) must be produced by using the overprint feature.

To trap a colored object that is sitting on top of another colored object:

- select the topmost object, and select Paint from the Style menu;

- if the object already has a stroke value, simply click on the Overprint checkbox in the Stroke option group;

- if the object has a fill value but no stroke value, click on the Process Color or Custom Color button, as appropriate, in the Stroke options;

- enter the same process color percentages or select the appropriate custom color to match the settings in the Fill options;

- highlight the Weight field, and enter a value between 0.8 (a thin trap) and 1.4 (a thick trap);

- click in the Overprint checkbox in the Stroke option group, but not in the Fill option group, then click OK.

When overlapping objects are assigned more than one color, only the colors that are not common to both objects are affected by the overprint feature. Colors that are common to both objects print as they normally would, with the topmost object masking the object beneath it. Because the monitor has no way of representing overprint colors, the trap does not appear on screen. It will, however, appear in the final printed results.

Editable PostScript

Hidden within the technical wizardry of Illustrator 3 is a possible solution to a major computer graphics problem: how documents can be exchanged between computer systems, especially those with dissimilar architectures. This is a crucial long-term issue for desktop publishing in color.

If only the raw content of the text of a document is required, without any formatting whatsoever, it can be boiled down to ASCII text and easily passed from one system to another. On the other hand, to treat the document as a high-resolution graphic for output on a distant computer system, it can be sent as a PostScript file. Unfortunately, the text represented by the PostScript file can't be edited without going back to the original application in which it was created. This makes it virtually impossible to make last-minute changes to the document.

One potential solution is editable PostScript. Previous versions of Illustrator could work only with text blocks smaller than 256 characters, and every character in the block had to be the same font. With version 3, Adobe's software engineers were able to provide directly editable text of any length, with individual formatting possible for each character. More important, they found a way to store both the content of the text and the PostScript outline code for each character.

Although this technology has not matured, it may represent an important direction in software design, leading to a more transparent way for people to exchange format-rich editable documents. Other industry groups are working on the same problem; these include a task force that is defining a Program Interchange Language (PIL) to enable people to embed graphic objects within other programs.

Adobe Separator

Adobe Illustrator documents that contain color can be printed as four-color and spot-color separations using the Adobe Separator utility that comes with Illustrator. The first time you run the program, Separator will ask you to open a PostScript file and a PostScript Printer Description (PPD) file.

Before the Adobe Separator program separates a document, it reads the specified PPD file, which provides information about the dot resolution, available page sizes, color support, screen rulings, and other parameters of your printer.

PPD files for various printers are supplied with Adobe Illustrator. Be sure to select the PPD file that matches the printer or imagesetter that will be using to print your files. (PPD files are text files containing PostScript language instructions, and can be modified by someone competent in programming with the PostScript language.) To ensure that the needed PPD file is always available (which speeds up the separation process), save a copy of the PPD file in the folder that contains your drawings.

Figure 6-11
The Adobe Separator dialog box gives you control over which inks print and whether or not they overprint.

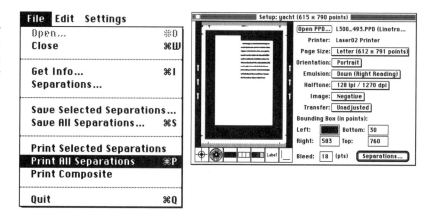

Separator contains a number of features that are handy for printing color-separation negatives; it displays the size of the *bounding box* (the outside dimensions of an illustration), and lets the user change the size. The trim marks and registration marks normally appear just outside the bounding box, but this can be changed by altering the dimensions of the bounding box.

The Separator dialog box allows you to print all the color-separation negatives using the default settings or custom settings. You may select one or any combination of color negs to be printed, or convert custom colors into their closest process color equivalents.

If your printer can selectively change the page size, Separator permits modifications to the page width and height in one-point increments. You can add offset (which moves the page away from the right edge of the printed sheet), and specify that the page is to be printed transverse (rotated 90°). Combining offset and transverse when outputting to an imagesetter packs three pages onto the same area of film usually used for just two, and avoids wasting expensive film.

Figure 6-12

Color separation negatives created in Adobe Illustrator, with registration marks, tint bars, star target, and dot gain indicator

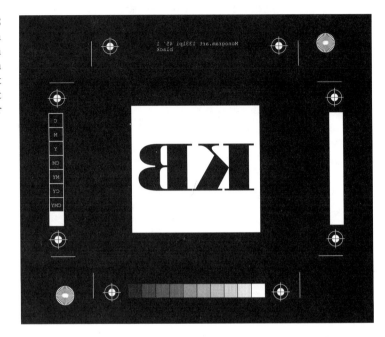

Each separation can be printed with registration marks, color bars, crop marks, and labels, plus a star target (for registration and image resolution), and a graduated screen (to check color accuracy and dot gain on the press).

When the Option key is held down while you are in the Separation dialog box, the Print One button changes to read Save One, enabling you to save individual separations to disk as PostScript language files. This makes it possible to print a very complex color graphic as four smaller files, which may be more easily transported to an imagesetter or service bureau.

Aldus FreeHand

Aldus FreeHand version 3 provides many of the capabilities of Adobe Illustrator, and adds a few of its own. For many users, a key advantage is that it can be used to draw and edit in the actual image, rather than in a wire-frame "preview" version that lacks color fills and patterns. You can create custom colors in the Library dialog box in the Color menu.

Figure 6-13
You can select colors in the RGB, CMYK, and PANTONE models.

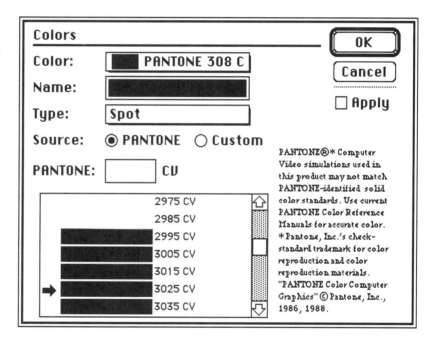

FreeHand lets you construct your drawing on more than 64 layers, which is helpful when working with a variety of custom colors. In addition to its built-in palettes of fill and line styles, FreeHand permits custom PostScript fills and lines to be specified by entering PostScript code in a dialog box. You can also add comments to the PostScript code as an illustration is created, so that when the code for the drawing is printed, each graphic element can be easily identified.

If you save your illustration as a template, it can easily be used as the starting point for other illustrations, with the same settings for artwork, lines, fills, and color styles already specified. A template can be opened, just as you open other illustrations.

Figure 6-14
FreeHand provides complete control over fill and line patterns, which makes it ideal for creating color traps.

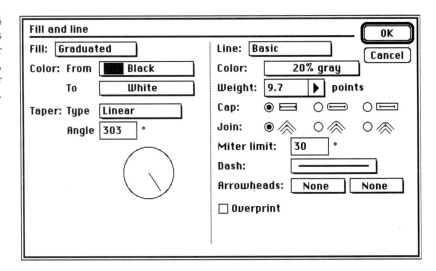

FreeHand supports spot color, including PANTONE Colors, and process color. Creating colored gradient fills in FreeHand is straightforward. Fills can be linear, logarithmic, or radial, and the angle of a fill can be specified. Gradients can blend between any two colors (or any two shades of gray).

Trapping

FreeHand lets you specify the color and thickness of strokes, so the outline of a letter can have a different color than its inside fill. This comes in handy for setting color traps to compensate for mis-registrations on press.

FreeHand's Element Info dialog box, its mathematical information bar, cloning feature, and overall positioning accuracy all work together in creating precise trap widths and alignment. You can also specify which colors overprint and which are knocked out, and can save user-defined fill and line styles for future use. For really finicky work, the Paste Inside feature ensures that graduated fills are positioned exactly inside the thin band of the trap.

When printing a FreeHand file that includes objects filled with White, you should note that the default White always knocks out of all other colors. FreeHand's default White is not a printing ink; it's the total absence of ink, which you can think of as the color of the paper. Because this white isn't an ink, it can't have an overlay, so it can't overprint other inks.

To produce a white that will overprint, one must be created. The default White can't be edited or removed, so use the Spot Color command to create a new color called something like "Snow white," which results in a white overlay that will overprint.

FreeHand's default White color also comes in handy when trapping a spot-color rule on top of a process color. One way to achieve this trap is to clone the line, reduce the size of the clone by a small amount (about 0.25 point) on all sides, color the clone default White, then put it directly behind the original rule. Because FreeHand's White automatically knocks out anything beneath it, the clone will produce the necessary knockout.

Custom PostScript fills

A wide range of preset line and fill options are built into FreeHand, but even more variety can be achieved by selecting the PostScript command in the Fill or Line menus. To create unique fill and line styles, enter PostScript code directly into the PostScript dialog box.

FreeHand comes with a good selection of predefined PostScript effects, but you are free to create your own, limited only by your capabilities as a PostScript programmer. PostScript lines and fills will not display on screen, but will print as described by the PostScript code. Note that complex fill patterns can take a very long time to output, especially on high-resolution devices.

Exporting from FreeHand to other applications

The Export command in the File menu enables you to export your FreeHand illustrations for use in other applications, in the form of an Encapsulated PostScript (EPS) file.

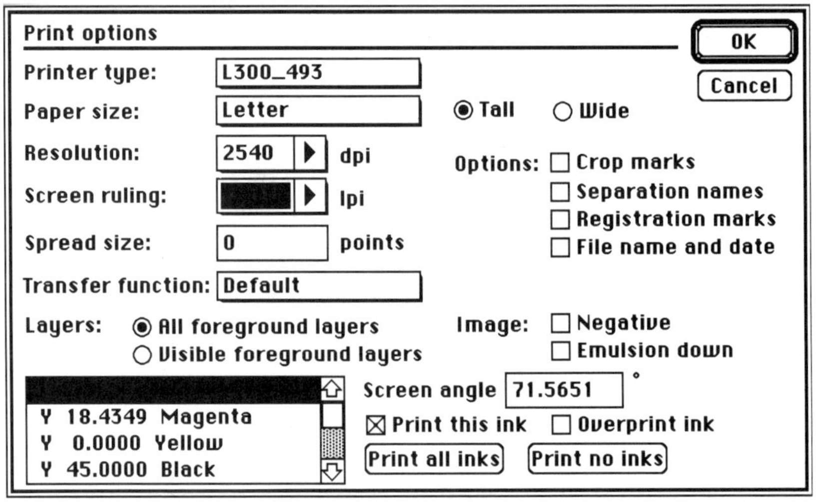

Figure 6-15
FreeHand lets you
control the parameters
for creating color
separations of your
work.

FreeHand is also capable of exporting an illustration as a PICT file with embedded PostScript. This enables you to paste the graphic in an application that does not support EPS. Because the PICT file contains embedded PostScript, the printer has the necessary information to print the graphic clearly.

To export a PICT file with embedded PostScript, select all or parts of the illustration, then press the Option key while choosing Cut or Copy from the Edit menu. This stores the selected elements in the clipboard, from which they can be pasted into another application.

When exporting from FreeHand, select the picture format appropriate to your needs. If you do not need a screen representation of the EPS illustration, select "None," and the image will appear on screen as an EPS bounding box only, but the actual illustration will print.

If you select the Macintosh picture format, a PICT screen version of the illustration is bundled along with the EPS file, which can be displayed by other Mac applications. Selecting the IBM PC option bundles a TIFF screen version with the EPS graphic.

Color separations

In the Print dialog box on the File menu, select Separations to tell FreeHand to print one page for each process color or one for each spot color. Click on "Composite proof" when printing to a color printer, or if you want to print all colors in black and shades of gray on a single page, so you can see all your illustration at once.

The Screen Ruling field in the Print options dialog box lets you use the default screen ruling settings (85, 100, 120, 133, and 150 lines per inch) or set custom screen rulings.

The Transfer function under Print options tells FreeHand how to match the densities of colors from the screen to their densities on the printed page. There are three density options:

- the Default option, which approximates what appears on the screen by quickly printing a 1:1 match, sufficient for general-purpose printing;
- the Normalize option, which matches color densities that might otherwise vary when you print the proof and final copies of an illustration on different printers—a 10 percent tint on a high-resolution imagesetter looks much lighter than a 10 percent tint printed on a desktop laser printer, and Normalize compensates for this difference;
- the Posterize option, in which FreeHand converts tints to one of four values (black, white, and two intermediate shades of gray), in order to create special effects.

Corel Draw

Corel Draw, from Corel Systems Corp., has a reputation among its users for being an intuitive and well-designed program that offers especially strong typographic effects. These include the ability to automatically align a string of text along a freehand curve, or to treat any character as a graphic that can be edited, enhanced, and saved.

Adobe PostScript font outlines are supported, as are fonts from most other foundries. Corel Draw also comes bundled with more than 3,000 clip art images from a dozen major vendors, and provides access to their complete libraries of more than 25,000 images. Draw supports RGB, HSB, CMYK, and PANTONE spot colors, and can output color separations on any PostScript printer.

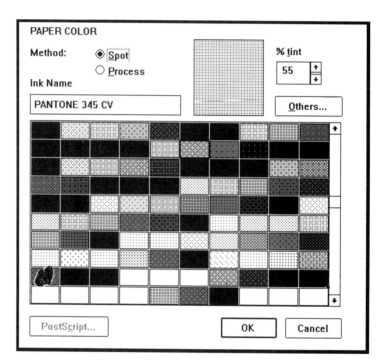

Figure 6-16
Corel Draw lets you specify colors in any of the main color models.

When creating illustrations, Corel Draw permits you to transfer the color of an object's outline and fill to a new object. When printing to a PostScript device, Draw also makes it possible to specify the number of steps for blends and set the halftone screen frequency to minimize banding (the appearance of unsightly steps or stripes).

Because Corel Draw uses the PostScript halftone screen function to create color separations, the screen function cannot be used to create special effects for spot colors. If a non-default screen function has been set for any CMYK objects, it is ignored. Separations will still print, but they won't include any special halftone screen effects.

To accurately specify colors with a program such as Draw, it's important to calibrate the output to the screen. When using a color PostScript printer, print the COLORBAR.CDR file from Draw's Samples subdirectory, then print the same file to disk and have it separated. Have a Cromalin or other proof made from the separations, and compare both with the colors as displayed on the screen. Better still, create your own test file with the process shades, blends, and other effects you most commonly use.

Spot and process colors can be mixed in a single image, and spot colors can be separated into their cyan, magenta, yellow, and black components, or output as an additional page for each spot color.

Corel includes extensive file import capabilities, including Adobe Illustrator EPS, AutoCAD DXF, GEM, CGM, Mac PICT, PCX, TIF, and Windows bitmaps (BMP), and works with the new 256-color displays. Corel graphics can be exported in a variety of formats, including EPS, Windows Metafile, CGM, GEM, VideoShow PIC, and SCODL (for slide film recorders). Corel Draw can also export files to the Macintosh in PICT2 or Illustrator format, and to IBM mainframes as PIF files (which can be translated to GDF format on the host).

Micrografx Designer

Micrografx Designer, from Micrografx, Inc., offers an extremely broad set of features with good color support, especially when the optional PANTONE spot color palette is added to the built-in RGB, HLS, and CMYK palettes.

Custom colors can be produced, and then saved and retrieved as custom palettes. Designer supports colored scanned images as

PCX or TIF files, which can automatically be traced and converted to editable color graphics.

Figure 6-17
Micrografx Designer
provides full-featured
color selection with
24-bit color PCs.

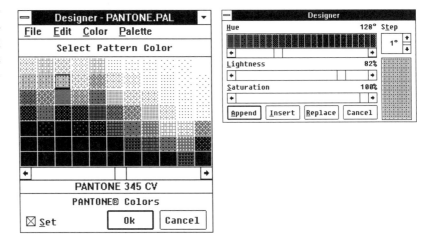

To prepare for high-resolution professional reproduction, Designer lets you print drawings as color separations, either as spot color or four-color process printing, complete with page labels, crop marks, and registration marks. Spot color and process color separations can be combined in the same printout. As shown in Figure 6-18, the screen angle for each of the CMYK separations must be precisely set, and the line screen selected that is appropriate to the paper and press being used.

Some of Designer's advanced color features, such as its ability to control the spread or overlap of different colors, are available only if the Micrografx version of the PostScript driver (MGXPS.DRV) has been installed. This driver, which is included with Designer, supersedes the one Microsoft provides with Windows, and increases speed and improves control of printing.

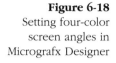

Figure 6-18
Setting four-color
screen angles in
Micrografx Designer

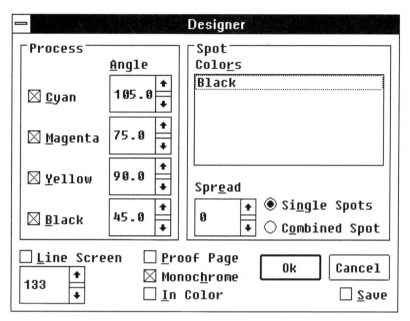

Arts & Letters

A third contender among Windows-based graphics programs is
Arts & Letters, from Computer Support Corporation, which distin-
guishes itself by using the metaphor of composition rather than
drawing. Arts & Letters comes with a library of more than 15,000
elements, or *artforms*, which can be combined into very complex graphics.

For example, instead of presenting ready-made clip-art illustrations of people, the program comes with a portrait gallery of
different head shapes, facial structures, hair, and so on, that
enable the professional artist or amateur to create a seemingly
infinite number of portraits. Composing an illustration in Arts &
Letters involves three steps:

- load all the symbols for the drawing onto the screen and
  color them to your specifications;

- compose your drawing by sizing, moving, and duplicating symbols;
- add depth by shading and blending various symbols.

Arts & Letters supports the RGB, CMYK, and HLS color models, and allows the user to define custom color palettes. Named color mixes can be included as styles, along with specific line and fill attribute settings, so that all these attributes may be applied instantly. Files can be imported (as 24-bit color) from TIF, PCX, GIF, and Targa formats.

Arts & Letters, at least in its current release, can perform color separations of graphics—but not of scanned images. You can select spot or process color separations, and specify the screen frequency and angle.

Drawing conclusions

Desktop drawing tools have opened a world of graphic creativity to a large audience, many of them people without formal artistic training. The ability to draw any shape, to color it any way, and to combine it with existing electronic artwork provides countless new possibilities for expression.

At the same time, these tools have revolutionized the work of professional illustrators. Never before have they had such a rich palette of tools, and never before have they been so intimately involved with producing the finished piece, not just creating it. The results of these trends are beginning to be seen everywhere, in advertising, industrial design, and fine art.

These drawing tools are essential because they provide the raw material for many of the illustrations that are created and separated on the desktop. During the next few years, these drawing programs will continue to evolve as creative tools for color publishers.

Desktop Color Imaging

"By convention there is color, by convention sweetness, by convention bitterness, but in reality there are only atoms and space."

DEMOCRITUS, CIRCA 400 B.C.

Images—photographs—are the most challenging aspect of color prepress.

Having examined drawing programs, in which lines and curves are used to create illustrations, we now explore the other visual domain, imaging, in which images are constructed from individual picture elements, or *pixels*. Be sure to read Chapter 5, which discusses the fundamentals of scanning, prior to reading this chapter.

It makes no sense to debate whether (pixel-based) images are better than (curve-based) graphics, because there is such diversity among the kinds of visuals you can create with each. In general, graphics programs are the best for many kinds of drawings, illustrations, and logos. Image programs enable you to paint with brushes and are essential for working with scanned photographs.

Painting on the desktop

All imaging programs operate by manipulating the pixels that make up an image. Within most programs, there are two main ways of working with pixels: you can scan and enhance existing artwork, or "paint" pictures "from scratch" with tools that mimic and extend the traditional artist's palette of brushes and colors. Some specialized programs perform only one part of the overall process, while others cover the entire image gamut from scanning to painting, enhancement, color correction, and separation.

Figure 7-1
The tool box in an imaging program, such as Adobe Photoshop, includes functions for selecting and modifying color pictures.

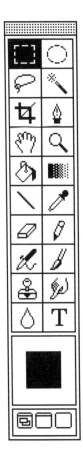

Digital painting tools have evolved to the point where artists and illustrators are putting down their brushes and picking up a pressure-sensitive stylus. When you paint in a pixel-based program, you change the colors of pixels. The number of colors available at one time depends on the amount of color information available for each pixel. On an eight-bit color system, you work with a palette of up to 256 different colors at one time. On a 24- or 32-bit system, you have a palette of more than 16-million *possible* colors, although no display system can show this many simultaneously.

A pixel-perfect toolbox

There is an overlap of tools and features between the leading imaging programs; most include:

- selection tools, such as the lasso (for selecting arbitrary shapes) and the rectangular and elliptical marquees (for selecting regular shapes);

- viewing tools, including the grabber (for scrolling through the image) and the zoom tool (for zooming in to do detailed work);

- fill tools, such as the paint bucket and the blend tool;

- painting tools, including the pencil, the line, the paint brush, the airbrush, and the rubber stamp (or clone) tool;

- editing tools, such as the cropping tool and eraser, plus effects including blur, sharpen, and smudge;

- a text tool, for adding text to an image.

Magic wands

In addition to the marquee and lasso selection tools, imaging programs often contain a *magic wand* tool that can be enormously useful when working with pictures: it allows the user to automatically select most irregularly shaped objects by using the changes in pixel values to recognize the boundaries between a foreground object and its background.

Clicking the wand on a particular color tells the program to select all adjacent pixels that are the same or similar color. By changing the sensitivity of the wand, you can control the extent to which neighboring pixels are included in the selection area. Once an area is selected, it can be cut, copied, or otherwise modified.

Figure 7-2
A magic wand tool lets you quickly select an irregularly shaped object based on the brightness of adjacent pixels.

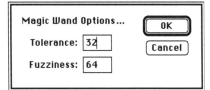

Brushes

How might Raphael, Rembrandt, or Monet have used the electronic paintbrushes in an imaging program? You can choose virtually any color, and create custom palettes of exactly the shades you desire. You can apply electronic paint with brushes that mimic traditional bristles, even to the point of simulating the effects of fade-out and drying.

Figure 7-3
Paint brushes

In ColorStudio, for instance, you can define your own "computed" pens, with control over variations in pen shape, paint spread, and even the rate of "animation" over which the radius of the pen stroke changes. A computed pen is a specification rather than a set pattern; it allows the user to vary the size and paint transparency from one state to another and back again during a single stroke. Computed pens are especially useful for giving work a "painterly" feel, especially when they are used with a pressure-sensitive stylus, rather than a mouse.

You can even select a set of pixels from an image and use it as a custom paintbrush, when you want to create a brush with a particular fixed shape or use a part of an existing image as a texture.

Type tools

You can create all kinds of wonderful colored type effects in imaging programs, but it's important to remember how they handle type. Unlike draw programs, which represent type as lines and curves, imaging programs treat type as if it's made up of pixels. As such, type is rendered at the resolution of the image (which is often lower than the resolution of your output device), and it can't be edited once placed. After you create and deselect the type, it becomes part of the image, and you can change the type only by editing the pixels that comprise the characters.

Anti-aliasing is a software technique for improving the quality of images by blending the edges of a bitmapped image into the surrounding colors. It is especially useful for hiding the sharp staircase edges often visible in bitmapped type. As shown in Figure 7-4, this makes the edges of each character seem smoother, so they blend into the background. To apply anti-aliasing to type, simply select the anti-aliased option in the Style menu. Anti-aliasing can be used only in pixel-based programs.

Figure 7-4
Bitmapped type without anti-aliasing looks jagged (left), but improves with anti-aliasing (right).

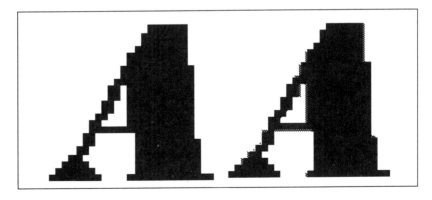

Image editing

Although imaging programs typically provide a wide range of painting tools for those wishing to create their own pictures from scratch, the primary use of most imaging software is for working with scanned photographs. The software can be used with photographs:

- to *enhance* images to make them clearer, or more easily reproduced;
- to *modify* images to create artificial visual worlds.

Before jumping into imaging, it's wise to keep in mind that many image manipulation operations take a long time, even on the fastest computer: be patient if your system seems to be preoccupied. And be prepared to use the Undo command to cancel the effects of a change that is in the wrong direction. If you save frequently, especially with incremental file names for each new version, you will be able to use a Revert command to dump the file you're working on and start anew with the previous version of the file.

A photograph is often enhanced by cutting away, or *cropping,* the image, or by changing its brightness and contrast to emphasize highlights or reveal detail. You can go further and create a composite image, bringing together bits and pieces from a variety of other pictures through the use of cutting, pasting, and cloning tools.

Color correction

There are many kinds of corrections you can apply to the color values in an image, to address disparities between the original or scanned image and the one you want to display and print. Color correction also allows you to compensate for deficiencies inherent in four-color reproduction: varying contrast between paper and ink; degradation of the original continuous-tone image as it is converted to a halftone or four-color separation; and contamination of process inks and their inability to match theoretical performance.

In addition to controlling brightness, contrast, saturation, and hue, you can make a variety of other adjustments, including equalizing the brightness values of colors, inverting colors, and converting a color image to black-and-white. When making color corrections, you will usually want to "preview" the changes on screen before applying them to your image. Although the screen may not provide a perfect representation of the corrected colors, it will at least show the direction in which color changes are being made.

One commonly applied correction is *color cast removal,* in which the hues in the image are remapped to remove effects caused by incorrect lighting in the original scene. For example, if the original was taken indoors under fluorescent lights on out-doors daylight film, the entire image will have a noticeable greenish cast.

White balance

To optimize the balance between highlight, midtone, and shadow areas, imaging programs let you specify the brightest point, or white balance, either manually or automatically. To set it manually in Photoshop or ColorStudio, select the eye-dropper (densitometer) tool, and point the cursor at one of the image's white highlights. Alternately, use the automatic white balance to let the software locate the brightest point.

Whatever the CMY values for that point (such as 1, 0, 2), they will be changed to 0 as the image is neutralized (its lightest points become pure white). The same operation can be performed to balance the black, by locating the darkest point in the image and neutralizing it with CMY values of 100, 100, and 100.

Filters

Both Photoshop and ColorStudio come with a variety of *filters*, which let you soften or sharpen the focus, apply special effects, fracture, offset, outline, or otherwise modify an image. Filters can be customized, saved, and reused with other images.

Figure 7-5
Filter menus in
Photoshop, ColorStudio

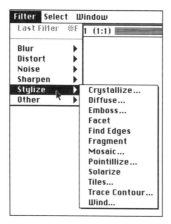
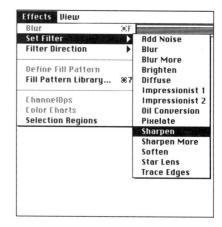

Many of the filters work by evaluating the brightness values of pixels in a selection, then changing the values. The programs typically work with one pixel at a time, evaluating its brightness relative to surrounding pixels and calculating its new brightness value, then moving on to the next pixel in the image.

Figure 7-6
Three views of the same photograph (center) show the effects of sharpen (left) and blur filters (right).

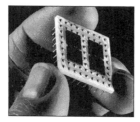
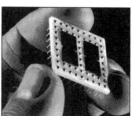
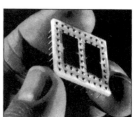

A sharpen filter, for instance, brings a selection into focus and improves image clarity by increasing the contrast between adjacent pixels. Likewise, a blur filter softens the image by reducing contrast between adjacent pixels. Photoshop also provides an unsharp mask filter that mimics the one used in traditional prepress production to enhance details in separations by producing exaggerated density at the borders of a color change.

Figure 7-7
You can apply a variety
of filters to any image,
such as Mosaic, Ripple,
Sphere, Find Edges, and
Trace Contour.

No Filter

Sphere

Mosaic

Find Edges

Ripple

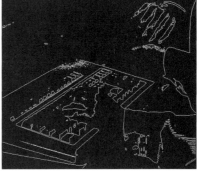

Trace Contour

Resampling

You can control the resolution of an image by *resampling* it, or changing the amount of information used in the image. Resampling allows you to discard image information that doesn't appreciably improve the output quality of the image.

The amount of information needed to produce an image depends to a large extent on the resolution at which you plan to output the image, how it was scanned, the quality you want to achieve, and the screen ruling used to produce halftones and color separations.

Figure 7-8
Resampling ignores a preset number of pixels, which provides a very good way to change the size or resolution of an image.

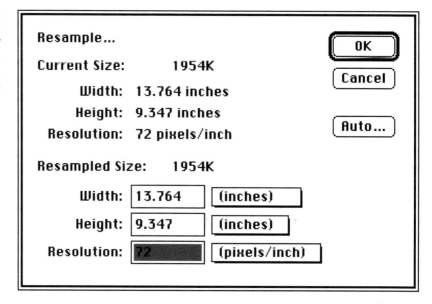

The benefit of resampling is that it allows you to work with the smallest possible file sizes, based on your device and quality requirements. Resampling can also save time if you receive *view files* from a color trade shop or service bureau to be used for position-only purposes during the design, layout, and approval process. Sometimes these files will contain far more color information than you need, because the trade shop may consider a 150 dpi image to be "position-only," even though a resolution only half this (75 dpi) is adequate for many layout purposes and results in files just one-quarter the size.

Color Separation

Traditional screen angles cause ink dots to combine together on the page into rounded shapes called rosettes.

In four-color process separation, every color in the original is broken into its cyan, magenta, yellow, and black components.

Color Proofs

A Color Key is made of four transparent layers, one for each process color, and provides low-cost proofs for color documents.

A traditional film proof such as a Cromalin offers the best color matching, but is relatively costly and requires that color separations be made beforehand.

A dye sublimation printer, such as the Kodak XL7700, provides a near-photographic quality that makes it appropriate as a proof in a number of color publication applications.

Halftoning Bitmapped Images

PostScript created digital halftones by grouping together pixels into cells; the number of pixels per inch should be about twice the screen frequency used, in lines per inch.

Changing Screen Frequencies

A series of images output at 2,000 dpi shows the effect of increasing screen frequency from 100 (left) to 130 (middle) to 150 lpi (right).
Photo by Jono Hardjowirogo

Color Trapping

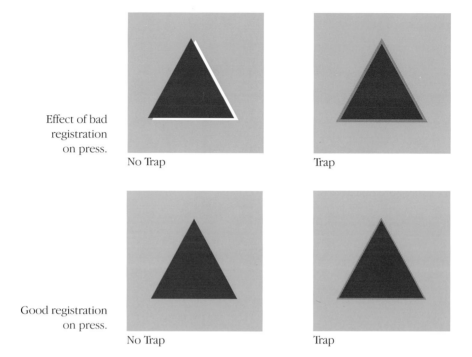

Effect of bad
registration
on press.

No Trap   Trap

Good registration
on press.

No Trap   Trap

Spot color graphic on a
spot color

Traditional method
(left)

Desktop method (right)

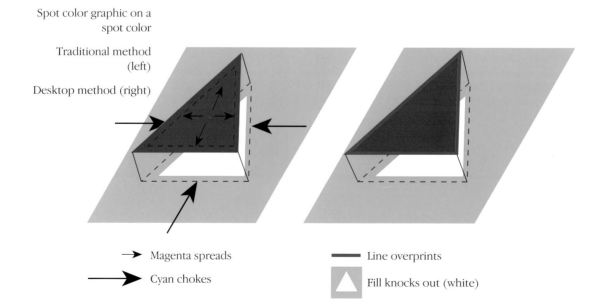

→ Magenta spreads

⟶ Cyan chokes

▬ Line overprints

◣ Fill knocks out (white)

Color Trapping
(continued)

Grayscale TIFF image
against a spot color.

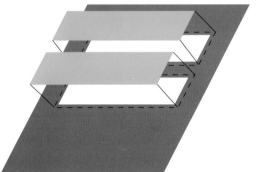

Spot color rule on
top of process color.

Process color type on
top of process color
background.

CorelDraw Art

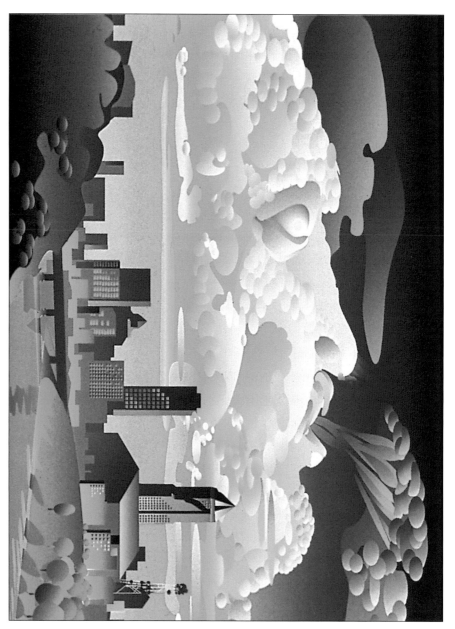

Cloudface, by Lloyd R. Hill, which won third place in the 1991 CorelDraw Design Contest.

Micrografx
Designer Art

A rough outline of a bicycle rider becomes a series of filled solids, then with complex shading becomes a realistic graphic. Created with Micrografx Designer.

**Adobe
Illustrator Art**

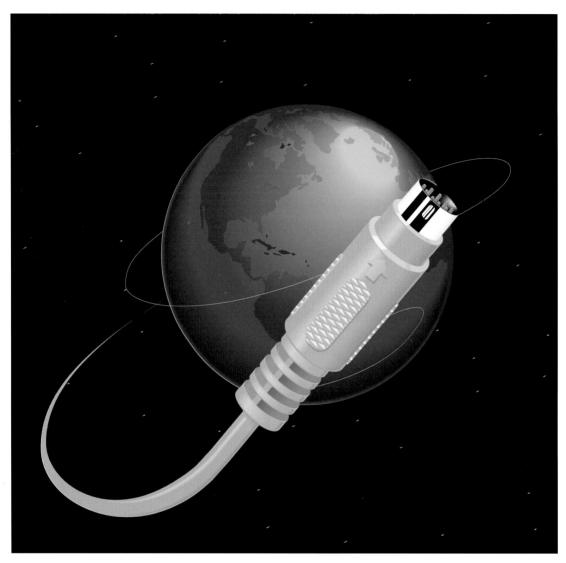

Serial World, by Courtland Shakespeare, WYSIWYG Studios—a dazzling example of what you can do with Illustrator.

It is not a good idea to resample down an image, for use on a low-resolution device such as a desktop laser printer, then resample up the same image for output to a high-resolution device. Every time you resample down, some color information in your original is deleted. If you resample up, *interpolation* is used to insert additional color information, resulting in an image that is not as sharp as the original. Interpolation fills in the missing information by comparing the color values of pixels adjacent to the pixel being calculated and averaging the results.

Drawing the line

Until now, it was convenient to make a distinction between images painted from scratch and those based on an existing photograph. Now it quickly becomes difficult to draw the line between the two. For example, adjusting the brightness or contrast of a photograph is considered a minor technical enhancement, rather than a modification of the picture content.

Figure 7-9
Changing the brightness and contrast of a photograph can bring out hidden details.

But if you change the brightness or contrast in only one region, it is easy to shift the overall message of the picture. Imaging programs allow us to do this and much more with relative ease, but in so doing they make it ever harder to precisely define the point at which a photograph becomes a painting.

Figure 7-10
A photograph can be modified electronically to resemble the brush strokes of a painting.

Color cast removal

An original photograph will sometimes have a color cast throughout, or in particular areas of the picture. Color casts can be caused by a number of factors, including improper lighting conditions and irregular processing of the film. Their presence will result in a reproduction with improper hue and contrast, and a lack of color saturation.

When assessing an original for color cast, always work with a 5,000 K lighting booth. Eastman Kodak makes a set of transparent color compensation (CC) filters that allow you to quickly determine the existence and extent of a color cast.

When color correcting an image for someone else, always check before removing a color cast during the scan, because he or she may want it partially or completely retained in order to create a certain effect. Once you've decided to remove the color cast, use the color correction filters to decide on the precise adjustment necessary, which can be applied during the scan.

The spectral sensitivity of a scanner is different than that of the human eye: the scanner sometimes confuses blue and green, leading to an image that is too blue and not green enough. The experienced color separator knows the problem, and compensates for it with the blue/green correction, in which a small amount of blue is removed during the scan and replaced with a small amount of green. You can do the same thing on the desktop.

Undercolor removal

In theory, color reproduction should be possible with just the first three process colors of cyan, magenta, and yellow. Because of unavoidable impurities in printing inks, however, in practice the use of black ink is necessary to add details and contrast.

One way to use black to best advantage is to remove some of the cyan, magenta, and yellow inks from the dark neutral areas of the reproduction to make room for a strong and rich black. This process is called undercolor removal, or UCR.

The major advantage of UCR is that it reduces the overall ink coverage on the sheet, thereby improving the ability of the sheet to hold onto the ink without smearing. A secondary benefit is that black brings out better detail and contrast in the photograph than is possible with process colors, and also increases image sharpness. Finally, the process color inks are more expensive than black, so UCR saves the printer money by reducing the amount of process ink required and substituting an appropriate amount of black.

The software used to control desktop scanners now has the ability to modify UCR, but that doesn't mean you should tamper with it. Calculating the correct amount of UCR is a complex procedure that must take into account the tonal properties of the original, as well as the printing method, paper, and ink. Unless you know exactly what you're doing, consult with a commercial print house before setting UCR, and follow its recommendation.

Gray component replacement

As we have seen, the black ink in process color reproduction is used mainly to assist the colored inks by providing better detail and contrast. But there's a further role that can be played by black ink, based on a printing method called *achromatic* color reproduction, or gray component replacement (GCR).

GCR is based on the theory that it is unnecessary to use cyan, magenta, or yellow to produce the black (or achromatic) component of an image: black ink can be used instead. When a color photograph is scanned with GCR, the gray component of a given color is removed and replaced with the appropriate amount of black.

The use of GCR results in a much greater use of black ink, with a proportionate reduction in cyan, magenta, and yellow inks. Benefits of GCR include reduced consumption of expensive colored inks, and less paper wastage at the make-ready stage, because of the thinner ink film. Finally, lighter paper can sometimes be used.

GCR also helps solve a major problem in process color printing—producing consistently neutral grays. In traditional process color reproduction, the neutral gray tones are created by delicately balancing the three process inks. A slight variation in the amount of any of them can result in significant color shifts. But GCR removes this problem: neutral grays stay neutral because grays are made primarily with black ink, rather than with a combination of cyan, magenta, and yellow. As with UCR, you should consult your commercial printer before applying GCR to an image.

File compression

The underlying physics of how computers understand pixel-based pictures has forced us to deal with files that are large, oversize, husky, big, extensive, gargantuan, jumbo, hefty, giant-size, immense, and humungous. As we saw in the chapter on scanning, a full-page color image in a magazine would take up 30Mb of disk storage and, in most cases, would be impractical to transmit by phone.

Our first line of defense against this problem is file compression. Getting complex images down to manageable size has become more and more important as desktop publishing moves toward increasingly complex graphics and greater use of color.

There are a variety of Macintosh and PC-based utilities available, such as StuffIt, ARC, and ZIP. These provide lossless compression, in which every byte in the original file is present in the file that has been compressed and subsequently decompressed. However, those usually have compression ratios of 2:1 and therefore lack the compression "power" required for the images manipulated in commercial prepress.

The emerging JPEG standard

The emerging standard in compression of *image* data is called JPEG, for the Joint Photographic Experts Group, a combined committee of the International Standards Organization (ISO) and the American National Standards Institute (ANSI).

Systems that use JPEG can compress image files to less than one-tenth their original size, so they can later be decompressed with little or no detectable loss of detail or color quality. This is a very significant improvement in storing images. It means that you have all the high-resolution color data you need while actually working with the image, but store on disk and transmit to other sites a compressed file with more than 90 percent of the data removed.

When the image is compressed 20:1, a color professional will recognize the loss in image detail and dynamic range, but most observers will not, especially in a high-contrast image. Although the JPEG standard is quite new, and the degree of compression that a given image can withstand varies according to its content (and the eye of the observer), it appears that, in general, almost nobody will be able to detect a 14:1 compression.

The JPEG standard specifies a "lossy" algorithm, or "non-loss-less" as it's often called, meaning that some image data is lost. However, the loss occurs only on the first compression and decompression cycle. Once an image has been compressed at the specified quality level, any subsequent compression/decompression cycle will be practically lossless.

The JPEG approach uses a compression method that is programmed to identify and ignore pixel information that contributes little to the overall quality of the image, such as that within any large area of mostly uniform color. At small compression ratios of 10:1 or less, these changes are virtually impossible to detect—as you can see in the color images on Color Page 19, which show the same photograph before and after moderate and heavy compression.

The first desktop products to provide JPEG compression and decompression include Macintosh software-only products, as well as those that make use of a NuBus card for improved processing speeds. Eastman Kodak's Colorsqueeze and Radius ImpressIt are software-only packages. Storm Technology's PicturePress is available as software, or as PicturePress Accelerator, a NuBus card that speeds compression. Neotech's Image Compressor is a hardware-software combination. Most of these programs also support plug-in modules that let you compress and decompress images from within Adobe Photoshop or Letraset ColorStudio, although in many cases these can take significantly longer than using the dedicated compression program.

Kodak Colorsqueeze is simple to use, because it opens PICT and TIFF files, displays them on the screen in either 24-bit or dithered eight-bit color, zooms in and out, and compresses images using one of three predefined compression rates (approximately 5:1, 8:1, and 15:1). If you transmit a Colorsqueeze file (to a service bureau, for instance), all the receiver needs is a copy of Kodak's free decompressor, which is available on many of the major on-line information services.

Radius ImpressIt, another software-only JPEG product, features a handy Preview window that lets you drag a slider to set the compression level to one of 25 different settings. It also lets you *subsample* at a 2:1 ratio—ignore every third pixel in a way that minimizes the resulting quality degradation. Compression rates vary with image content, with the highest compression selection resulting in a rate of about 100:1, while the lowest produces about 3:1 compression.

Neotech's Image Compressor uses software in conjunction with a NuBus card containing the CL-550 JPEG compression chip from C-Cube Microsystems. You simply install the card in a slot and drag a Startup document (INIT) into your System folder.

One of the more interesting features of Image Compressor is an image archiving application called Image Browser. Instead of opening image files directly, it scans a selected disk, folder, or group of folders for TIFF, PICT, and its own files, and then displays thumbnails of these in a window. You can save and update browser files, customizing them for various collections of images.

Image Browser offers four compression levels, and is speedy because compression takes place in the specialized C-Cube chip. You can compress one or more images by selecting them from within the browser window—although you may want to backup your files first, because the program automatically overwrites the existing version of a file.

PicturePress is another compression package available with a NuBus card, and also available in a software-only version. It offers four preset levels of compression, and adds capabilities targeted at professional users, such as the ability to directly manipulate the variables controlling the JPEG algorithm. You can customize the quantization tables for chrominance and luminance, choose independent vertical and horizontal subsampling rates, and generate custom Huffman-encoding tables, which compress more data, albeit at slower speeds.

Most users probably won't want to customize their quantization tables, but this is a valuable tool in the hands of a skilled professional. By controlling the amount of quantization applied to the chrominance and luminance, acceptable quality with higher compression rates can be achieved than would otherwise be possible. For example, an image with little contrast but a wide range of colors can lose more luminance data and less chrominance data than a high-contrast image in which a few tones predominate.

At this point, the potential of the JPEG approach remains constrained by the fact that the technical standard has not been entirely ratified by the ISO (International Standards Organization) and ANSI (American National Standards Institute), although the proposal is in its final stages. Unfortunately, this means that a file compressed with any of the four leading packages cannot currently be decompressed by another. It seems certain that all the major vendors will support the final version of the JPEG specifications, but until then, these products should be regarded as transitional.

One reason it's important to use a product that is completely JPEG-compatible is that PostScript Level 2 supports JPEG-compressed images sent to PostScript laser printers. Decompression takes place in the printer, which means document transmissions take much less time.

Another factor that enhances performance is selective compression, in which lower compression ratios (and hence better image quality) are used for the parts of the image that contain the area of interest, while higher compression ratios are used for image portions that contain less important elements. In a typical shot for a sales catalog, for example, the product would be less compressed (higher quality) than the backgrounds. This feature is built into the JPEG++ specification in PicturePress from Storm Technology.

Hardware-based compression

Most users will find it more cost-effective to use software-based compression tools, but those willing to pay for extra performance will want to investigate the new hardware-based compression products coming to market. The first generation of desktop compression boards are still not widely used, but chip producers are now shipping to board manufacturers a compression chip that can compress or decompress a typical color image in a few seconds or less. With chips like these, plus some standards for how compressed files should be stored, it becomes practical to store large image files on floppies, to move them around on networks, and to transmit them over telephone lines. The ultimate goal remains to perform such operations in real time, so that compact files on disk can be instantly viewed and edited at their full resolution on screen.

All in all, compression technology and the JPEG standard are on the verge of greatly simplifying image storage and transfer for color desktop publishing. However, whatever the other benefits of compression, you have to accept that it will not improve times for the actual manipulation of images, because the files have to be decompressed before they can be manipulated. The performance issue will be solved only through ongoing speed improvements in computers and in programs for displaying and manipulating images.

Adobe Photoshop

Adobe Photoshop is a powerful Macintosh image processing program with versatility that allows it to be used as a paint, prepress, color correction, and darkroom program—all in 24-bit color. Photoshop lets you start with scanned photographs, slides, electronic artwork, or from scratch. You can paint originals with soft-edged brushes, or with custom brushes, textures, and patterns. Airbrush, cloning, and rubber stamp tools further increase flexibility in retouching photos. You can also blend, layer, or fill multiple images for mosaic, photo-realistic, or impressionistic effects.

Figure 7-11
Photoshop color picker has an "excess gamut indicator" in the top right corner (an exclamation point within a triangle) to warn that the specified color cannot be printed with any combination of process color inks.

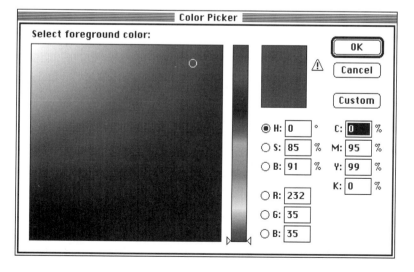

For most users, Photoshop presents an overwhelming richness of features. The tools are intuitively designed, and can easily be fine-tuned. A novice user can create really nifty effects within the first few hours, and often gain a level of basic competence with a few days or weeks of practice. Yet the expert user will find enough controls and combinations to keep busy for years.

Photoshop 2.0 has added support for on-screen CMYK editing (rather than RGB), a feature previously seen only on high-end systems. By editing CMYK values on screen, you improve color accuracy between the scan, the display, and output. CMYK scans don't need to be converted to RGB for display, then converted back to CMYK for output.

The new version of Photoshop also includes a Bézier selection tool, plus the ability to import Illustrator artwork into Photoshop at any resolution using *anti-aliasing* to soften the imported artwork's edges. You can also create accurate duotones, monotones, tritones, and quadratones with any PANTONE or process color ink and preview the result on screen and in color.

Other new features include custom color dithering, on-screen editing of tonal values, support for pressure-sensitive tablets, and the ability to calibrate separations to match specific monitors and output devices.

Image size is virtually limitless

Photoshop works with *virtual memory*, swapping required RAM to and from your storage device, so you can edit images of virtually any size. Photoshop has very robust file import and conversion features. You can import and export Encapsulated PostScript (EPS), PICT resources and files (including 32-bit), TIFF, Scitex, MacPaint, TGA (Targa), PIXAR, Pixelpaint, Compuserve GIF, and Amiga IFF/ILBM. It even supports Thunderscan, for all those color enthusiasts creating separations from the roller of a dot-matrix printer.

You can view and edit images in a variety of color and black-and-white modes, with the default mode determined by the image: grayscale images appear in monochrome and color images in RGB color.

Figure 7-12
Photoshop Mode menu, with options for converting between color modes

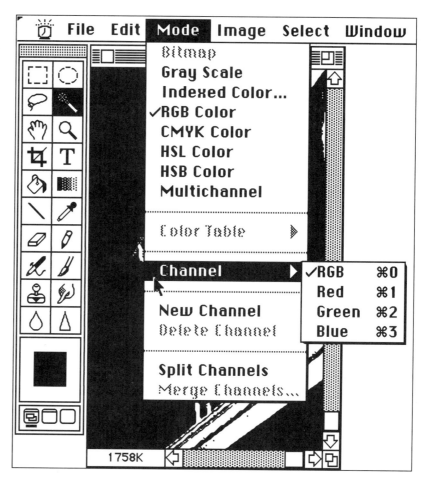

You can override these defaults for special effects. To colorize a black-and-white photograph, for example, you change the mode from grayscale to RGB; to create color separations, you change from RGB to CMYK.

Photoshop's full range of filters and painting, drawing, and selection tools provide a tremendous degree of artistic control and precision. Filters include sharpen, edge sharpen, blur, Gaussian blur, despeckle, motion blur, add noise, diffuse, facet, star lens, mosaic, trace contours, and convolution. And if none of these quite fit the bill, you can create custom filters, or buy them from third-party vendors. You can print separations directly from

Photoshop, or save them in Encapsulated PostScript (EPS) format for placement in graphics and page layout programs.

Some graphics applications, such as Adobe Illustrator and Aldus FreeHand, use the EPS format to transfer drawings between programs. PostScript print files can't be displayed on any screen (except a NeXT computer with Display PostScript), but an EPS file bundles the PostScript code with a low-resolution screen preview—a PICT file on a Mac and a TIFF file on an IBM compatible.

Figure 7-13
Photoshop dialog box to set screen angles and frequencies

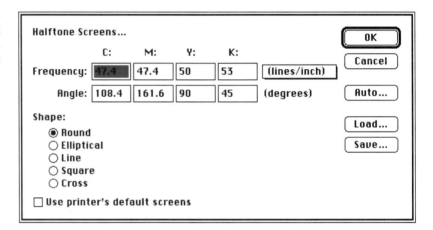

The preview allows you to place the image on the page with appropriate sizing and scaling, and gives you an idea of what it will look like when it is printed. Another export option in Photoshop allows you to save a CMYK document as five separate EPS documents for placement in DCS-compatible page layout programs such as QuarkXPress.

Photoshop lets you print to any PostScript color or black-and-white printer, with control over halftone frequency, screen angle, and dot shape. Another important output feature is "intelligent resampling," which lets you reset resolution or image size to values appropriate for printing.

Photoshop contains a very sophisticated automatic selection tool called the "magic wand," which lets you quickly distinguish even very complex objects from their backgrounds. A variable "feather edge" helps you select arbitrary regions, and you can add to, subtract from, and refine your selections. If you make mistakes while defining the area to select, Photoshop lets you go back and reduce or enlarge the selected area.

Image enhancement in Photoshop

In addition to providing control over brightness and contrast, Photoshop also permits you to work with a *histogram* of the image, to help you visualize the effects of the changes you specify. A histogram plots the color value of pixels in the active channel of an image against the total number of pixels with those values in the channel.

Figure 7-14
Photoshop's Histogram window helps you visualize the prevalence of light or dark tones in your image.

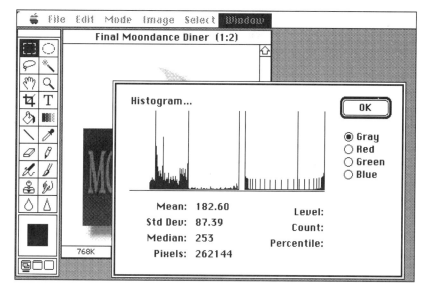

When you point the cursor at a specific part of the histogram, Photoshop displays the color level (from 0 to 255) for that point, the total number of pixels at that level, and the percentage of pixels with color levels darker than the level on which the pointer is currently positioned. The left side of the histogram shows the pixels with dark color values (near 0), the middle section those with medium color values (near 128), and the right section those with light color values (near 255). The Y-axis represents the number of pixels with that value.

Figure 7-15
Photoshop allows you
to control the tonal
qualities of an image
with the Curves dialog
box.

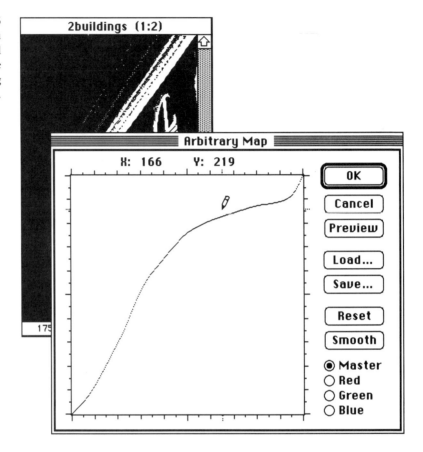

Photoshop also lets you modify the *gamma,* or midtone, values in an image without substantially changing the highlights or shadows.

Channels

Among the most powerful features in Photoshop is the *channel* capability, with each channel similar in concept to the individual plates used in the four-color process. A bitmap and a grayscale are single-channel images; RGB, HSL, and HSB images have three channels, and CMYK images have four channels. Additional channels (up to 16 in all!) can be added to manipulate the image and to store *masks*, which isolate part of the image so it can be modified without altering the rest of the picture. This leaves plenty of room for experimenting.

Masks

Channels are especially useful for creating masks. If you want to manipulate a specific part of an image while leaving the rest untouched, you simply create a new channel in which the image is converted to black-and-white. It is very easy to use the magic wand tool to select a discrete white area. You then change everything except your selection to solid black, thus creating a mask.

Figure 7-16
Photoshop's masks let you isolate the foreground elements so the background can be edited independently

Once the object is selected, the mask channel can be reincorporated into the full-color editing channel, and the defined object will remain highlighted as the current selection. You can then modify the selection any way you want, completely independent of the rest of the image.

In creating a mask, the magic wand tool often does the hard part of the job—distinguishing between the shades that are included in the selection from those that are background. The masking procedure then photographically isolates the area of interest.

Trapping color images

In theory, the kinds of detailed, multicolor images you can create in Photoshop should be among the most difficult to trap, because of the complex shapes and ever-changing combinations of foreground and background colors. In practice, Photoshop simplifies the trapping process.

Figure 7-17
Image menu Trap
dialog box

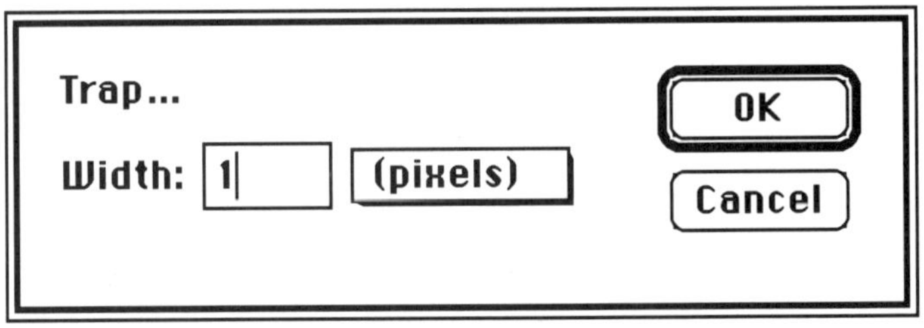

```
┌─────────────────────────────────────────────┐
│                                               │
│   Trap...                    ╔═══════════╗    │
│                              ║    OK     ║    │
│   Width:  [1|]   (pixels)    ╚═══════════╝    │
│                              ┌───────────┐    │
│                              │  Cancel   │    │
│                              └───────────┘    │
│                                               │
└─────────────────────────────────────────────┘
```

First, an image is selected and converted from RGB to CMYK mode. Then Trap is chosen from the Image menu and the size of the trap is specified—Photoshop does the rest automatically.

Plug-in modules

Adobe has wisely opened up Photoshop to third-party software and hardware vendors by making it easy to add plug-in software modules with specialized abilities, such as scanner control or background image compression. To install a Photoshop plug-in, simply drag its icon into the folder containing Photoshop.

Among the plug-in programs is Aldus Gallery Effects, a library of professional-quality special effects for grayscale and color images. It provides 16 "master effects" that look hand-created, yet can be applied to any image—effects like watercolor, charcoal, graphic pen, dry brush, and emboss. Each of these effects includes individual controls that you can preview; you can save up to 25 custom settings per effect.

In addition to the many image filters provided with Photoshop, you can devise your own by experimenting with the values in the Image Filters Custom dialog box. You create special effects by changing the brightness values of pixels according to a mathematical convolution kernel that you specify. For example, you can define a filter that displays a selection in high relief or a filter that creates a motion blur effect.

As shown in Figure 7-18, the filter uses a grid consisting of text boxes, with the grid acting as a kind of template that is applied to each pixel in the image, one at a time. The center text box in the grid represents the current pixel, the one whose new brightness value is currently being calculated; the text boxes around it represent the pixels surrounding that pixel.

Figure 7-18
To develop Photoshop filter sets of your own, experiment with variations of any of the numbers in the matrix.

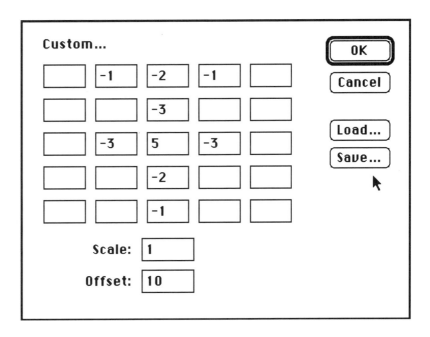

The values you enter in the text boxes apply a designated weight to the pixel represented by that text box. If you enter a high value, that pixel is heavily weighted and is more influential in the brightness calculations than pixels that are assigned lower values. To save time when playing with different custom filters, use the Command-Option-F keyboard shortcut to return directly to the custom filter dialog box. Filters can be saved and loaded in other documents.

Letraset ColorStudio

ColorStudio software brings professional prepress color capabilities to the Macintosh, through all phases of the design process. It allows you to:

- create original color illustrations;
- scan and input existing prints, slides, and drawings;
- retouch color photos;
- assemble montages and composite images;
- proof and color-correct images for separation and printing.

Figure 7-19
Letraset ColorStudio paintbrush palette, showing custom brushes

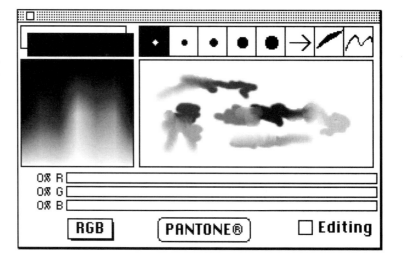

ColorStudio supports 32-bit color—full 24-bit color plus an eight-bit mask layer with 256 levels of transparency. You have 16.7 million colors at your fingertips, and can choose between all the major color models—RGB, CMY, CMYK, HSV, and the PANTONE MATCHING SYSTEM. Color images can be input from scanners, video capture boards, and high-resolution Crosfield data tapes.

As with Photoshop, ColorStudio works internally with all 16.7 million (24-bit) colors, even if you have only an eight-bit video card—but, in that case, only 256 colors can be displayed at any one time. For the most accurate image display with an eight-bit card, use the Color menu's Recompute command every once in a while or choose Apple Set Preferences and click on Auto Recompute.

Figure 7-20
ColorStudio provides complete control over screen angles and frequencies, as well as other output parameters.

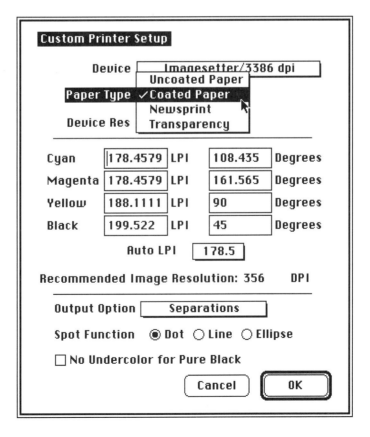

The ColorStudio paintbrush lets you pour color into shapes, open areas, and image segments, using a library of predefined and user-created patterns. The paintbrush includes a "paint with part of image" feature, which allows you to transfer graphic elements between images, and a "spectrum" command for cycling the tool through the entire color spectrum as you paint.

ColorStudio comes with a variety of image processing filters, such as blur, diffuse, sharpen, soften, and harden. The program can correct for distortions in scanned images caused by the mechanical limitations of various scanning devices. Corrections to color values can be made globally during the scanning process, or made later to either the entire image or just to portions of it, in 1% increments. ColorStudio also works with all Photoshop filters and scanner drivers.

For output, you have complete control over parameters for paper type, line screen, color, dot, and screen angle. A color correction screen lets you display separate on-screen "plates" for each color (cyan, magenta, yellow, and black), as well as a preview of the image as it will appear on the selected output device.

Colormap transfer function

The Colormap feature in the Color Correction window permits you to control how colors in a scanned image are reproduced on screen and saved in a ColorStudio file. It lets you adjust, or color correct, image colors to compensate for deficiencies in the scanned original, or to balance the colors between images photographed under different lighting conditions. It also provides control over the image's dynamic range, to help bring out detail in the highlights and shadows.

Colors in the scanned image are mapped to screen colors by the four *transfer lines* in the Colormap, one each for cyan, magenta, yellow, and overall brightness (C, M, and Y together). The transfer line initially lies at 45°, giving a one-for-one correspondence between scanned and displayed colors. In other words, for each color, the shadow areas, midtones, and highlights on screen match those in the scanned image as closely as possible.

Transfer lines can be straight, curved, or a mixture, and you can drag the lines as smooth curves, or paint freehand transfer lines. Once you've achieved the desired results, you can apply them over the entire image or any selected portion of it. You can save the transfer line patterns for use with other images, making it easier to correct multiple images that require the same kinds of adjustments.

Figure 7-21
Initially, the transfer lines show an exact correspondence between scanned and displayed colors. The transfer curve starts out straight, but is often modified into a curve to produce better tonal compression.

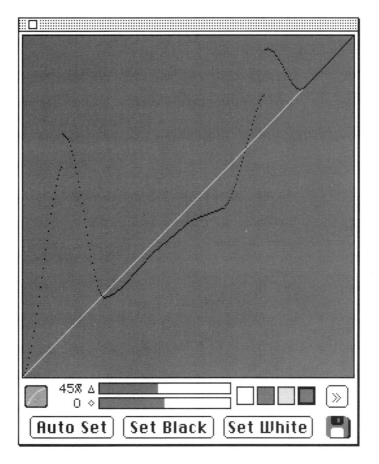

As shown in the set of color pictures on Color Page 21, straight transfer lines tend to show more visually abrupt changes of color value than curves. The standard way of working with transfer lines is to change them into *gamma curves*, to allow smooth variations in value while achieving changes in contrast and brightness. The gamma curve is concave, for an original in which highlights must be enhanced and shadow areas brightened and given added contrast. A convex curve would be used for an original requiring additional contrast in the highlight values while giving shadow areas reduced contrast.

In the examples shown, all four transfer lines are lying along the same path, but ColorStudio lets you re-map each of the transfer lines independently, giving you complete control over they way the image is rendered.

Editing mask

ColorStudio provides a flexible eight-bit mask layer that works as a stencil to isolate and protect portions of images being altered. The mask layer can also be saved and printed later separately as a fifth plate for spot varnish or a spot color. In this respect, the current version of ColorStudio is not quite as flexible as Photoshop, in that you have only the single mask channel to work with at any one time, as compared with the 12 additional channels available in Photoshop. ColorStudio's unlimited selection regions help compensate for this.

Figure 7-22
The Mask Options window in ColorStudio lets you work with a floating selection, either from the active image or pasted from another image.

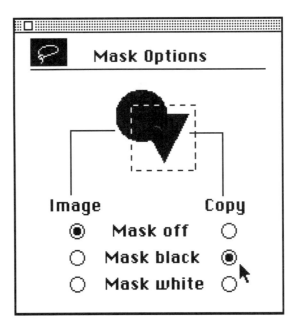

The Mask Options window allows you to control how masking effects are applied in the image. The buttons for the Image icon (a square enclosing a circle) determine how the mask in the image takes effect on any floating images which overlay it. The buttons for the Copy icon (a square enclosing a triangle) determine how the mask in a floating copy affects the appearance of the floating image.

The Shapes annex

Shapes is a PostScript drawing environment for enhancing ColorStudio images, which permits you to draw and build objects in Shapes' separate drawing layer and render the design into ColorStudio's image and mask layers or leave it as a printable PostScript layer. Shapes adds a third layer (PostScript lines and curves) to ColorStudio's paint layer and mask layer (bitmaps).

It adds seven new tools to ColorStudio's toolbox, including a Bézier curve pen, a freehand drawing tool, and a variety of geometric shapes. Shapes is based on the idea of *rendering,* in which images are merged into the ColorStudio image or mask layer at the resolution of the image, optimized for print or video.

Figure 7-23
The Shapes toolbox adds lines and curves to ColorStudio.

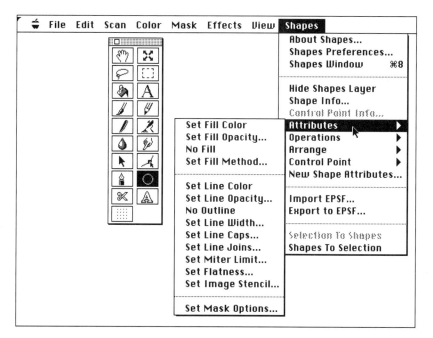

You can import EPS files from Illustrator or FreeHand, with complete control over color and outlines, and import any PostScript font outline with control over Bézier points.

Shapes also lets you control the opacity of EPS lines and fill colors. You can render semi-transparent text over bitmap images, an effect previously available only on high-end systems.

Shapes lets you use colors from the ColorStudio palette or match a color in the image. You can change any object by stretching, scaling, rotation, adding control points, cutting, coloring, and combining with other objects.

Trapping

Unlike Photoshop, the current release of ColorStudio does not have an explicit trapping command. Trapping is achieved through anti-aliasing, which is effective but imperfect because it doesn't always blend lines that are perfectly vertical or horizontal.

To use anti-aliasing with Shapes, first create the ColorStudio image, then use Shapes to either create objects or import an encapsulated PostScript (EPS) file. Select Render to Paint Layer from the Operations submenu, and ColorStudio converts the shapes to a bitmap, anti-aliasing the objects in the process.

Aldus PhotoStyler

Aldus PhotoStyler is the first full-function 24-bit color imaging program that runs on IBM-compatible computers under Windows. Other software vendors are rapidly bringing similar Windows programs to market, and what started out as an all-Macintosh domain is rapidly spreading to PCs.

PhotoStyler provides photo-realistic image enhancement capabilities for processing 24-bit color, grayscale, and black-and-white images. It takes full advantage of the advanced features in Windows 3.0, including virtual memory, which removes any practical restrictions on the size of an image or the number of images that are displayed at the same time.

Although PhotoStyler will run on any Windows-capable computer, it should properly be run on a fast 80386 or preferably an 80486-based system, with 4Mb or more of RAM. It works with VGA, XGA, 8514, and any eight-, 16-, or 24-bit display that supports Windows.

Figure 7-24
PhotoStyler lets you work with multiple color images on IBM compatibles running Windows.

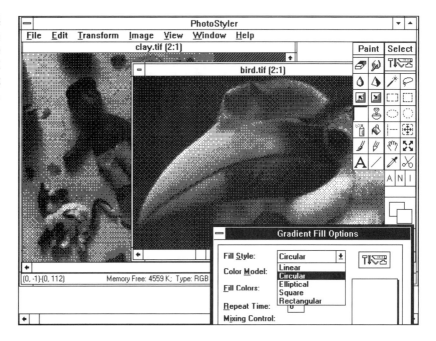

An extensive array of tools is available for color correction, conversion, separation, image editing, retouching, and composition. Built-in filters include sharpen, blur, edge trace, add or remove noise, emboss or relief, mosaic, motion blur, pinch, whirlpool, and so on, and you can define and save custom filters. A "magic wand" tool lets you quickly select parts of an image to create masks, which can be added, subtracted, or inverted from other images.

PhotoStyler also provides control for pasting images through the Merge Control command, which allows you to specify the opacity of the selection before it is pasted to the underlying image. The Compute command is one of PhotoStyler's most powerful features, enabling you to combine channels to form duotones, mezzotints, and other special effects.

PhotoStyler comes with drivers for most popular desktop scanners and laser printers, plus export filters for dye sublimation printers such as the Nikon CP-3000 and Kodak XL7700. It supports all Windows-compatible and PostScript printers. Files can be imported and exported as TIFF, Targa, EPS, PCX, BMP, and GIF.

Figure 7-25
PhotoStyler provides photo-realistic image enhancement capabilities for processing 24-bit color, grayscale, and black-and-white images.

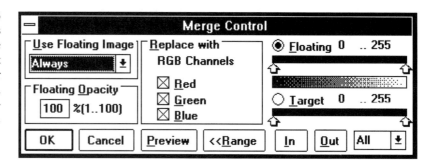

For producing color separations, PhotoStyler provides control of screen frequency, angle, and shape, plus the ability to set black generation for undercolor removal and gray component replacement. Like Adobe Photoshop and Letraset ColorStudio, PhotoStyler uses an open architecture that allows for future developments in scanning, file transfer, and image compression technologies, through support for "plug-in" modules.

Image-In-Color

Image-In-Color is a color version of Image-In, which was among the first black-and-white imaging programs for IBM compatibles. It runs under Windows 3 and provides a complete set of tools for editing and color-separating VGA, SuperVGA, and 24-bit color images.

You can control the pressure, density, and size of all retouching tools, such as the pencil, paintbrush, and airbrush. Items in an image can be moved or cloned.

The program supports RGB, HSV, and CMYK color models, and uses advanced color reduction algorithms and palette optimization functions for quick and precise color selection. You can display histograms of any image, with full controls for editing the color map. Color separation controls include GCR, UCR, and press gain compensation.

Image-In-Color supports all popular scanners, and works with Wacom pressure-sensitive tablets. Files can be imported and exported to and from Image-In-Color using most desktop publishing programs, in a variety of file formats, including TIFF, EPS, PCX, BMP, GIF, and TGA.

Color image conversion

Many potential color publishing applications are thwarted by the unavailability of image data in an accessible format. Color image conversion programs, such as ChromaTools from Videotex Systems, solve such problems. ChromaTools can be used for color publishing, multimedia, picture databases, and CD-ROM libraries.

ChromaTools converts TGA (Targa), PCX, GIF, TIFF, and VST images to TGA, PCX, GIF, TIF, VST, and color PostScript. It converts images to all PC screen modes including Super VGA, VGA, EGA, CGA, and Hercules. ChromaTools features multiple color reduction algorithms, optimized palette reduction, and multiple dithering patterns, all of which allow you to get the best possible conversion. It includes tools for sizing, cropping, and re-scaling, plus filters, spot meters, and user-programmable modules.

The future of color correction

The human eye has an uncanny ability to detect color imperfections in any reproduction, especially for "memory colors"—trees, sky, water, and people's faces.

Color correction of images is as much an art as a science—as anyone who has tried it has learned. When a single color image appears on a page, the reader's eye will quickly adapt to the content of the image, unless its colors are unusual.

However, when two or more images appear together on a page, much greater care must be taken to ensure that the memory colors are consistent from picture to picture. This ideal, which is very important to the uninterrupted perception of the reader, is difficult to attain unless the photographs were taken on identical film, in the same lighting and exposure conditions. Furthermore, accurate color correction has required calibrated monitors and carefully controlled viewing conditions. These are both becoming more widely used as part of the overall growth of color publishing.

In the high-end prepress world, experienced scanner operators have learned how to alter the colors as they are being recorded to compensate for differences between original photographs. The imaging applications described in this chapter provide the technical capabilities for color correction, but only a skilled color technician has the judgment needed. One of the greatest impediments to the effective use of desktop color is the lack of such expertise. Clearly, a new generation of color experts will have to be trained.

EFI Cachet

Until that happens, the most ambitious attempt at solving color correction problems has been the Cachet program for the Macintosh from Electronics For Imaging (EFI). The software is accompanied by a book containing reference pictures, plus a disk of the corresponding scanned images used to print the pictures. You operate Cachet by viewing two images on screen—the subject photo you wish to color correct, and one of the reference photos. Your task is to make the subject photo look like the reference photo.

One of the advantages of this approach is that you don't need a calibrated monitor and controlled room lighting: as long as the subject photo looks like the reference photo on screen, it will print with the appropriate colors.

Figure 7-26
Cachet lets you control contrast, color saturation, and tonal curves by comparing a subject image with a reference image on screen.

Cachet lets you manipulate contrast, color saturation, and tonal curves directly, although most novice users will prefer Cachet's "picture palette" approach. In addition to the subject photo, Cachet displays on screen six alternative versions of the same image, each slightly different. For example, if your original image is too dark, you select "lightness" from a menu, which then displays three progressively lighter and darker versions of your original image.

One of these six alternates is probably closer to what you have in mind than the others; clicking on that image applies its levels of brightness adjustment to the subject image. The six alternate images are then updated to present a new range of progressively lighter and darker choices.

Figure 7-27
By selecting one of six alternate versions of an image, the nonexpert user can perform sophisticated color separations.

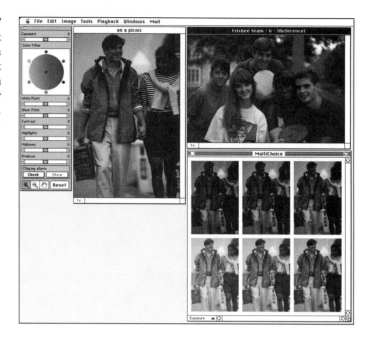

Selecting from the multiple-choice picture palette automatically updates the values in the various brightness, contrast, and other color controls. Therefore, as you use Cachet, you begin to learn what effect each of the traditional controls would have on a given image.

Cachet also lets you mask any portion of the subject image by using a lasso tool to define the general area, then refining the selection area by picking a color from the image and allowing the program to include in the mask all pixels that have a similar color. Once you have defined a mask, you can adjust the colors within it to match a range of colors in the reference picture, or set the color of an object in your subject image to match a specified PANTONE Color.

All of Cachet's color manipulation tools make use of EFI's Eport color server, a database of device characterizations with software that translates screen colors into their hard copy equivalents. The Eport database includes characterizations for many popular color printers.

Using the Eport data, Cachet can warn you when a color you have requested is outside the gamut of the selected printer. This gives you two choices—either switch to a (more expensive) printer with a wider gamut, or do nothing and depend on the Eport software to map any out-of-gamut colors into the gamut of the selected printer.

The EFI Eport color server is among the first of a new generation of color management products, but it is not the only contender.

Kodak Color Management System

Kodak recently unveiled the Kodak Color Management System (KCMS), a set of tools and utilities that provides consistent, high-quality use of color across software applications, computer platforms, and peripheral devices. Because computer devices currently use different color spaces and have unique characteristics that alter the reproduction of color, there is no guarantee that colors in a photograph displayed on a computer screen will look the same in, for example, a print of the same image.

Kodak's color management system works in two ways. It provides consistent and efficient processing of color data between software applications and hardware devices. Also, it provides device calibration, comparing and, if necessary, fine-tuning a device's actual reproduction of color with its expected reproduction of color.

The system includes a developer's toolkit, user environments (initially for DOS, Windows, SunOS, and Unix 5.4), device profiles (for popular scanners, displays, and printers), and calibration tools. The Kodak color management system is designed to be independent of any particular device or operating system, and is compatible with Kodak's PhotoYCC color space and other color spaces such as RGB, CMYK, and CIE.

The end of photography as evidence of anything

To paraphrase Democritus, there are no colors, only pixels and space. We've become jaded during the past few years by ads showing artificial worlds in which cars fly through outer space and people walk inside computer chips. To create a picture that will sell a product, commercial artists have used specialized imaging tools that were formerly available only on high-end systems, but are now accessible from any desktop.

These tools provide users with the ability to create visual worlds that would be difficult or impossible to create in concrete reality. After all, if the ad calls for a tiger stepping out of a courier package, it's easier to shoot each image element separately and glue them together electronically than to ask the tiger to hold still while you adjust the lights. These synthetic worlds appear so real, in fact, that an international group of photographers and editors recently met to debate the use of a circled-M symbol similar to the circled-C © copyright symbol, to designate an image as being modified or a montage.

Without such a designation, it is virtually impossible to detect many of the changes possible with digital photography. And although modifying an image may be standard practice in the advertising industry, many observers question whether it should have any role at all in news photography.

Recently, newspaper readers were startled to see the well-known World War II picture of Roosevelt, Stalin, and Churchill at Yalta—with Sylvester Stallone behind them, listening intently! Although that meeting took place in 1945, well before the movie star was born, there was nothing in the quality of the photo—no unexplained shadows or awkward lighting—to mark it as a fake. The message was obvious: with computerization the camera does, indeed, lie—or, at least, it can be made to lie persuasively.

Such capabilities are very new, and our framework for dealing with them has not kept pace. Many questions remain unanswered:

- Should a news magazine's photo editor retouch a shot of the queen of England because the camera angle makes it look as if a tree is growing out of the royal nose?

- Should retouching be used at all in a daily newspaper?

- Is a renowned geographic magazine within its rights in moving the Great Pyramid of Cheops over a little so it fits better on the cover? Should it be required to tell its readers the image was modified?

There are no simple answers to these questions, but the issue of reality versus photography is worth careful consideration—before we quickly forget which is which. Afterall, with desktop imaging it's not just a question of where we draw the line, but how we find that line again once it's been seamlessly smudged into the background.

Desktop Color Page Layout

*"This whole color revolution isn't about technologies—
it's about content development."*

PETER FINK, IMAGESETTER RESEARCHER

Color page layout is where everything comes together—the graphics, images, and type—to create the complete pages and publications that will be seen by the reader. It combines meticulous control over positioning huge volumes of type with the ability to import and color separate a wide variety of drawings and pictures.

QuarkXPress, Aldus PageMaker, Letraset DesignStudio, Ventura Publisher, and other page layout programs are similar in that all of them provide the typographic tools you need to produce a single page or an entire 1,000-page publication. But they are very different in terms of what they can do with color graphics and images, and for most color publishers the differences are crucial.

This is not to suggest that any one program is better than the rest, but that different users will find some programs better suited to their requirements than others. Among the parameters that must be considered in assessing color page layout programs are the quality of typography, support for graphics and images, and ability to create color separations. This chapter explores not only the page layout programs and their color capabilities, but the emerging standards for semiautomatic links between desktop publishing and high-end prepress systems.

Color page layout

To produce pages on the desktop, some features are so essential that all the major page layout packages incorporate them in some form or other. These include typographic control, support for different color models, integration of various text, graphic, and image files, and the ability to create color separations.

Fonts

In the early days of desktop publishing, access to high-quality fonts was a big problem. It still is, but the challenge now is to select an appropriate typeface or two from the *literally* thousands available.

Figure 8-1
Typography is the language of design.

Once you've selected your fonts, they must be positioned precisely in the page layouts. All the major programs provide control over *leading* (the space between lines), *kerning* (the space between specific pairs of characters for a good fit, particularly at larger point sizes), and *tracking* (overall tightening or loosening of letter spacing that affects all characters equally). But the programs differ in the level of control they provide over each of these parameters. Some make you select from just a few levels of tracking, for instance, while others allow you to set any values you want, in tiny increments.

They also differ in their ability to rotate type, with some able to do so only in 90° increments, while others can rotate text (and even graphics) in increments of 1/1,000th of a degree.

There are also some type effects, such as gradient fills or the use of type to mask parts of an image, that are difficult or impossible in a page layout program. They can be created in an illustration or imaging program, then exported as an EPS file to be imported into the page layout.

Figure 8-2
Adobe Multiple Master font technology allows you to create all the intermediate variations between any two versions of a typeface.

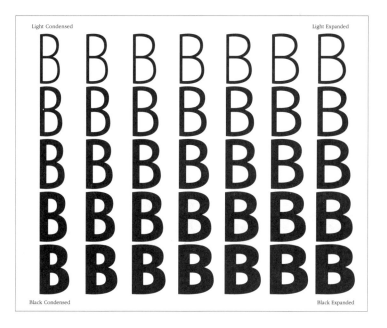

In the near future, page layout programs will support Adobe Multiple Master font technology, which uses two or more variations of a typeface (such as a compressed and an extended version) to automatically calculate all the intermediate variations in the face. Each variation is *optically scaled*, rather than simply linearly stretched, so that the thickness of stems and the shapes of serifs are modified in order to maintain the essence of the original typeface.

Support for multiple color models

The type and linework in a layout can be colored using any of the color models supported by your application program. Virtually all provide support for RGB, HSB, CMYK, and the PANTONE MATCHING SYSTEM.

For best results, use the color model appropriate to the task at hand:

- If the piece is going to be printed as a four-color process job, specify all the colors, from the beginning, in terms of their CMYK values. Use a process color guide, such as those available from Focoltone, Trumatch, and PANTONE (their new process color guide).

- If the piece will be printed with spot colors, specify each color in terms of its PMS number or other solid color standard. You can start with the PANTONE Color library when defining spot colors and, if the one you need is not available, define a custom color using any of the color models. Your printing company can then apply a pre-mixed or custom-blended ink for that spot color.

Color Stripping: In House or "Export"?

Desktop color is not a single tool or technique—it is an approach. It encompasses prepress solutions in which the desktop component varies according to the requirements of each job: some projects can be produced entirely from the desktop while others require that page layouts created on the desktop be integrated with images scanned and corrected on conventional high-end prepress systems.

For example, one can use desktop graphics and page layout programs to create all the type and linework, including *keylines* (boxes that show where images are to be placed). The photographic images are scanned using conventional color prepress systems, then stripped into position by hand during the film assembly stage.

The newest scanners and imagesetters allow you to perform the entire color separation process on the desktop. However, if you are greatly concerned about image quality, and have not yet mastered the skills of color production, you may be well advised to make use of the services of a professional color house for scanning the original images and separating the final film.

In effect, you are letting the professionals perform the most difficult and hardware-intensive part of the color prepress process; for some users, that approach will result in higher quality and lower costs than scanning and separating color images on the desktop.

Maximum savings are achieved because you create and modify the type, graphics, and page design, using desktop color page layout software. Maximum quality is attained because the really difficult color imaging part of the job is being performed by highly trained professionals using extremely expensive equipment.

Linking desktop and high-end systems

Chapter 9, on Color Electronic Prepress Systems, describes the proprietary links to the desktop provided by each of the major vendors of high-end prepress systems. But before considering those high-end tools, it is important to understand the connections between them from the desktop point of view.

Essentially, it all comes down to PostScript. From the earliest days of desktop publishing, PostScript defined a standard device-independent way of handling typography. With desktop color, PostScript is emerging as a similar standard, especially with recent enhancements (PostScript Level 2) in screening algorithms that eliminate moiré patterns.

Most page layout programs can't perform color separations, while the separation programs lack the typographic and pagination features of the layout programs. To date, two main protocols are being used to bridge the gap between different software packages—DCS and OPI.

Figure 8-3
Flow chart of PostScript
code being generated
by your application and
interpreted in the
output device

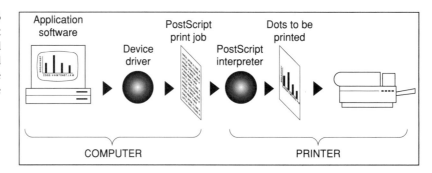

The similarities and differences between the two will be of concern to any desktop publisher working with color, whether adding a single spot color to a company newsletter or producing a snazzy full-color catalog with high-quality photographs.

Desktop Color Separation (DCS), was introduced by Quark in 1988, as part of QuarkXPress. The Open PrePress Interface (OPI) specification was introduced by Aldus in April 1989. Both standards have been published, and developers of other page layout programs are free to adopt them. Indeed, beginning with version 3, QuarkXPress files are both DCS and OPI compatible.

Although different in many ways, both specifications exist for the same reason: to produce plate-ready color separations of entire publications, including photographs. DCS is a desktop-only solution, while OPI offers paths to both desktop and high-end systems.

Desktop Color Separation (DCS)

DCS is the simpler of the two protocols, being designed just for desktop work. QuarkXPress can already generate process separations of encapsulated PostScript (EPS) images and page elements colored in XPress, so DCS is required only when separations of color photographs and other continuous-tone images are needed.

For example, to produce a publication containing color photographs, you simply scan each color photo with a desktop scanner either directly to DCS format, or to produce a TIFF (tag image file format) file, which you then separate using a DCS-compatible program such as Photoshop, ColorStudio, or

PhotoMac. This gives you five EPS files for each TIFF—one main file plus one file each for the cyan, magenta, yellow, and black separations. The main file includes a low-resolution screen image, information for printing a composite page proof, and a set of comments that link the file to the four separation files.

Figure 8-4
Schematic of workflow with Desktop Color Separations (DCS)

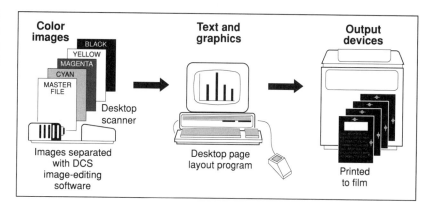

You then import the main DCS file for each image into a DCS-aware page layout program, such as QuarkXPress or DesignStudio, which can produce color separations of text and graphics. When the layout is finished, simply print separations from the page layout application to any PostScript-language imagesetter—your application will read the DCS comments attached to the main files and replace each main file with the four corresponding separation files. The resulting output is full-color separations, plate-ready for your commercial printing company.

Open PrePress Interface (OPI)

OPI is a standard file format that was originally designed for transferring information from color desktop publications to high-end prepress systems, so that stripping and rework costs could be minimized. It has emerged as the only way to get separations from PageMaker, which, unlike XPress, currently separates only spot color overlays.

The development of OPI continues the work Aldus has done to encourage standards for the publishing industry. A few years ago, when desktop publishers struggled with a maze of incompatible formats for bitmapped images, Aldus spearheaded a group (including Microsoft and all major desktop scanner manufacturers), that agreed on the TIFF standard.

Since then, TIFF has become an ever-evolving standard that has grown to incorporate color information and file compression, with other innovations on the way. Later, when similar problems began to arise in linking desktop publishing programs with high-end color prepress systems, Aldus developed and published the OPI specification to provide a standard link between the two worlds.

Figure 8-5
Schematic of workflow with Open PrePress Interface (OPI)

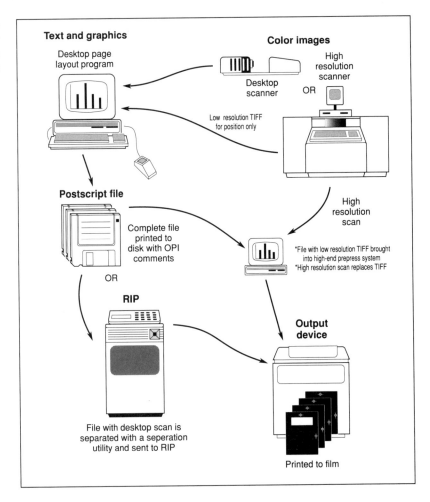

You can create files that conform to the OPI specification with PageMaker 4.0, DesignStudio 2.0, QuarkXPress 3, and other applications such as FreeHand.

To produce the same color publication as you did with DCS, you scan each color photo on the desktop to produce a TIFF file or, for higher quality, pay a color prepress shop to scan your original on its drum scanner as a high-resolution image while providing you with a low-resolution TIFF file for screen display. Instead of separating the images at this time, as you would with DCS, you place the TIFFs directly into an OPI-compatible page layout program such as PageMaker.

While in your page layout program, you can also specify color page elements as desired, and import any other color EPS or TIFF files. When the layout is complete and you are ready to produce separations, print the file to disk, which saves it in OPI format. OPI consists of PostScript-language comments that provide information about the placement, sizing, and cropping of color images included in the publication.

You then use an OPI-compatible separation utility, such as Aldus PrePrint or SpectreSeps PM, to generate the separations from the OPI file through a PostScript-language imagesetter. You can also upload the file to an OPI-compatible prepress system from Agfa Compugraphic, Chelgraph, Crosfield, Diadem, DuPont-Camex, Eastman Kodak, Hell Graphic Systems, Howtek, Networked Picture Systems, or Screaming Technology.

If you print separations through an OPI-compatible high-end color prepress system, the low-resolution versions of the TIFFs will automatically be replaced by their high-resolution counterparts. In either case, the resulting output is full-color separations of the entire page, plate-ready for your printing company.

Relative strengths and weaknesses of DCS and OPI

Both DCS and OPI have their advantages and disadvantages. DCS produces five EPS files per image, thereby consuming more disk space than OPI, which must store only one TIFF file per image. Because the DCS method uses pre-separated images, any changes you make to the images means they must be separated and placed again. With OPI, photographic images can be altered after the page layout stage but before separations are made.

Because DCS works only with pre-separated images, you must commit to specific separation parameters (such as paper type and press characteristics) before beginning the page layout. These parameters, however, may change during the design process, perhaps requiring you to separate and place the DCS images again. This is not a problem with OPI, which works with unseparated images.

Both DCS and OPI allow you to combine desktop-published documents and color photographs on the same set of plate-ready separations. DCS works well as a desktop-only solution, but closes the possibility of combining desktop layout with high-end color output.

OPI offers significant flexibility as a post-processing tool that lets you choose whether to use desktop color technology for a quality mid-range solution, or color prepress technology for a high-end solution. However, the fact that it requires the user to write each publication to disk, rather than reading the application's data files directly, limits OPI's acceptance in many production environments.

Together, these specifications are making it easier for desktop publishers to include color in their documents, and to have a greater level of confidence that the final printed piece will look right, with no surprises.

Aldus PageMaker

Aldus PageMaker is the package that began the desktop publishing revolution when it was introduced in July 1985. Since then, PageMaker has undergone numerous revisions, adding more features each time while retaining its intuitive look and feel.

Version 4 of PageMaker, which is available for the Macintosh and for IBM compatibles running Windows or OS/2, is based on the pasteboard metaphor familiar to traditional layout artists. In addition, it incorporates some of the long-document features, such as index and table of contents generation, that have made Ventura Publisher popular.

Color support in PageMaker

PageMaker allows you to produce spot color separations directly, but requires a post-processor—such as Aldus PrePrint or Adobe Photoshop on the Mac, or Publisher's Prism or PhotoStyler on the PC—to handle four-color separations of photographic images.

PageMaker lets you define color using four different methods—CMYK and PANTONE for process and spot-color definition, plus RGB and HLS for convenience in working with other color domains. No matter which method you use, PageMaker can translate as needed to create process or spot colors.

Just as paragraph styles make up a publication's style sheet, the colors you define make up a publication's color palette. (If you are stuck with a monochrome monitor, all colors appear as black, white, or perhaps shades of gray. A color monitor, however, will simulate your chosen colors as they will appear when printed.)

Your publication's color palette automatically contains three colors—Paper, Black, and Registration. Paper refers to the color of the paper you will be printing on; its value is the only one you can change. Black refers to a preset and unchangeable color value. Registration refers to objects, such as crop marks, that are to be printed on each separation.

PageMaker lets you apply colors to imported bitmapped images, but not to vector graphics. Boxes, circles, and ovals can be filled with colored shades or patterns but, because PageMaker allows only one color per object, a pattern must have the same color as the bounding box. PageMaker maintains a color name tag that associates a color with every object, and changing the value of that color will change the color value of all objects tagged with it.

When printing separations from PrePrint, be careful with the names of the colors being used in the file, because PrePrint uses the spelling and punctuation of the color name to determine whether it is the same as another color. When you use more than one application program, chances are colors will be named differently.

Figure 8-6
You can edit colors in PageMaker using a variety of color models.

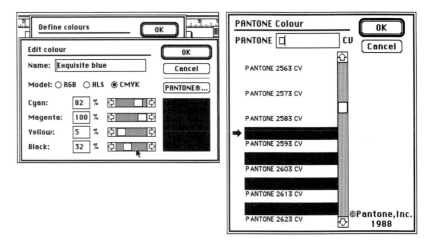

If the names of the colors are not the same (including capitalization and punctuation), they will print on separate spot-color overlays. In particular, note that PANTONE Color names are abbreviated differently in PageMaker and FreeHand. If you're working with a PageMaker publication that includes placed FreeHand illustrations containing PANTONE Colors, make sure the color names are the same in both PageMaker and FreeHand.

In addition, when defining process colors in PageMaker, the CMYK percentages you enter in the Edit Color dialog box must be the exact percentages your print shop will use. To define process-color equivalents in PageMaker, use the Edit Color dialog box to choose the color you want from the PANTONE Color library, then select one of the other color models (such as CMYK), thereby converting the PANTONE Color's definition.

Knockouts in PageMaker

PageMaker can print spot-color overlays with or without knock-outs—knockout overlays eliminate the need to remove the first color underneath an overlapping object—for example, a 20% screen in the area beneath the logo. This may save your printing company the time required to remove the screen in the cutout area, although it's best to check with them first. PageMaker does not provide control of trapping, so if registration is not tight, gaps will show between the knockout and the background colors.

Another potential problem to look for concerns the difference between solid blacks in FreeHand and in PageMaker. FreeHand defines its black as a process color, while PageMaker defines all colors as spot colors, including those created using the CMYK model in PageMaker.

The spot color Black represents all the black objects in PageMaker; likewise, all the blacks in the FreeHand EPS file are shown as Process Black. To print all the blacks on the same separation, highlight the spot color Black from the ink list in PrePrint, and then select Convert Ink to Process. This converts all the blacks in the separation file to process blacks and it prints them on the same separation.

If you create spot-color separations by printing directly from PageMaker, any PICT, TIFF, or EPS graphic is printed in whatever color it was assigned in PageMaker. However, if you use Aldus PrePrint to create separations, you can separate color TIFF and color EPS graphics (though not PICT graphics) into their intrinsic colors.

Beginning with PageMaker version 4 for the Mac, you can now compress these files as you place them, by using a weird combination of keystrokes. After selecting the file name of a TIFF image (color or grayscale), hold down the Command and Option keys for two seconds while clicking OK. To get the maximum level of compression, also hold down the Shift key (or get a friend to hold it down for you). To decompress a file, hold down just the Command key as you open the file.

Managing links

Many users find PageMaker's ability to manage links valuable, especially if they are working with color publishing. The Links command in the File menu brings up a list of all the text and graphics files that have been imported into PageMaker from other application programs.

Figure 8-7
PageMaker Links
dialog box

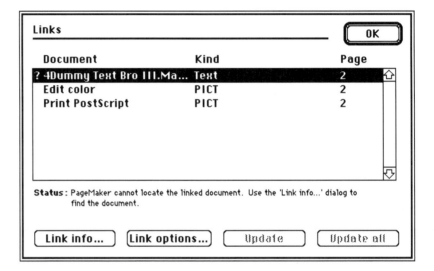

File names are listed with file type and the page number in the publication, opposite which are symbols to indicate whether the file is linked to an external file that has been modified but not updated in the publication, whether the item is linked to an external file in which both the internal and external files have been modified, and at least three other conditions.

To create process color separations with PageMaker Mac, print to disk by clicking the PostScript button in the Print dialog box. The PostScript file can be opened and separated in PrePrint or any other program that supports OPI.

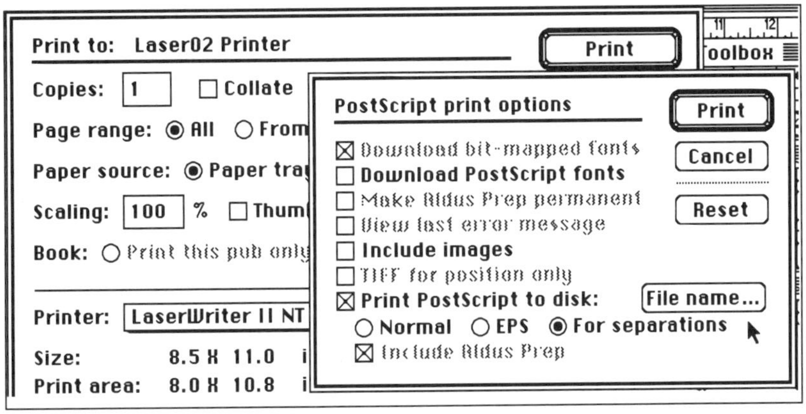

Figure 8-8
PostScript button
in the PageMaker
Print dialog box

QuarkXPress

Many desktop publishers consider QuarkXPress second to none in its color features. It permits the user to apply color to characters, lines, and rules, to box backgrounds and frames, and to imported black-and-white pictures. You can apply only those colors contained in a document's color palette, but can quickly add new colors to a palette. You can edit existing palettes, and append colors from other documents' palettes. When you create a document, it automatically includes the default color palette, which you can fine-tune to your taste.

The preset default color palette contains nine colors: black, white, red, green, blue, cyan, magenta, yellow, and registration. The registration color enables you to print characters and items to which it is applied on all color separation films. You can apply the registration color to cut or fold marks, for example, so they appear in the same position on every color separation film when you print a page. The default on-screen display color for the registration color is black.

You create and edit colors using the Edit Color dialog box (the Color command in the Edit menu), which enables you to use a color wheel or numeric fields to create colors.

You can specify color using any of four methods: PANTONE, HSB, RGB, and CMYK. You can begin by selecting a PANTONE Color and edit it using another color model. To apply color to characters and pictures, use the Color command in the Style menu; to items, via the Color pop-up menu in the Item Specifications dialog box; and to rules, via the Paragraph Rules dialog box. You can switch from one color model to another while creating or editing any color. In QuarkXPress 3.1, you can do all this in the new Colors palette. You can switch from one color model to another while creating or editing any color.

Figure 8-9
QuarkXPress Edit Color
dialog box

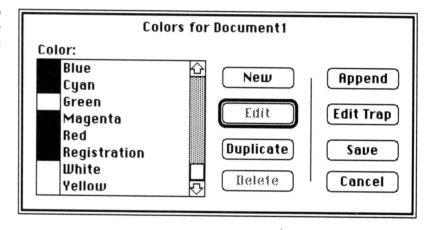

If you modify a color after applying it to characters or items, QuarkXPress automatically updates the color wherever it is applied, according to the changes you have made.

When you create or edit a color, you can specify it as either a spot color or a process color. QuarkXPress prints items that have been given a spot color on an individual spot color separation plate; items to which you apply a process color are printed on four process color separation plates. Note that if CMYK is the selected model, you can specify a color using the definition fields only, rather than the color wheel.

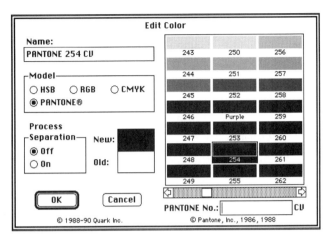

Quark has recently upgraded to version 3.1 of QuarkXPress, adding a number of new features:

- There are three new floating palettes for colors, style sheets, and trap information, which keep oft-used controls at your fingertips.

- You can now specify the color of margin guides, ruler guides, and baseline grid lines displayed on color monitors. TIFF and RIFF format images can now be previewed in the Get Picture dialog box.

- You can apply color to text, pictures, lines, box backgrounds, and frames, and specify two-color blends for box backgrounds. In addition to PANTONE Colors, the Trumatch and Focoltone process color matching systems are now supported.

- The XPress Data file is no longer part of QuarkXPress. Kerning table and tracking table information, hyphenation exceptions, and custom frame information are now saved in the XPress Preferences file, which is stored in your QuarkXPress folder. Unlike the XPress Data file, the XPress Preferences file does not have to be included when you send a document to a service bureau for printing.

Trapping in QuarkXPress

Trapping is handled somewhat differently in versions 3.0 and 3.1. To specify trapping values for colors in QuarkXPress 3.0, select the Colors dialog box in the Edit menu. Selecting Colors when no document is open changes the trapping values for colors in the program's default color palette.

In the Colors dialog box, select from the Color list an object color for which you want to specify trapping values. Click on Edit Trap to display the Trap Specifications dialog box. QuarkXPress 3.1 provides a trapping palette that can be displayed on screen at any time, offering even more precise control over complex trapping situations. It also allows you to set traps for each object, rather than just for a particular color.

Figure 8-11
Edit Colors—Trap
Specifications

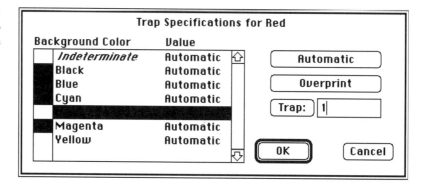

The scroll list displayed in the Trap Specifications dialog box shows the trapping values specified for the object color selected in the Colors dialog box and each of the colors in the Background Color list. The Value column displays the trapping value specified for each background color, with Automatic indicating that the object color and the background color's trapping relationship is determined by the program's built-in automatic trapping algorithm. Overprint indicates that the object color is not knocked out of the background color's separation film. A numeric value indicates a trap value has been specified between the object color and the background color.

To specify a trap amount between the object color and the selected background color, enter a value in the Trap field and click Trap. You can enter trap values from -5 to 5 points, in increments of .001-point (although, in practice, trap values are usually kept within -1 to +1 points).

A negative trap value chokes (reduces) the knockout area on the background color's separation film; a positive value spreads (enlarges) items on the object color's separation film so that they overlap the background color.

The automatic trap value for a given combination of object and background colors is determined by the amount of black in the two colors. The object color and background color are first converted to CMYK values, and the black values of the two colors are compared. If the black value is greater in the object color than it is in the background color, the background color is choked. If the black value of the object color is less, the object is spread. The amount of trapping is determined by the difference in the two black values.

Trapping is a complex subject, worthy of its own book. But it is sufficient here to explore a few operating principles that determine how QuarkXPress creates the trap in a number of common and not-so-common situations.

- If the background of an object is Indeterminate (containing multiple colors, as in a color photograph), automatic trapping knocks out the object's background without trapping;

- Color characters are always trapped to the background of the text box that contains them.

- Process colors are trapped according to the CMYK values associated with their color, although they print on the process separation film.

- If you specify a negative trap value between an object color and the Indeterminate background color, text to which the object color is applied will not be choked, but will be knocked out of the background color without any trapping. All other items of that object color will be choked by the Indeterminate background color.

If you want two characters or items of the same color to be trapped differently against the same background color (in XPress 3.0), create two colors that are identical except for the name and the trapping values associated with them. Version 3.1 eliminates the need to do this.

Using XTensions

XPress is *extensible*—if you know how to write computer programs in any common language, you can write custom Xtensions, either for your own use or for the commercial market. Among the Xtensions currently available are:

- Visionary, from Scitex, which provides a link between desktop page layout with QuarkXPress and high-end imaging on a Scitex color prepress system;

- XData, from Em Software, which automates the production of recurrent documents by taking data from any database or spreadsheet file and mapping it through a template in XPress, thereby producing hundreds or thousands of customized documents;

- CopyFlow, from North Atlantic Publishing Systems, which allows you to keep track of all the text files, graphics, and images you use in QuarkXPress documents, and to print reports based on their use;

- SpectreSeps QX, from Pre-Press Technologies, which adds the ability to create four-color separations of color TIFF images directly from QuarkXPress.

This is merely a taste of what is available, and the number of useful extensions available is sure to grow as the user base expands. To use an extension, simply copy the extension file into your QuarkXPress program folder and launch QuarkXPress. That's all there is to it. Once it's loaded, an extension's features—new windows, menu commands, tools, and so on—are seamlessly integrated into XPress. The kerning and tracking editor that is bundled with QuarkXPress is one example of an extension that many people have used.

Quark also sells a package called QuarkXTras, which includes extensions that support various popular scanners. It also includes the Super XTension, which adds a number of important features such as graphics retrieval and printer calibration.

Sending XPress files to a service bureau

In QuarkXPress 3.0, to be certain your document will print properly, you must provide your service bureau with some files in addition to the QuarkXPress document file you want to output:

- the XPress Data file, which contains custom tracking and kerning tables, hyphenation exceptions, and any frames you create using the Frame Editor;
- high-resolution picture files, such as any EPS, TIFF, or RIFF picture files needed to print pictures imported into the document.

This has also been eliminated in version 3.1.

Color separations from QuarkXPress

To print color separation films directly from QuarkXPress, select Make Separations in the Print dialog box, which activates the Plate pop-up menu. You can print one color separation film, or *plate* as Quark calls it, at a time, or print color separation plates for all colors specified on the page.

If you will be using QuarkXPress to make separations of full-color photographs, you must use a DCS-compatible program to create the color separation files. Among the DCS-compatible programs available are Adobe Photoshop, Letraset ColorStudio, and Pre-Press Technologies' SpectrePrint Professional.

Working with DCS separations

As previously mentioned, QuarkXPress works with color images that have been pre-separated using the DCS specification. A DCS-compatible scanning program or color separation package creates five files for each image: a DCS master file containing a low-resolution PICT version of the image for screen display, and four color EPS separation files, one each for the image's cyan, magenta, yellow, and black components.

You import the DCS master file into QuarkXPress using the Get Picture command, after which you can position, crop, and scale the image as desired. When you print a document that contains a DCS picture, QuarkXPress uses the color separation information contained in the four DCS separation files to output the process color separation plates with the color image correctly positioned and sized.

The DCS master file contains information about the location of the four color-specific separation files. If you move the master file or separation files from the folder or disk in which you saved them when you originally created the separations, the path names specified by the master file will no longer match the files' actual locations.

In this situation, XPress will look for the DCS files in the folder where the QuarkXPress document you are printing is located. Although some users will rely on this as a way out of the missing file dilemma, a better approach would be to plan the file names and folders at the outset, so that you don't force yourself into data shenanigans such as editing the DCS master file. If QuarkXPress is unable to find the high-resolution files in either of these locations, it will print the low-resolution versions of any pictures whose high-resolution files were not found.

QuarkXPress performance note

The most common cause of sluggish performance in QuarkXPress is lack of available memory. The program requires at least 2 megabytes of RAM, but 4Mb would be an absolute minimum, and 8Mb to 16Mb would be more appropriate, for documents containing photographic images. For memory-intensive tasks such as text rotation and image scaling, increasing the amount of memory available to QuarkXPress results in a significant improvement in speed.

One way to increase the memory available to QuarkXPress is to hide all unused extensions. When XPress starts up, it looks for extensions in the program folder and runs any it finds, including import/export filters, the Kern/Track editor, and any third-party extensions. Because each of these adds to Quark's RAM requirements, you should hide the extensions you are not using by creating a folder within your QuarkXPress folder and placing them in it. You can bring them out later if you need them.

If you are running under MultiFinder or System 7 and have more than 2Mb of RAM in your machine, you can increase the partition size allotted to QuarkXPress. Without QuarkXPress running, select its program icon and choose Get Info from the Finder's File menu. Enter the amount of memory you want to allocate to QuarkXPress in the Application Memory Size field in the lower portion of the Get Info dialog box.

Letraset DesignStudio

Letraset DesignStudio is a full-function Macintosh page layout program that can handle all phases of the publishing process, from concepts and thumbnails through roughs and proofs, right to four-color separations. DesignStudio supports all the major color models, including RGB, HSV, CMYK, and PANTONE

DesignStudio lets you rotate text, graphics, and other design elements in increments of one-tenth of a degree. It features advanced typography with precise control over kerning, leading, runarounds, hyphenation, horizontal and vertical justification, and three levels of tracking. One useful feature is a Glossary that lets you store recurring text or graphic elements for instant retrieval and placement in your publications.

DesignStudio allows you to display and print text and graphics in full 24-bit color, as RGB, HSV, CMYK, or PANTONE Colors. It can provide output for proofing, comps, and roughs as well as separated film for reproduction. It supports the use of Letraset Printer Description (LPD) files to take full advantage of the capabilities of specific PostScript printers.

DesignStudio has one very handy feature for color publishers that is currently lacking in all other programs—an automatically generated list of all the fonts and pictures used in your document, for your own use or to be provided to your service bureau.

Letraset supports the use of Annexes, add-on modules that install in DesignStudio's folder to extend its functionality. There are five Annexes bundled with DesignStudio, for kerning, tracking, and other specialized functions, and additional Annexes can be purchased from Letraset and third-party developers.

Separator Annex

The DesignStudio Separator Annex produces full-page color separations from DesignStudio documents output to PostScript color imagesetters. DesignStudio was the first program on the Mac to separate all the elements on the page, including color TIFF, RIFF, PICT2, and EPS files, in addition to text and graphics created in DesignStudio. It uses the CIE color model for converting RGB data to CMYK, and includes undercolor removal (UCR) and gray component replacement (GCR), plus tone and saturation compression.

With the Separator Annex, you can also specify settings for paper type, dot gain, and screen ruling. Text and graphic elements can be designated for either spot or process separations, and trapping is supported, including the ability to define chokes and spreads for specific elements.

Ventura Publisher

Ventura Publisher is one of the most powerful publishing programs available: it has shifted the focus from laying out individual pages to automating the production of recurrent documents.

Ventura is available in four editions, but at the present time only the Windows edition includes substantial color capabilities. The editions of Ventura Publisher for DOS/GEM, OS/2, and the Macintosh support spot color but not process color. You can assign spot colors to any text, paragraph tag, or line graphic, and create spot color separations ready for reproduction. You are limited to eight spot colors, which is more than you would want to create in any event.

For those using the DOS/GEM version of Ventura, one way around the program's color separation limitations is to import color EPS files into Ventura and print them to disk as PostScript, then separate them with a third-party utility such as Publisher's Prism.

To work with full-color images, you need Ventura Publisher 4 for Windows, which supports 24-bit color files in TIFF, EPS, DCS, and PCX formats. Ventura 4 allows the use of optional extensions for scanning and separating fully composed pages with all text, illustrations, and photographs in place from within Ventura. It works with all major color models, including RGB, CMY, CMYK, HLS, and PANTONE.

Figure 8-12
Defining spot colors in the DOS/GEM version of Ventura Publisher.

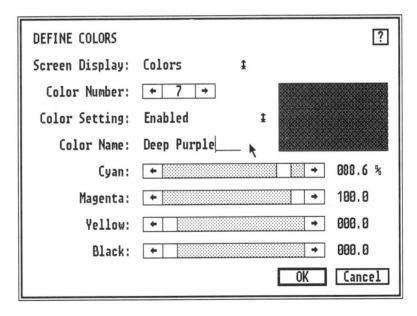

Ventura Scan is an extension that permits scanning from within Ventura Publisher, using most popular scanners. It saves images in TIFF format, and lets you preview a low-resolution scan, then crop and color correct it before scanning directly to disk or into a Ventura frame.

Ventura Separator is also an extension, designed for publishers who want to separate complete Ventura pages with all text, illustrations, and scanned images in place. It provides control over brightness, contrast, sharpening, and color saturation, plus custom screen angles and frequencies for optimal color separations on any output device.

Ventura ColorPro is a professional color correction and separation package that includes most of the features found on high-end systems, including tone curve correction, color correction for scanner deficiencies and ink impurities, compensation for press gain, gray balance adjustment, undercolor removal and addition, gray component replacement, and unsharp masking. Ventura ColorPro can be run from within Ventura Publisher or as a standalone application under Windows.

Ventura PhotoTouch is a professional image editing program that can be run either within Ventura or under Windows. It provides tools for retouching and masking color and grayscale images of any size, with an assortment of filters to sharpen, blur, or modify the hue and saturation of any selection. To maximize speed, Ventura PhotoTouch records your changes while working in low-resolution mode, then automatically updates the high-resolution image. It supports RGB, HLS, CMY, and CMYK color models, and works with EPS, DCS, BMP, TIFF, DIB, Targa, and Scitex CT files.

Ventura 4 contains a few other features of particular relevance to publishers, especially its support for Dynamic Data Exchange (DDE) and Object Linking & Embedding (OLE). These two protocols allow you to build links between Ventura and other software programs, such as Microsoft Excel, Word for Windows, WordPerfect for Windows, Corel Draw, Micrografx Designer, and Charisma.

Version 4 also boasts improvements Ventura users have been clamoring after for years, such as a built-in spell checker (with an 88,000-word dictionary); search and replace of text, attributes, and tags; and an Undo command.

Separation software

Because many color graphics and imaging programs provide insufficient control over the color separation process, a variety of add-on programs have emerged, designed specifically for color correction and separation. These range from simple separation utilities to full-function color correction packages with features comparable to those found on high-end systems.

Most specialized separation programs are currently available only on the Macintosh, though that is changing with the recent popularity of PCs' running Windows. For many PageMaker users, Aldus PrePrint is popular as a separation utility, providing a reasonably good set of controls. Other professional color publishers might prefer to pay for the extra features found in Pre-Press Technologies' SpectrePrint Pro.

SpectrePrint Pro

SpectrePrint Pro from Pre-Press Technologies is a professional color correction and separation program for the Macintosh, providing a powerful range of controls comparable to those found on high-end scanners. It provides control over undercolor removal and addition, gray component replacement, and tonal range and gradation for each of the process colors. It allows access to gray balance curves that let you precisely control neutral tones, and lets you compensate for press gain, as well as specify halftone screen frequencies and angles.

A built-in monitor calibration feature gives you a fairly accurate on-screen view of how an image will look when printed with the selected paper stock and inks. Color value readings taken with the program's digital densitometer accurately reflect the results you will get on film.

Aldus PrePrint

Aldus PrePrint is a Macintosh color separation program that adds to the capabilities of layout programs such as PageMaker, and illustration programs such as FreeHand. PrePrint lets you generate quality four-color separations of text, illustrations, and photographs—directly from the desktop. You can separate an entire publication at once, without splitting it into single-page files. Alternately, you can start with one or more TIFF image files, or any color file saved in the PostScript/OPI format.

You can output color separations to any PostScript-compatible imagesetter, or as black-and-white or color composites to a PostScript printer. Files can be printed to disk for transport to your service bureau, and image masks can be included in your separations for use with traditional stripping methods.

With PrePrint 1.5, you can print pages in any page range, and print them page-by-page rather than color-by-color

PrePrint now supports DCS and CMYK TIFF files, and can directly separate any PostScript-language file that conforms to Adobe's document and color-separation conventions, and includes OPI comments for photographs.

Figure 8-13
PrePrint dialog boxes

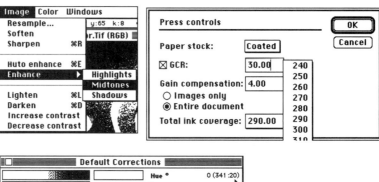

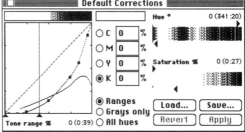

Aldus PrePrint provides a broad set of enhancement controls that let you soften, sharpen, lighten, or darken an image, increase or reduce its contrast, and increase or decrease the

color saturation. These filters are applied over the entire image, and have been preset within the program at levels that should prove optimal for most images. You have slightly greater flexibility with the control for enhancing highlights, midtones, or shadows, and with the color balancing control, which allows you to specify the neutral tone to which the rest of the image should be balanced.

This approach greatly simplifies the use of a color manipulation program by using "expert systems" within the software to replace the friendly, experienced color technician whose expert eye can look at four pieces of separated film and immediately detect a subtle color cast and the correction required.

To some users, PrePrint may seem limited because the user can apply these transformations only globally—there is no way to "touch up" an image by making subtle local modifications. And the image controls are all pre-set, using values Aldus derived from visiting hundreds of prepress houses and observing highly skilled people at work on everyday images.

However, it's important to keep in mind that PrePrint is intended for processing images, not for creating or enhancing them, and was therefore designed for a different audience than a program like Adobe Photoshop.

How does PrePrint fit into the typical production cycle? After creating your publication in an OPI-compatible program, print the file to disk as a PostScript-OPI file for separation. The OPI file is opened in PrePrint, where it can optionally be enhanced, before being printed as separations. Images saved in RGB TIFF format can also be imported into PrePrint for enhancement and color separation.

How to use PrePrint

To use PrePrint, first print your publication to disk from your page layout or graphics application. In PageMaker Mac, choose the For Separations option in the PostScript Print Options dialog box, thereby creating a file with a .SEP extension that a separation program such as PrePrint can use to create the separations.

When printing a .SEP file from PageMaker, make sure the Include Images option in the PostScript Print Option dialog box is *unchecked*. Because you'll link to the high-resolution scan in PrePrint, there's no reason to have PageMaker include the image in the .SEP file. OPI ensures that all the sizing and cropping you've made to the low-resolution version in PageMaker is included in the .SEP file, and will be applied to the high-resolution version when you link the image in PrePrint.

The PostScript-OPI file can contain text, artwork, and links to TIFF or DCS images. Whenever you place a TIFF or DCS image in your publication, PageMaker displays a low-resolution version of the image on the screen and establishes a link between the publication and the high-resolution file. When you print the publication to disk for separations, PageMaker saves the link information in the PostScript-OPI file so that PrePrint can locate the high-resolution image to use in printing the actual separations. PrePrint 1.5 provides default dot-gain compensation, total ink coverage, and UCR based upon the user's choice of paper stock. The user can further modify these settings.

When printing separations, PrePrint normally knocks out any ink that underlies another. However, to reduce trapping problems, you can specify that one ink is to overprint others. PrePrint lets you select precisely the best screen angles and rulings for each ink, to minimize moiré patterns. You can print any spot color as either a process or spot color, set the total ink coverage, and tell the program to compensate for the paper stock being used.

Figure 8-14
PrePrint workflow
schematic

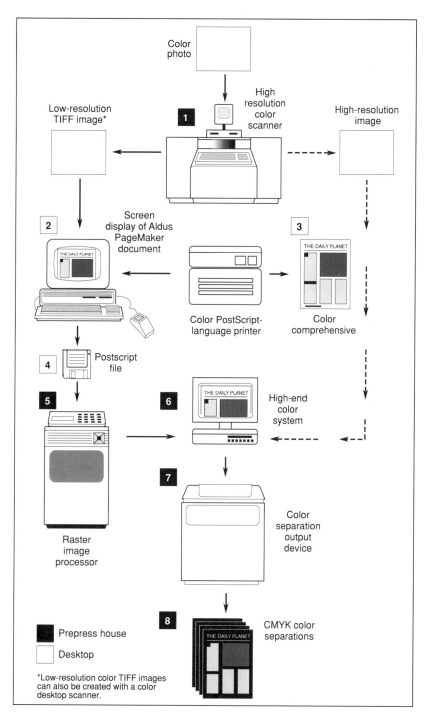

PrePrint uses information, from the PostScript Printer Description (PPD) and Printer Description Extension (PDX) files, to create the separations:

- PPD files, developed by Adobe or your printer manufacturer, contain screen angle and line ruling information designed to reduce the potential for disruptive moiré patterns in printed documents;

- PDX files, developed by Aldus, include information for imagesetter calibration to optimize output from the targeted imagesetter.

Aldus PrePrint can give you separations with near-magazine quality color photographs. For a final version that rivals the color images in magazines of professional quality, you may want to use PrePrint for all but the color photographs and send the job out to a prepress house to separate them. If the prepress system supports PostScript as well as OPI, you may be able to separate the entire publication using the prepress system, which saves money by creating only one set of film.

Otherwise, create two copies of the PostScript file, one for the PostScript service bureau and one for the prepress house. The two resulting sets—one for your PageMaker publication and the other for your color-separated images—can be positioned quickly because of the registration marks on both sets of film, making final stripping much easier.

Calibrating PrePrint

The importance of calibration has been mentioned before, but warrants a few more words. For a number of device-specific reasons, most PostScript devices vary in they way different dot densities are measured and printed. This means, for example, that a requested 30 percent tint (from your application) may actually print at 35 percent (on the imagesetter) when the film is measured with a densitometer. This slight difference can be crucial when doing color separations, because PrePrint converts each color into halftone dots on an individual separation.

An uncalibrated imagesetter will lead to surprising color shifts on press, as colors can shift noticeably with as little as 2–3 percent difference in dot densities, especially when the colors consist of significant portions of each process color, or when a specific tint percentage is crucial to a certain spot color. PrePrint gives you control over the gray calibration process with a PDX Editor HyperCard stack, which lets you modify your output device's PDX file directly.

When you take your work to a service bureau, as described in Chapter 10, make sure that they use a PDX file calibrated for your job. If you decide to create the separations yourself by using PrePrint to write the job to disk (as .PS files), you should get a copy of the service bureau's calibrated PDX files for their output device. PrePrint 1.5 supports external imagesetter calibration packages, high-quality image resampling, and user-adjustable color conversion tables.

SpectreSeps

Pre-Press Technologies makes SpectreSeps PM, a program that adds continuous tone capabilities to documents created using Aldus PageMaker version 4. A PageMaker user can now place pictures directly into PageMaker publications and, with all other page elements in position, four-color separate them to a PostScript imagesetter.

PrePress Technologies also makes SpectreSeps QX, which is an Xtension that adds similar color separation functions to Quark XPress.

Adobe Photoshop

People who think of Photoshop as primarily a painting or image enhancement program are missing its capabilities for color separating any color TIFF or EPS file. You can use Photoshop in conjunction with just about any page layout program simply by including your color images and graphics in the page, then writing the page to disk as a PostScript file, which can be opened and color separated in Photoshop.

Another option is to use Photoshop to color separate any image in CMYK mode into five separate EPS documents for placement in page layout programs supporting the DCS specification.

Letraset ColorStudio can also be used this way for color separating any color TIFF or EPS file.

Publisher's Prism

The Publisher's Prism program from InSight Systems will color separate any PostScript file, and provides complete control over line-screen frequencies, screen angles, dot gain, and UCR.

It consists of two parts: a PC-based program running under DOS or Windows, and a 75 Kb program that is downloaded to your PostScript output device (printer, imagesetter, or interpreter). The PC-resident program combines the parameter settings you specify with the PostScript page description to create four files, one each for the cyan, magenta, yellow, and black images. The printer-resident program prints out each separation as a separate page.

Figure 8-15
Publisher's Prism
provides a complete set
of color controls.

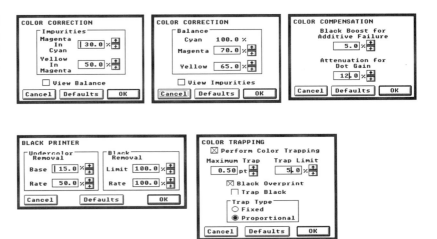

Publisher's Prism provides a rich assortment of controls, including color correction, compensation, balancing, and trapping.

The Settings Summary shows all the parameters selected, and can be printed, saved, and loaded for use with other images.

Figure 8-16
Publisher's Prism lets
you print a Settings
Summary of all
parameters.

```
SETTINGS SUMMARY                        Gray Scale Correction: OFF
  Paper: letter/portrait                Color Correction: ON
                                        Magenta Balance = 70%
Crop inside left edge 0.75 in           Yellow Balance = 65%
Crop inside right edge 0.75 in          Undercolor Rem. Thresh. = 15%
Cropped Width = 7.00 in                 Undercolor Removal Rate = 50%
Scaled Width = 7.00 in                  Black Removal Limit = 100%
Width Scale Factor = 1.0000             Black Removal Rate = 100%
Crop inside bottom edge 0.75 in         Additive Failure Comp. = 5%
Crop inside top edge 0.75 in            Dot Gain Compensation = 10%
Cropped Length = 9.50 in                Trapping: Proportional
Scaled Length = 9.50 in                 Maximum Trap = 0.50 points
Length Scale Factor = 1.0000            Trap Limit = 5%
                                        No Black Trap
No Bleed          No Rotate             Black Overprint
Left Indentation = 0.25 in
Bottom Indentation = 0.25 in                    Screen Angles:
Positive, Right Reading                 Cyan    = 15    Yellow =   0
Screen Frequency = 133 lpi              Magenta = 75    Black  =  45
Annotation:
  [Cancel]    Input: none
              Output: d:\prism\jgraham.CNF                    [ OK ]
```

Desktop color in every document

Page layout combines the words and drawings and pictures. It's the part of the process in which the designer has free reign to create not just graphics but entire pages and books.

With the addition of full-color separations to the desktop publishing process, the shift from black-and-white to color is almost complete. Now you can integrate color type, graphics, and pictures as part of the publication of all kinds of documents.

Software vendors have had to solve a variety of complex technical problems in order to build programs capable of color separating complete documents from the desktop. But the whole color revolution is about *content*, not technologies. In other words, now that color page layout tools are here, the big question is what we'll do with them.

Color Electronic Prepress Systems

"We all know what light is; but it is not easy to tell what it is."
SAMUEL JOHNSON

Color electronic prepress systems (CEPS) are specialized computers used for scanning, enhancing, retouching, correcting, and color separating full-color artwork and photographs. They have become indispensable for producing high-quality color in publishing, advertising, and packaging.

They are referred to as high-end both in terms of their price and performance. These systems are the basis of many recent innovations on the desktop, such as cloning, the magic wand tool, and color maps.

Only twenty years ago high-end prepress was the "coming revolution," threatening to displace traditional camera-based color separations, but today its own future is threatened by lower-cost systems on the desktop.

The high-end color prepress systems explored in this chapter are comparable to the emerging desktop color systems, but with a few differences:

- they are usually faster, sometimes a lot faster;

- they have greater resolution and dynamic range, and hence higher quality;
- they are more complex to operate;
- they can handle larger original and output sizes;
- they cost more, often a lot more.

In the past decade, the market for high-end professional color systems has been shared primarily by four companies: Hell, Scitex, Crosfield, and Screen. Their customers have been the color houses—also known as film houses, color separators, or trade shops—where photographs are scanned, combined with page layouts, and color separated.

Typically, the owners of a color house have invested millions of dollars in hardware—specialized prepress equipment, most of it from a single vendor whose products are often completely incompatible with those of other vendors. For instance, a scan performed on one brand of scanner might not work with a competing brand of film recorder, because the pixels were shaped as rectangles instead of squares.

A further complication is the emergence of increasingly capable mid-range systems such as Kodak Prophecy, Agfa Pix, and others, which use standard Unix-based computers as workstations.

A successful color house has also invested substantial money in training the people who operate the equipment. The prepress process requires many skilled, highly paid technicians precisely cutting, aligning, and taping pieces of film.

This chapter is concerned with high-end and mid-range prepress systems and the color houses that use them. It includes information on each of the major vendors, as well as their links to the desktop. It also describes the services and operations of a typical color house, with suggestions for desktop users who want to integrate high-end color into their publications.

Figure 9-1
Advanced electronic
prepress station, with
peripherals.
Courtesy of Scitex
America Corp.

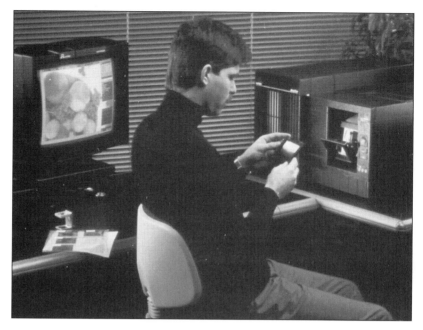

Evolution of color separation technologies

To provide a context in which to explore the ever-changing products in the professional prepress market, consider how the color separation process has evolved. A person entering the color prepress industry in the 1960s would have learned how to create color separations "in the camera"—through the photographic process, using a reprographic camera. This involved literally dozens of different steps, and often as many pieces of film.

Analog scanners, which store and manipulate color data as varying electric voltages, became increasingly common in the 1970s and '80s. In the late 1980s, analog scanners began to be replaced by digital scanners that manipulated the data as discrete zeros and ones, and offered connectivity to high-speed digital computers. Today, digital scanners and the high-end prepress systems they work with have become the standard tool for making color separations.

Although it may take some time, desktop color separation will inevitably be the next stage in this evolution. In 1990 more than 80 percent of the color separations in North America continued to be produced on analog systems, with fewer than 20 percent created on high-end color prepress systems from the four major vendors. The percentage generated on the desktop was too small to be measured, but these proportions are shifting rapidly, and it seems likely that desktop separations will dominate, even if it takes a few years.

The color house

Although color houses provide a diverse assortment of value-added services based around the prepress process, their bread and butter comes from making *quads*—sets of four color-separated films, ready to be stripped into *flats* from which the printer will make the printing plates that go on the press.

Most large prepress houses run 24 hours a day, cranking out color separations and stripping them together. Just as the night shift ships its last set of quads, the couriers start arriving with raw material for the day shift—new negatives, new layouts, new problems.

The production manager and his or her assistant receive production reports from the night shift supervisor, along with any noteworthy dockets, and in consultation with the sales department, prepare a schedule for the day.

They have at their disposal some very expensive equipment and highly skilled scan operators, layout artists, and film strippers, all of whom must be able to work under the daily pressure of deadlines and inevitable breakdowns.

A large group of production managers supervise and coordinate all aspects of the work flow. At any one time, there may be more than a hundred jobs in various stages of production, from initial scanning and page layout through client approval and final output. A variety of customized forms are attached to the job docket at different stages, such as color correction or image assembly, so the client can be billed correctly for the work performed.

Everything gets scanned

Most jobs begin with preparation of the artwork for scanning. Although an increasing number of originals arrive as 35 mm slides, other formats, such as 4"-by-5" color transparencies and hard-copy photographs up to 8"-by-10", are also common.

Transparencies are preferred over reflective art because they tend to maintain a greater dynamic range during the scanning process. The originals are cleaned and carefully mounted on a plastic cylindrical drum, which is loaded into one of two different machines.

Figure 9-2
A drum being loaded on a scanner. Courtesy of Scitex America Corp.

In a modestly equipped color house, the drum is loaded directly onto the scanner, where it is pre-scanned or simply probed to determine the proper densities and other parameters.

The scanner operator uses a keyboard or control panel to enter the appropriate scanner instructions, the final scan is performed, and the image saved to disk or tape.

In a medium-sized or large color house with more expensive equipment, the drum is first mounted on a pre-scan station. The operator determines all the operating parameters for the particular job, then transfers them to the scan station across the local area network.

In many color houses, each scanning drum is identified by a bar code, so that as soon as it is mounted on the scanner, the job parameters are loaded and run, and the image data are stored on magnetic tapes or disk packs.

Type is scanned into the system from a black-and-white *mechanical* or typeset galley, or arrives as PostScript code, which is uploaded to the high-end system and raster image processed, or *ripped*, so that it becomes part of a pixel image. (One exception to this is the Screen approach, in which type is not ripped, but instead is married on-the-fly to the output recorder, where it takes priority over the image.)

Often, before the layout artist can integrate the type and scanned images into the rest of the page, the images must be cleaned up with retouching tools. This is accomplished by zooming in on individual pixels with pencil, brush, or eraser. At the same time, the operator will compensate for any global or local color casts, and will touch up any small problems.

Cycle of proofs and approvals

Once the page layout is complete, a proof is generated to be shown to the client for approval. Despite the emergence of desktop color design, high-quality proofing remains more important than ever because mistakes can be incredibly costly. Even a relatively small color print job can cost tens of thousands of dollars, and printing bills in the millions are not unusual. A few hundred or thousand dollars spent on proofing can represent good economy.

The question these days is whether to go with film proofs or with the new direct digital color proof (DDCP) methods. A film proof, such as a Cromalin, MatchPrint, or FujiPrint, is made through exposure to each of the cyan, magenta, yellow, and black film negatives, and is based on the very film from which the plates would be made.

As its name implies, a direct digital proof is made directly from the digital color data generated by the application program, and can be produced from either a high-end or a desktop system. The important feature of a digital proof is that it is made before the colors have been separated to film. This makes digital proofs cheaper than film proofs, not only because the proof itself costs only about half as much (typically $50 rather than $100), but also because every time viewing a proof causes you to make changes, you've saved the expense of throwing out an entire set of film separations.

The trade-off, of course, is quality. To obtain any kind of critical color matching, most people buying prepress services would much rather be looking at a film proof than at a direct digital proof because of quality. Even this could rapidly change, however, with the emergence of new direct digital proofing methods, such as 3M's Digital MatchPrint, which costs a few hundred thousand dollars and produces stunning output.

Assembling pages into flats

Although more and more color pages are being produced from the desktop, the assembly of pages into printers' flats, ready for plate-making, remains largely a handcraft procedure. One reason is the cost of a film recorder that can output an entire 25"-by-40" piece of film at once. Another is that, at least with desktop color separations, a composite file that large will take hours to print, and may not print at all.

Each flat must be carefully planned before it is stripped up, so that pages appear in the correct order after binding and trimming, and to ensure that color pictures appear where color inks can print them. This process, known as *imposition*, must be accurate and precise, or the consequences can be disastrous. For publications that are stapled (saddle-stitched), each spread must be a slightly different width, to account for the *shingling* that occurs when the publication is folded shut.

A skilled film stripper at work is quite a sight. Small metal clips are inserted into the punch holes in each piece of film, and pieces of film and rubylith (masking material) fly here and there as the stripper uses a razor-sharp knife (or a computerized ruby cutting machine) to cut each element precisely to size. Little pieces of tape hold the various components together. When all the elements for each flat have been stripped together, it is ready for plate-making, which is the responsibility of the printing company

Working with a color house

If you're buying prepress services, there are a few guiding principles that can save time and money. Indeed, when Ben Franklin observed that "time is money," he might have had in mind today's color houses. Turnaround times have been halved in most metropolitan film shops during the past few years, with three-day or four-day service replacing the old one-week turnaround. Of course, you can get complex color corrections, proofs, and separations overnight if you're willing to pay the cost.

When using the services of a color house, it is important to understand the basis on which they charge; failure to do so can be an expensive mistake. Many color houses use semiautomatic systems in which the operators hit a control key to mark the start and finish time for each element of each job. If you ask for a certain effect without specifying a time or dollar limit, you may get the effect you're looking for, but at a price that will leave you in shock.

One way to increase throughput when using the services of a color house is to set up your originals precisely so you can scan directly into your page layout, thereby reducing film stripping costs.

If you're working on a project with long lead times, negotiate with your film supplier early in the game, to get discounts not available on last-minute deadlines. Another way of saving money without giving up quality is to work out an annual commitment with your color separators, in which they gain a steady stream of work at predictable times and you get improved service and predictable costs.

Components of a prepress system

In order to provide such a diversity of prepress services, the color house must make a substantial investment in specialized computers and peripherals.

Processor

Image processing is a very computation-intensive application, requiring the constant recalculation of colors for millions of pixels; therefore, high-end prepress systems are built around powerful processing chips. From their inception, all of the high-end systems have bascd on proprietary and mutually exclusive hardware and software, structured and optimized for image manipulation in different ways. The main requirement for central processors is speed, both internally and in communication with the rest of the system.

Storage

During the past two decades, high-end systems have used a variety of mass storage formats, evolving from tape to disk and back to tape again. Early prepress systems stored images on large reels of nine-track magnetic tape (magtape), each of which was capable of storing less than 100Mb of image data (much less in the earlier models).

Magtapes were superseded by magnetic "disk packs" capable of storing 300Mb, and offering much higher storage and retrieval speeds. Magnetic hard disks are still widely used as a primary storage medium in many color houses, and tape is still the backup medium.

Some color houses use erasable magneto-optical drives, which come in 650Mb cartridges, although more are opting for tape-based solutions, such as digital audio tape (DAT), which have a capacity in excess of 2,000Mb.

Pre-scan

Because of the cost of the scanner, color houses have the option of using a *pre-scan* station to measure density values and set up the parameters for each job before it gets scanned at high resolution. The original is first mounted on a clear plastic cylinder, or drum, which is loaded onto the pre-scan station, where measurements are taken of the size, position, and color content of each original.

The drum is then loaded onto the scanner itself, the scanning parameters are retrieved from a floppy disk or across the network, and the scan is performed and saved to disk. Pre-scanning is especially important when trying to march colors to an actual product or sample, and when there are hundreds of similar originals to be scanned.

Scanner

The principles of high-end scanning are identical to those discussed in Chapter 5 for desktop scanners, although the scanners themselves are different in a few essential ways. The first big difference is resolution: after dealing with typical desktop scanning resolutions in the 200 to 300 dpi range, it's refreshing to move to scanners where 4,000 dpi is the low-resolution setting.

More important, high-end scanners are capable of a dynamic range that puts the desktop units to shame. They can scan an original with a difficult range of contrasts and, within limits, capture detail in both the highlight areas and the shadows. A desktop scanner, with its more narrow dynamic range, is usually forced to drop the shadows to black in order to maintain any detail at all in the highlights. Even with this expanded dynamic range, it still remains important to have a human operator set the color controls to emphasize which parts of an image are to be accentuated.

High-end scanners can work with much larger originals than desktop units, often with poster-sized reflective art up to 20-by-24 inches. Typically, they also operate at much higher speeds, rotating in excess of 800 revolutions per minute.

Because of the time and skill required during the scanning process, the most widely used cost-savings measure in color prepress is *ganging*, in which more than one color separation is made at the same time. All the elements to be scanned must be in the same form (transparencies, prints, or original artwork), and all must be sized to the same percentage during input. Most important, the color content of the shots must be similar.

In some kinds of color separation, the person operating the computer controls is trying to make the color look realistic, and this usually entails balancing the overall cast to a single color element. In pictures of people, this color element is usually flesh tones, while in landscape photography it is often the color of trees, water, and sky. (In some kinds of ad photography, realism is the last thing they're after.) In product shots, the most important factor is the color fidelity of the image to the actual product. Ganging works best when the operator has all scenics, all people shots, or all product shots.

Furthermore, all images in a gang must be free of overall color casts, or any color casts present must be uniform throughout all the images. The highlight areas of each image in the gang should be checked to ensure they are uniform in weight, density, and color cast. If an experienced color separator suggests you break a large gang into two smaller ones to allow for cast correction, it is almost certain to be cheaper in the long run to pay for two good scans than for one that is compromised.

Output

The output from the color prepress systems is generated on a *film recorder*, sometimes known as a laser plotter. Film is generally output as quads, or sets of color separations.

Unlike many of the PostScript imagesetters used to output desktop color separations, all high-end film recorders are based on a rotary drum design, rather than on a flatbed. Punch registration systems are used to hold the film tightly to the drum during exposure, to ensure tight alignment between separations. The halftone screening is usually generated through built-in proprietary hardware, although in many cases the screening algorithms are licensed from Hell Graphic Systems.

The other main difference is speed: high-end film recorders are typically two to 20 times faster than most PostScript imagesetters.

Network

In designing a desktop computing environment, it is often useful to focus on the applications at first, then worry about networking them later. That doesn't work with color prepress, especially at the high end, because cost demands the monitoring of the number of separations completed each hour.

To get those separations out, each component in the prepress system must be tightly linked across a local area network. And there are usually a number of components: rather than use general-purpose workstations for different tasks, most vendors sell highly specialized stations for each aspect of the process. For example, in order to keep the main scanner busy full-time, a color house may have one or more specialized pre-scan stations, which have limited functions but are much less costly than their full-functioned relatives.

Among many prepress users and vendors, the Ethernet network is evolving as a standard. A central PC, Mac, or Unix-based server handles communication between the various specialized devices on the network. Network speed is of the essence, because of the size of image files.

Software links

To take advantage of desktop flexibility and high-end color imaging, many publishers are using software links—programs and protocols that connect the two domains. Software links such as Hell ScriptMaster, Scitex Visionary, and Crosfield StudioLink, are being sold by high-end prepress vendors as a means of including their scanners and film recorders in the desktop color production process.

They share a common workflow. Original art is scanned on a high-end scanner and saved as both high-resolution and low-resolution files. The low-resolution files (which are much smaller and more easily handled) are transferred to the desktop computer, where they are used for position only (FPO). The page layout artist can crop, scale, and rotate any image in real time, because the position-only files are so small. The final page layout is transferred to the high-end system through the software link, where the low-resolution image files are automatically replaced with their high-resolution equivalents, prior to output of color separations on the high-end film recorder.

Hell Graphics Systems

Hell Graphic Systems, a pioneer in color electronic prepress, is now part of the Linotype-Hell Company. Their high-end DC3000 prepress systems have taken the idea of specialization to the limit, with the scanning process now involving three workstations in addition to the scanner itself.

The ChromaScale is used for setting up and defining the job, and specifying the recording and scanning parameters such as enlargement, reduction, and rotation, as well as standard color corrections. It plots to acetate to show the proper work area and angle of each image. The ChromaMount P320 is then used for mounting all the originals—reflective, transmissive, or both—at the correct angle. Next, the ChromaSet P330 station is used for interactive color correction based on the original images, with definition of coordinates for scanning.

Once these steps have been completed, the scan itself can take place. The prepared drums can be automatically scanned by the ChromaGraph S3010 scanner, using the values stored on disk during the preparation stage. The S3010 provides controlled positioning of the scanning head, and adjustment of aperture and focus.

Hell offers two models of electronic page assembly stations. The Hell ChromaCom 1000 is an entry-level electronic cropping and assembly station that works with the Hell ChromaGraph scanners. The ChromaCom 2000 is a full electronic image processing station.

Finally, the ChromaGraph R3020 or R3030 film recorder produces the finished separations, which can be automatically exposed onto roll film in daylight mode, with automatic mounting and removal of the film. Relieved of the tedious job of preparation work, the high-speed scanner and recorder break through the bottleneck that too often hampers the productivity of midsize and large film houses.

ScriptMaster desktop link

Hell believes that desktop publishing linked to high-end prepress will become the standard means of color production in the 1990s. ScriptMaster translates PostScript applications files created in any PC or Macintosh program into ChromaCom files. Supported applications include Aldus PageMaker (PC and Mac), Ventura Publisher, Aldus FreeHand, Adobe Illustrator, and QuarkXPress.

The Unix-based workstation that Hell uses to run the PostScript interpreter can also be used as an AppleShare server, allowing a Mac user to share files over a network, as well as via modem.

The ScriptMaster/OPI version of the program supports the Open Prepress Interface standard, allowing the exchange of image data between a desktop computer and the Hell system, plus the ability to convert a Hell scan into a low-resolution TIFF file for import into a desktop layout program. ScriptMaster passes data from the desktop publishing program as an EPS file through the Hyphen software to the Hell M-series computer. The Hell operator receives the page data and formats it for film generation. With OPI support, the image is received as a mask, along with information on cropping, scaling, and positioning. This eliminates steps in page assembly on the high-end system. Special image enhancements, color correction, or retouching continue to take place on the Hell ChromaCom station.

ScriptMaster can translate files from high-end publishing and typesetting systems such as Interleaf Publisher, MagnaType, and BestInfo Wave4. It supports tints, spot color, overprint borders, and color matching with art created on the desktop.

Crosfield

Crosfield Electronics Ltd. is a division of DuPont Imaging Systems, responsible for building advanced prepress workstations and peripherals.

The Lightspeed Color Layout System (CLS), a graphic design system based around the Macintosh II, lets you create, revise, and enhance designs, and streamline production by capturing design specifications for transfer to color prepress systems. Designs can include color photography, line art, illustrations, logotypes, and text.

A 300 dpi scanner is used to capture reflective art and transparencies, which can then be cropped, moved, and resized while being integrated into a layout. Colors can be specified according to their RGB, CYMK, or PANTONE values, and you can create custom color palettes for precise color specification and mixing.

Version 2.5 of Lightspeed CLS adds the ability to import EPS files, and to save files in OPI format for linking to high-end systems. The links to Crosfield Prepress have been improved, allowing larger page sizes, automatic assembly of CLS pages on Crosfield Studio systems, and faster RIP speeds.

StudioLink desktop connection

StudioLink version 2.1 is a generic PostScript interpreter that supports the Open PrePress Interface (OPI). StudioLink is based on the concept of "image reservations"—you work with low-resolution TIFF preview images generated by StudioLink on a Macintosh, and have the high-resolution version of those images positioned automatically on a Crosfield Studio system.

StudioLink is compatible with page layouts from Crosfield's Lightspeed Color Layout System, Letraset's DesignStudio, QuarkXPress, Aldus PageMaker, and other applications that comply with OPI. You can now download and rasterize Adobe Type 1 fonts (in addition to Type 3 fonts).

StudioLink is built around the Scripter/PS PostScript interpreter, which rapidly converts text files to high-resolution raster data for page assembly; exposes film of fully composed pages with type, line art, and high-resolution color images for proofing and printing; and employs sophisticated halftoning algorithms and laser dot generating hardware to ensure consistency, color fidelity, and repeatability between separations.

The StudioLink hardware platform is a Sun workstation with a minimum of 12Mb of RAM. By using a software RIP, Crosfield assures portability across a range of high-performance workstations.

Scitex

Scitex sells a complete line of high-end color prepress components, and was among the first companies to develop links to the desktop, through its Visionary product.

Smart Scanner

The Scitex Smart Scanner is a flatbed CCD color scanner that offers setup and scanning times considerably shorter than those of traditional drum scanners. It handles transparencies and reflection copy from 35 mm to 8-by-10 inches, using specially designed cassettes that make mounting quick and easy—with no taping, oiling, vacuum, or time-consuming alignment.

During pre-scans, the Smart Scanner analyzes the original and automatically adjusts for highlight and shadow points, film type, and overall tone. Working at a Scitex Softproof workstation, the operator can quickly perform image cropping, sizing, and rotation via pull-down menus.

Productivity can be increased with the background scanning feature. All transparencies required for a page are pre-scanned; while that batch is scanned in the background, the images for another page are pre-scanned. Smart Scanner performs each high-resolution scan without further operator intervention, although it provides a wealth of digital color correction features to interactively modify tone and color. These include unsharp masking, undercolor removal (UCR), and gray component replacement (GCR).

Scitex also makes the SmarTwo PS, a compact CCD color scanner for transparencies from 35 mm up to 2.25-by-2.25 inches. The SmarTwo PS provides direct RGB and CMYK data input to a Macintosh or PC, and can scale images from 20 percent to 1,700 percent.

Star stripping workstation

The new Star stripping workstation represents a first for Scitex—an IBM PS/2-based product in what started out as a Macintosh-oriented field. The Star is a complete page assembly workstation that operates interactively with the Scitex system and shares tasks with other workstations.

Continuous-tone files can be sent from the Scitex system to the Star station before or after retouching and color correction. After stripping and execution on the Star, the composite continuous tone and line-art files are transferred to the Scitex system for output on a film recorder.

In addition, Star uses an Adobe PostScript interpreter to ensure complete compatibility with the desktop. PostScript files from all major desktop publishing and graphics programs are interpreted, merged, and edited on the Star, then transferred to the Scitex system as continuous tone and line-art files.

The Scitex Prisma color image editing and page makeup system is used for heavy-duty retouching tasks and complex layouts. The color capabilities of the workstation include continuous tone creation, global and local gradation, color correction, enhanced airbrush, interactive ghosting, and gray component replacement—in 16 million colors.

Figure 9-3
Scitex Star PS/2-based stripping station. Courtesy of Scitex America Corp.

Visionary desktop link

The Scitex Visionary design layout system consists of a 68030-based Macintosh running a QuarkXPress with an Xtension optimized for working with Scitex systems. Once your design has been perfected and approved (and then corrected just one more time), you can transmit it—with all the page elements in place—to a color service bureau that has a Scitex Response prepress system. The low-resolution screen images are replaced with their high-resolution originals, then separated to film.

Visionary now supports 24-bit color PICT and TIFF files, which can be generated in Mac applications and placed in the Scitex system without loss of quality. Files created and scanned on a Scitex system can be converted to TIFF or PICT format for downloading to the Mac, where they can be used with popular page layout programs.

Early versions of Visionary could read and write only those files in its own unique format, and did not work with ordinary QuarkXPress files. This has been remedied: because Visionary is now an Xtension, it can read and write QuarkXPress document files.

Visionary Interpreter for PostScript (VIP)

Visionary Interpreter for PostScript (VIP) is a Macintosh software application, developed jointly by Adobe and Scitex, that converts PostScript files into Scitex format. It is sold as an option to the Visionary Gateway.

Version 3 of the Visionary software incorporates the features added to XPress 3, such as an enhanced user interface, object grouping and rotation, element libraries, and the ability to view any number of pages as a spread. In addition, a routine has been included that generates a script of image attributes whenever an EPS file is incorporated into Visionary. The VIP program interprets this script and RIPs (raster image processes) the EPS file, eliminating the manual record-keeping formerly required. It then automatically sends processed files to an attached Scitex production system.

At the Gateway site, illustration and graphic files, which have been created and saved in any PostScript application, may be translated into high-resolution, high-quality Scitex format. These files are transferred through the Gateway into the Scitex Response system, where they may be further manipulated prior to film output on a Scitex laser plotter. According to Scitex, VIP is fully compatible with all PostScript font libraries, and conforms to Adobe's "red book" standard.

In 1991, Scitex introduced a workflow process called automatic picture replacement (APR), which allows images to be scanned at high resolution on the SmarTwo PS scanner and archived to removable media. A low-resolution view file is generated at the same time, translated into PS Image (a Scitex EPS format), and transferred to a Macintosh for positioning during page layout. While page layout is being performed, the high-resolution file is read directly to the Scitex PostScript RIP, VIP/2.

When the layout is complete, a PostScript file of the page is created and also sent to the RIP. During the interpretation process, the low-resolution image is automatically swapped with the high-resolution image, and the complete page is output on the Dolev PS imagesetter.

Screen

Screen (formerly Dainippon Screen), is the largest vendor of prepress systems in Japan, and is a leading graphics art supplier worldwide. Their comprehensive prepress product line includes page make-up stations, scanners, scanner peripherals, mask cutters, process cameras, step and repeat machines, assembly and stripping stations, film processors, printers, plate-makers, and proof presses.

The Sigmagraph 2800 electronic page make-up system is their leading color prepress system, designed for high-volume production environments. It comprises more than a dozen separate components, which the film house integrates according to its specific requirements. The processor unit is integrated with a disk unit containing up to eight hard drives, each with a formatted capacity of 640 Mb.

The root of this multi-tasking system is the Disk Unit Controller, or DUC. The DUC is a sophisticated switching unit that allows the system to match up any hard disk with any workstation. This eliminates file copying from drive to drive to execute functions.

An image workstation handles retouching, silhouetting, interactive cropping and assembly, and special effects. A graphics workstation uses a separate 32-bit processor to handle files containing line-art, tints, and logos. An image data executing station moves image post-processing tasks off-line, so the image workstation operator can continue with interactive work while output file creation is underway.

An inter-system communicator station transfers data files between various networked devices, and includes magtape functions for offline image transfer and storage.

Re-writable Magneto Optical Disks are available for this workstation to eliminate the use of tape completely. The communicator station is compatible with the DDES UEFOO (ANSI/1T8.1-1988) standard, allowing free exchange of image data with other DDES-compatible systems.

Screen recently introduced the ISC-2010 color image scanner, which offers a maximum resolution of 6,400 dpi and can upload data directly to a Macintosh, PC, or UNIX-based workstation. It can scan black-and-white and color originals from 35mm up to 10-by-11 inches, and uses four photo-multipliers to ensure maximum dynamic range. Data from the ISC-2010 can be output in RGB mode as color TIFF or PICT files, or in CMYK mode as an EPS file, all in 8-bit per color format.

The IGR-2020 output recorder uses a highly stable, long-life, 10 beam laser diode as the exposure light source. It can output standard screen rulings, from 65 to 200 lpi. Output resolution is 2,000 dpi, 2,540 dpi, and 3,500 dpi. Output size is 15.5-by-24.1 inches, therefore easily handling a two page spread of 11-by-17 inches.

Screen's DTP development division is Island Graphics, which has released Screen's Sun Sparc 2 based, color retouch/page assembly system product.

The EPA is capable of receiving Postscript files as EPS format and ripping them to DS format for merging with high resolution images. The ECR has all of the standard retouch functions as well as the option to work in RGB or CMYK. It performs all functions in real time at full resolution. The ECR is also capable of processing a low resolution TIFF file and porting back to the MAC for image placement. Optical disk technology is also available for this product.

The two monochromatic flatbed scanner products SCREEN has to offer are the Scanica SF-323 and SF-123. Both scanners utilize

CCD technology with the 323 using a single 10,000 pixel CCD. Both also have the ability to SCSI interface to the MAC platform and send full-resolution black and white images to the MAC hard drive. These scanners both have special effect and high resolution text scanning capabilities, as well as the ability to operate in a full-daylight office environment by means of a film transport to processor option.

Generic desktop-prepress links

RIPLINK

The RIPLINK system, from Screaming Technology Inc., consists of seven software modules that construct a bidirectional pathway for information between Macintosh-based page layout programs and Hell, Scitex, or other DDES-compatible electronic prepress systems.

- RIPLINK READ allows the user to send high-quality continuous tone scanned images from standard prepress formats into the Mac, via tape or disk.

- RIPLINK RIP processes any PostScript document into a prepress linework file at any resolution, while establishing the proper run-length code for the Hell, Scitex, or DDES-equipped system.

- RIPLINK WRITE takes linework files from other RIPLINK products or Scitex Handshake files and outputs to Hell ChromaCom, Scitex Handshake, or DDES format linework or continuous tone files.

- RIPLINK CONVERT accepts a linework file from RIPLINK RIP or a Handshake continuous tone file, and exports a CT2T tape file.

- RIPLINK OPI allows prepress page instruction files to be produced at the desktop, by supporting the Aldus OPI

PostScript extensions for image name, cropping, scaling, rotation, and position.

- RIPLINK TRAP works with any desktop file, which it will auto-trap to the width specified, using a knowledge-based routine, to spread visually lighter colors into adjoining darker colors.

- RIPLINK TIFF lets you scan line-art originals on high-end prepress drum scanners, with the resulting images stored as 1-bit (black-and-white) or 32-bit (color) TIFF linework files.

RIPLINK is significant because it is generic, and cheaper than the proprietary solutions.

Hardware Links

The desktop-to-prepress links discussed so far have been software programs and protocols. However, for some users all these products are constrained by the fact that the scanned images continue to be stored on high-end magnetic tape or disk packs, rather than directly on the desktop.

But a new trend is beginning to emerge, based on products that use *hardware* links to connect desktop microcomputers directly to high-end scanners. A variety of companies have released hardware links that connect microcomputers (usually Apple Macintoshes) with high-end scanners. These products, which share many similar features but have a few key differences, include:

- Color GateWay, from AGS Associated Graphic Systems;
- Scan-Link, from Diadem;
- CC Mac, from Linotype-Hell;
- SpectreLink, from Pre-Press Technologies;
- RIPLink Direct, from Screaming Technology.

The key feature shared by these products is that each acts as a *bi-directional on-line interface* for transferring high-resolution images between drum scanners and desktop computers.

Let's take that one step at a time. Each product provides an *interface*—it connects desktop microcomputers with high-end scanners. This connection is *bi-directional*—scanned files can be saved on the desktop hard disk, and images that have been corrected or enhanced on the desktop can be output on the high-end device. (Most high-end scanners are both input and output machines—after scanning an image, they can record the resulting separations onto film.) Finally, most of these products are designed to be used *on-line*—the image is transferred directly to the desktop hard disk as it is scanned, rather than requiring an intermediate storage device, such as magnetic tape.

By combining the quality of the high-end scanner with the flexibility and ease of use of a Mac or a Windows-based PC, hardware links offer the best of both worlds.

SpectreLink

SpectreLink consists of a bi-directional SCSI interface that mounts in the cabinet of any analog Hell scanner, a NuBus SCSI card and 600Mb hard disk that are installed in a Mac, plus a high-speed cable to connect the two. Interfaces are currently available for Hell 340, 341, 350, and 399 scanners, with image data output as TIFF (CMYK or RGB) or Scitex CT files.

SpectreLink handles only the continuous-tone image data, not text and linework, and is designed primarily to reduce stripping costs. For example, an image can be scanned on the Hell scanner through the SpectreLink interface, then color corrected and manipulated on the Macintosh, then integrated into a page layout before being output directly to a Scitex film recorder.

With SpectreLink, the scanner operator sets up the scan as usual, making the required adjustments for UCR (undercolor removal) and GCR (gray component replacement). Indeed, any parameters that can be set on the scanner's keyboard can also be set directly from the Macintosh. Because the image data go directly from the scanner to the Mac, performance is not constrained by either the processor speed or by the amount of memory available.

A key component of the SpectreLink system is the SpectrePrint Pro color correction software, which can be purchased separately. According to many color professionals, SpectrePrint Pro is the first desktop program to provide a level of functionality previously available only on high-end prepress systems. For instance, it provides automatic color correction for most scanners by measuring the scanner calibration target and mapping it into the output color space of the printing process.

Color GateWay

The Color GateWay Graphic SubSystem uses a high-speed VME bus to connect Macintoshes to Hell, Royal Zenith and Screen digital color scanners, as well as ECRM Autokon black-and-white scanners. It is based on the concept that high-resolution image files should never be transferred across the network—low-resolution view files are created in the Color GateWay for use in desktop page layout programs, then replaced by their high-resolution equivalents prior to output.

Color GateWay connects to the color computer inside the scanner, or directly to the hard disk in the Hell ChromaCom page makeup station. Color corrected scans are sent to the Color GateWay as CMYK TIFF files and stored on a 740Mb (or larger) hard disk; a SCSI connection allows archiving to tapes, disks, or other back-up media. Low-resolution view files are created automatically, and transferred over the network for use in applications programs supporting the Open Prepress Interface (OPI) or Desktop Color Separation (DCS) protocols. Color GateWay uses SpectreScan and SpectrePrint Pro software for scanning and color separations, plus Adobe Photoshop for retouching (of high-resolution images).

Following the automatic blending of the page layout with the high-resolution scan, the complete file may be sent to any PostScript output device or passed at SCSI speed to a PostScript RIP within Color GateWay. The Color GateWay twin-disk RIP will process PostScript files while simultaneously recording to the ECRM Pelbox or to a PostScript imagesetter.

Scan-Link

Unlike products that connect the scanner directly to the Mac, Scan-Link uses an IBM-compatible computer as a control and storage unit. It can be configured with a variety of storage devices, including fixed or removable hard disk packs, erasable optical disks, and removable tape or disk cartridges, with capacities ranging from 45Mb to 2.2Gb (gigabytes, or billions of bytes).

Scan-Link is not designed to produce low-resolution view files for page layout and approval—it generates full resolution TIFF images, which can be manipulated or color-corrected using programs such as Adobe Photoshop and Letraset ColorStudio. Once image enhancement is complete, the resulting file can be output through two different methods: it can be exported through Scan-Link for conversion to CMYK format for output on a high-end film recorder, or it can be integrated with text and linework in a desktop publishing program and output on a PostScript imagesetter.

RIPLINK Direct

Unlike products that connect a Macintosh directly to a drum scanner, RIPLINK Direct connects the Mac to the hard disk in the high-end prepress system. RIPLINK Direct is currently available in versions for Scitex and Hell color prepress systems, with support for other systems in development.

For color houses with Hell prepress systems, RIPLINK Direct connects a Macintosh to the 300Mb Control Data SMD hard disks commonly used in Hell installations. It provides fast uploading and downloading of files to and from the SMD and Macintosh. Files originating on the desktop are written seamlessly to the SMD disk in Hell disk format, and files from the Hell system are easily read on the Macintosh. The connection between the Mac and the high-end scanner is through a General Purpose Interface Board (GPIB), with a cable that plugs directly into the scanner.

Screaming Technology recently announced RIPLINK Composite, which enables final pages created on the Macintosh using off-the-shelf page layout software to output directly to a high-end film recorder.

CC Mac

Linotype-Hell's hardware link is called CC Mac, and it enables Hell ChromaCom data disks to connect to a Mac's SCSI port in order to provide a bi-directional file transfer link. Its main function is to take high-quality scans from a Hell scanner and transport them to the desktop, using a MegaShuttle 765Mb removable drive as a file transfer medium. Pages composed in a desktop page layout program can also be processed through a Macintosh-based software RIP, transferred to a ChromaCom workstation, then output on a large format Hell-Linotype drum recorder.

Which link is best?

There are a variety of factors that must be assessed in order to determine which of these hardware link products might be most appropriate to your requirements. For example, some products assume you own a complete high-end prepress system, while others require only the scanner. This could be an important difference for a service bureau or in-house publisher wanting to add high-quality scanning. If you already own the desktop equipment, you could purchase a high-end scanner, perhaps secondhand, along with the hardware link.

Price is another variable. It's difficult to compare the cost of these links, because of significant differences in hardware requirements. CC Mac, for instance, uses removable hard disk cartridges as the file transfer medium, whereas Scan-Link uses an IBM-compatible computer as the intermediary.

Hardware links between the desktop and high-end scanners are a new and potentially significant innovation in color publishing, because they combine the quality benefits of high-resolution scanners with the flexibility and control of desktop page layout systems.

Mid-range systems

Mid-range systems, as their name suggests, fall somewhere between desktop and high-end systems in their capabilities and cost. They are usually based on one of three "standard" platforms—IBM compatibles, Macs, and Unix-based systems.

Kodak Prophecy system

A new contender in the mid-range domain is the Prophecy workstation from Eastman Kodak Company, which strives to bring professional-quality color to the desktop environment, for about half the price of the traditional high-end systems.

The Prophecy is designed for the entry-level user, and is based on industry-standard Unix-based microcomputers. It uses a full WYSIWYG interface, and connects with a variety of low-to-high-resolution input scanners, as well as to all PostScript-compatible output devices.

To configure a complete PostScript prepress system, the Kodak Prophecy workstation acts as a color image server to a network of Macintosh computers using off-the-shelf desktop publishing software. The color workstation receives high-resolution images that are sent as low-resolution files to the Mac for cropping, sizing, and positioning in page layout programs such as Aldus PageMaker, QuarkXPress, and Letraset Design Studio.

Low resolution proofs can also be output at this point using PostScript-compatible color proofing devices. The completed page layout, including text, graphics, and images, is returned to the Kodak workstation, where the low-resolution images are replaced with high-resolution files for output.

High-resolution images can come into the system from a variety of devices, including the Optronics ColorGetter, Screen 2010, Sharp JX-600, or any other device generating RGB TIFF files.

The system allows the Kodak workstation to perform high-resolution color image editing and retouching, tone and contrast correction, gray balance control, image sharpening or blurring, selective color changes, cloning, masking, and rotation. It incorporates a number of productivity enhancing features such as multi-tasking, which allows simultaneous input, retouch, and output color image files.

The Prophecy's support for device-independent color, using the CIE model, is an important feature of the system. Because the color on the monitor more accurately represents the color on the final output, color visualization and calibration across the system can be maintained, which is imperative in any system that brings color to the originator. Accurate color throughout the production process saves time and money by reducing the need for remakes, and has the potential to eliminate conventional off-press proofing methods.

Agfa PIX

The PIX system is Agfa's color image processing workstation, offering commercial-quality color retouching, image manipulation, and color separation capabilities. It is based on a SUN Microsystems 386i workstation running under Unix, enhanced with a custom display board.

The system features 16Mb of memory, two 760Mb internal hard disks with a 150Mb streaming tape backup, and a 16" color monitor with 1,024-by-1,024 pixel resolution. PIX uses the Open Look graphical interface to create a flexible and easy-to-learn mouse- and menu-driven system within a windowing environment.

PIX handles color retouching, masking, image collaging, color adjustment, and special effects. It can output images directly as four-color separations from high-resolution PostScript output devices, such as the Agfa SelectSet 5000 or competing machines from other imagesetter vendors. Completed images can also be exported to the new Agfa Catalyst color composition and page layout system for incorporation in other documents prior to output, or for export to QuarkXPress.

Transparent and reflective art is scanned into PIX, at which point the operator can take the continuous tone data and correct the tone curve, adjust image sharpness, or perform other functions such as rotation, scaling, or screening. Color retouching effects include an electronic airbrush, and tools for masking, collaging, and cloning. Other special effects include vignettes, embossing, dithering, posterization, and image distortion. For output, PIX provides control over parameters such as gray component replacement, undercolor removal, and dot-gain compensation.

Agfa Catalyst

The Agfa Catalyst station is used for page layout and composition, and can be linked with the PIX color workstation as part of Agfa's integrated ColorScape system. The Catalyst comes with 8Mb of memory, expandable to 16Mb. Theoretically, the Catalyst workstation could be used on a stand-alone basis to output PostScript color separations. However, most people will use it in conjunction with PIX or with Macs and PCs.

Catalyst and PIX were designed to work together over a Sun Ethernet TCP-IP network, so that images scanned and retouched at the PIX workstation can be easily incorporated into pages at the Catalyst station. It can also be configured with Macs and PCs, importing graphics and images in encapsulated PostScript or TIFF format, and text in ASCII or WordPerfect files.

Catalyst can output PostScript color separations of all job elements, including spot or process separations of imported color EPS and TIFF files. Naturally, Agfa hopes those separations will be output on an Agfa imagesetter, although any high-resolution PostScript output device can be used.

Networked Picture Systems

The Page Express program from Networked Picture Systems runs on an 80486-based computer with 16Mb of RAM, and can work with scanners and systems from Hell, Scitex, Crosfield, and Screen. It allows the color house to electronically strip all high-resolution line work, text, and continuous tone images into final pages, complete with PostScript graphics and high-resolution pictures.

Precise traps can be specified for all page elements, including chokes and spreads for text, and CMYK or PANTONE Colors assigned to any element. High-resolution images can be color corrected, combined, masked, and retouched, using a variety of brushes and filters, including sharpen and blur.

High-resolution color-separated files can be input or output via nine-track magnetic tape or through a hardware interface to scanners and film plotters, in a variety of common formats including Hell ANSI, Crosfield, Scitex Response (R-3000) and CT2T, DDES, and TGA (Targa).

NPS also makes Link Express, a 486-based interface to high-end prepress systems. Link Express can transfer and RIP PostScript files from Macintosh and PC-based publishing systems, and connect to high-resolution line art scanners. It also converts and color calibrates formats between different prepress systems, and connects to a variety of high-end color scanners and film plotters.

Quantel Paintbox

High-end design studios and ad agencies often want to create extremely high quality electronic paintings, so they invest in a Quantel Paintbox. This mid-range color imaging system is built around a dedicated 32-bit processor with specialized graphics controllers that Quantel claims operates at more than 1,000 MIPS (million instructions per second). There are more than 200Mb of hardware image storage and 1Mb of system memory, plus gigabytes of high-speed mass storage.

All work is viewed through the display memory buffer, or *store*, from the working store, which always carries a fully processed image. The result is that you always see exactly what will be output, without post-processing prior to output. An example of the remarkable effects you can create with a Paintbox is shown on Color Page 24.

Each Paintbox image has a working area of 5,400 x 3,700 pixels. Paintbox is supplied with an ultra-high-resolution 28" monitor, which displays 1,920 x 1,035 pixels (about twice the current high-resolution PC XGA standard of 1,024 x 768).

The Paintbox excels in freehand painting and illustration, allowing you to create artwork either completely from scratch or in combination with scanned images. A wide range of functions are available, such as soft edge masking, wash, tint, blur, shade, and sharpen.

The Paintbox is ideal for photo retouching, photo montaging, special effects, and creation of original artwork. Any retouching task such as scratch removal, color replacement, or background extension can be undertaken with instant magnification to the individual pixel level. Completed images are provided as digital color separations on industry-standard magnetic tape for production of transparencies or color separation films.

The long-term significance of links

From their established positions at the high end, the makers of professional color workstations have seen the beginnings of the desktop color revolution with a mixture of hope and trepidation. They hope that by bringing their products downstream, they can capture a significant number of first-time color users. But they are justifiably concerned about the long-term prospects for their bread-and-butter market—the professional color house.

The price-performance ratios for microcomputers continue to drop dramatically: now you can have a mainframe's number-crunching power on the desktop. And it is becoming increasingly attractive to create products to meet the needs of a growing market for color.

There are other factors that favor the decentralized desktop approach. Software innovation is a human creative activity, not a business process. The desktop software industry has refined its ability to design, produce, and distribute powerful programs, and already has distribution channels to the first-time color market through existing desktop publishing and graphics products.

The high-end prepress vendors and color houses want to believe that links will be a permanent part of the new color landscape—that no matter what happens with type and illustration, the color images will always be scanned and separated at the high end.

At the other end of the spectrum are the brave new color practitioners whose impulse is to do it *all* on the desktop. Perhaps it's extreme to believe that links are nothing more than a temporary way of taking advantage of the last vestige of high-end value added. However, as desktop micros continue to surpass the performance of minis and mainframes, it is reasonable to expect that industry-standard micros will be used as the front end for all publishing activities, regardless of whether they include professionally scanned or separated color.

The future of high-end prepress systems

Depending on who you ask, five years from now high-end systems will play a vital role, a small role, or will not be a factor in color production.

- A lot of people will pay for higher quality than is possible on the desktop, according to those who defend the future prospects of high-end color prepress. Their plan is to master the new digital technologies that are rapidly changing the age-old printing trade. In their view, traditional systems will continue to offer such significant quality and speed advantages that the impact of desktop color will be minimal.

- A small part of the market will always be willing to pay for ultimate quality—for example, a car manufacturer who needs to know that the paint colors in an ad are just right. But according to desktop progressives, this is the only part of the market that will continue to use high-end systems, while everyone else uses desktop tools.

- None of the color separations produced five years from now (or at least a portion too small to measure) will make use of traditional high-end components, according to the radical proponents of "total desktop" color systems. Quality and throughput issues are rapidly being solved, and the cost-effectiveness of desktop color will rapidly force high-end vendors out of the market.

Whichever of these three scenarios is closest to your personal interpretation, keep in mind the plight of those who own and operate the color houses. Given the rapid pace of change, what should they buy to keep up? How can a transition to desktop tools be best accomplished? What role will the high-end systems play?

The color prepress market is extremely capital intensive: vendors sell specialized workstations for every task, from mounting the transparency to stuffing the finished film in an envelope. For the owners of a prepress house, ultimately, the cost per separation becomes a function of speed.

And speed is what separates desktop systems from high-end systems. Whether this separation is light-years away, or just a few years away, remains to be seen.

Output Service Bureaus

*"The darkness is no darkness with thee
but the night is as clear as the day."*
THE BOOK OF COMMON PRAYER

Service bureaus are companies that provide computer output in a variety of forms—as film separations, slides, transparencies, and color proofs. They are equipped to take PostScript files created on the desktop and, from them, generate high-resolution film ready to be reproduced by offset litho or other printing methods.

Imagesetters—high-resolution laser printers that translate electronic files into paper "camera-ready" pages or directly into film—are the service bureau's basic equipment. For black-and-white publishing, the imagesetter normally creates a single piece of film or paper per page. For publishing with spot color, it produces a piece of film or paper for each color. Full-color graphics or images require four pieces of film.

Service bureaus have been an essential element in the success of black-and-white desktop publishing, because they provide high-resolution output at a reasonable per-page cost to those who would never be able to afford their own imagesetters. Some bureaus also provide related services such as image scanning, file conversion, and page layout.

With the rapid proliferation of desktop color, many service bureaus are determined to remain at the technological forefront while, of course, others will lag behind.

An understanding of imagesetter technology may seem of little use to you, given that imagesetters will probably not have a place in your workspace—not when they are priced at more than (at the high end, a great deal more than) $50,000. Many of the 4,000 service bureaus already in operation in North America probably provide satisfactory service. But your understanding of imagesetter technology may someday help you buy your own imagesetter. And until then, the information in this chapter will help you choose the best bureau, monitor how well it serves you, and ensure that it maximizes the quality of its separation films. This chapter also provides operating guidelines for selecting and working with a service bureau, so that you sidestep potential technical and communications problems. Much of this information will also be helpful if your company has an in-house service bureau that operates its own imagesetters.

One of the main trends throughout the world of desktop publishing has been to have the designer accept ever-increasing responsibility for the production process. Only a few years ago, this would have been unthinkable: the designer was expected to hand the original art over to graphic arts professionals, who assumed total responsibility for rendering it properly in the printing process.

Now the writer, illustrator, designer, and layout specialist may well be the same person, one who turns the work over to a service bureau only at the film separation stage, and hands the film to a printer to offset litho thousands of copies. It is therefore essential that the designer understand and accept more responsibility for what happens at the service bureau.

If the printed piece is of poor quality, the client isn't going to care that the designer is convinced it was the service bureau's fault. In effect, the designer working with computers has accepted responsibility, not just for aesthetics, but for the realities of getting the printed piece through the color production process.

Imagesetters

An imagesetter is a precision photographic printer that uses a laser to expose photosensitive paper or film, which is then processed chemically. Imagesetters produce an intermediate by-product (the exposed film), which laser printers do not.

Figure 10-1
The Agfa ProSet 9800 features a dual-beam imaging system to improve halftone accuracy.
Photo courtesy of Agfa Corporation.

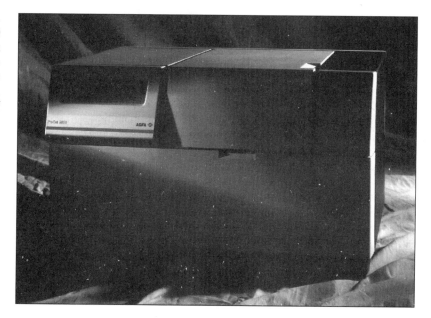

An imagesetter requires highly skilled operators, especially for color work. There are some smaller and less expensive imagesetters targeted at design studios, but these lack the precision necessary for producing color separations, not to mention that they use desk-sized liquid chemical processors.

Until quite recently, imagesetters were designed primarily for monochrome output, and were generally ill-suited to producing process color film. A major problem was repeatability—because they used imprecise mechanical feed methods, a dot produced on one separation was often displaced slightly from the same dot on another separation.

Imagesetters must clearly lay a dot of light in a specified position, with an accuracy of at least .003 inches, and be able to lay another dot just as precisely on the next piece of film. Building an imagesetter is a difficult task: not only must it work with great precision, but it has to be fast enough to record many jobs each day—a color house can't make money if it outputs only one or two sets of separations per day.

The imagesetter market has evolved quickly, going through three generations in five years.

First-generation imagesetters, such as the Linotronic 100, used a flatbed imaging area, with a capstan roller system pulling the photographic medium through the machine. They provided sufficient quality for type and spot color work, but lacked the resolution, precision, and repeatability necessary for process color reproduction.

Second-generation imagesetters, such as the Linotronic 330, improved the imaging and transport mechanisms to provide acceptable resolution and repeatability for many kinds of non-critical color documents.

Third-generation imagesetters use rotary drum technology, rather than a flatbed mechanism, and typically provide sufficient precision and repeatability for any color publishing application. This category includes the Linotronic 630, Agfa Compugraphic SelectSet 5000, Optronics ColorSetter, Scitex Dolev PS, Scangraphic Scantext, and Purup ImageMaker.

How imagesetters work

Although the details may vary between manufacturers, there are certain operating principles shared by virtually all imagesetters. In describing the workings of imagesetters, this chapter refers to their output as film, although the output medium can be either photographic film or resin-coated (RC) paper (or even plate material).

It is essential for the color publisher concerned about quality to understand the technical details involved in operating imagesetters. This means understanding the machine itself, the photographic media, and the chemical development process, especially the digital halftones that are crucial in color reproduction.

There are three main components to an imagesetter system, apart from the computer on which the pages are created: the raster image processor (RIP), the imager, and the film processor.

Let 'er RIP

The RIP converts the PostScript code from a desktop publishing system into a format acceptable to the imager. It takes the lines and curves that make up graphics, plus the bitmaps that make up halftones, and renders them as a series of pixels matched to the resolution of the specific imager being used.

The RIP begins by breaking the PostScript file into individual objects, which it processes one by one until it has built a complete high-resolution bitmap. The RIP then passes the bitmap to the imager, where a marking engine generates the actual spots on the paper or film. In other words, the RIP is the link between the electromagnetic domain and the material domain—the bridge between the pure abstraction of the digital halftone and the hard cold world of precision photography.

The major concerns with RIPs are speed and halftone quality. Service bureau operators in particular are concerned with the speed of the RIP, especially for color work, because CMYK separations require the production of four times as many pieces of film as black-and-white.

In many cases, the speed of the RIP is the determining factor in the overall speed of the imagesetter. This explains the intense research and development devoted to RIPs, and the on-going debate about which manufacturer's is the fastest. The original Linotronic 100 was sold with the RIP 1. The Linotronic 300 was sold with either the RIP 2 (also called the Atlas RIP) or the RIP 3 (the Atlas Plus). Nowadays, the Linotronic 330 is sold with an even faster RIP 4 or RIP 30. Despite the fact that every new generation of RIPs has meant faster speeds, imagesetters still are

Somewhat slower than the high-end prepress systems described in the previous chapter.

Because the overall speed of a RIP is also a function of the amount of RAM it contains, the trend in recent years has been to increase the RIP's memory so that it doesn't hold back the rest of the system. Other factors that govern RIP performance include the speed of its hard disk and the speed of the network.

Although most RIPs perform their calculations with specialized chips and circuit boards, others do all the work in software, and run on standard microcomputers, such as Macs and IBM-compatible machines. In recent years, the performance of software RIPs has increased to the point where they are serious competitors to many hardware RIP vendors. Software RIPs are also commonly used in slide file recorders and digital proofers.

The laser imager

The laser imager, often called the *recorder*, typically weighs hundreds of pounds and takes up as much space as a medium-sized photocopier. It connects to the RIP circuitry through a cable, and receives the image of each page as raw computer code, which it converts into a series of tiny pixels. On the top or front of the imager, a panel display lets the operator select the desired resolution and other parameters.

One common type of imager uses lenses and mirrors to modulate (turn on and off) a tiny beam of light from a gas laser, thus converting the data into pixels exposed onto photosensitive paper or film. Another type of imager uses a simpler laser diode that it modulates electronically. Most current imagesetters are based around lasers that generate a spot about 20 microns (a micron is one millionth of a meter) in diameter.

All laser beams have some light that falls outside their nominal width. In lasers with a 20-micron beam, this leads to a broad fringe around each pixel. By contrast, the 10-micron beam used in the latest generation of imagesetters produces a crisper dot that is less susceptible to unwanted pixel growth.

In general, PostScript imagesetters tend to produce digital halftones with a *hard dot* that is crisper and more sharply defined than the *soft dot* characteristic of halftones created with traditional photographic techniques.

Accuracy and repeatability

In addition to spot size, two other variables are crucial to the performance of the laser imager: accuracy and repeatability. Accuracy refers to the imagesetter's ability to place a pixel in precisely the correct location, and is typically plus-or-minus 2 microns on an imagesetter designed for color separations.

Repeatability is a measure of the imager's ability to place a pixel in exactly the same location, time after time, and is typically less than plus-or-minus 25 microns over the full exposure area of the imager. Repeatability is essential for producing color separations because to create accurate colors, the halftone dots in the cyan, magenta, yellow, and black films must be precisely positioned with respect to one another.

Although a number of factors contribute to the accuracy and repeatability of an imagesetter, mechanical design is one of the most important for producing consistently high-quality color separations. The first generation of PostScript imagesetters use a flat-bed design, in which a roller-feed mechanism (capstan) pulls the unexposed film from the cassette, holds it flat during exposure, and pulls it into a take-up cassette for processing.

More recent designs have replaced the rubber rollers with a system of precisely aligned pins and holes, thus providing better control over the positioning of the film. They have also replaced the flat bed with a rotating drum, to ensure uniform distance between the laser and the film, and to minimize distortion of the halftone dots.

The media (photographic film and paper) are specially designed for imagesetting, and are sensitive in the part of the color spectrum emitted by the laser, which varies between manufacturers. There are countless subtle differences in the properties of the leading photographic films, whether from Kodak, Fuji, Agfa, or other manufacturers. Similarly, there are subtle but important differences in the response curves of the various processing chemicals commonly used. These result in measurable differences in the exposure times required, and in the resulting dot densities. Many service bureaus have eliminated the problem of film and processor variability by standardizing on a single brand.

Most PostScript desktop laser printers are based on the concept of a *frame buffer*, in which part of the printer's RAM is used to image an entire page in memory and dump it all at once to the marking engine. By contrast, most imagesetters use a *band buffer*, with thin strips of data rasterized and sent to the imager, one after another.

This usually works fine, but it can be the source of banding errors (sharp white or black lines evident in tints and photographs), if the transport mechanism in the marking engine does not start exactly where it left off. Indeed, any disruption of the photo medium as it moves through the marking engine will usually result in banding or other damage to part of the image.

In most imagesetters, the media are stored in two cartridges: an input cartridge for unexposed media, and a take-up cartridge for media already exposed to the laser beam. After a job has been exposed, the film is cut and the take-up cartridge removed from the imagesetter and inserted into the photo processor.

The processor

In some service bureaus, the humble processor is treated with disdain, as if film processing has become a routine activity for even the most simpleminded human or machine. In fact, nothing could be further from the truth—the processor determines dot densities.

When creating color separation films, a change in dot size of less than three percent—in any one or more of the films—will result in a noticeable reduction in color fidelity. Yet variations of five percent or more occur all the time in some service bureaus, either because the bureau lacks the deep-path chemical processors, or staff lack the knowledge to operate them in a stable and consistent manner.

The photo processor uses a three-stage system. The film is first bathed in developer to darken only those areas of the film exposed to the laser beam. The film then passes through a bath of fixer, which stops the development process, stabilizes the blackened areas, and dissolves unexposed light-sensitive material from the film. Finally, the film is washed with water to remove the final traces of chemicals, and heated to remove moisture. The dried medium—film or resin-coated paper—is then cut into individual pages, either automatically or by the operator.

Virtually all high-end service bureaus now use "deep-bath" processors that automatically replenish the different chemicals as they are needed. On some models, you can actually hear the injectors being squirted to freshen the chemical cocktail when a cartridge of film or paper is inserted for processing.

The concentration and temperature of the chemicals determine the rate of reaction. The object is to maintain a consistent temperature and chemical balance in the developer and fixing solutions: even a small change at this stage can markedly affect the density of the separation films.

The crucial concentration is not in the solutions, but in the microscopic layer of solution adjacent to the film's emulsion. This is why precision agitation is an essential part of photo processing. If your service bureau's processor has "hot spots" where agitation is reduced or eliminated, the film it produces will show distinct variations in density across its width. Knowledgeable service bureau operators make it a rule that no one is to adjust the temperature or rate knobs on the processor—some going so far as to keep the controls under lock and key.

Despite recent innovations that have considerably cleaned up the photo processing area, this is still the messiest aspect of high-resolution output. Although progress is being made in dry film processors, it will be a few more years before they are commercially available, so in the meantime we are stuck with liquid chemicals.

Figure 10-2
A deep-bath photo
processor
Photo courtesy of
Agfa Corporation.

Leading imagesetter vendors

The first company to exploit the emerging desktop publishing market in the mid-1980s was Linotype (now Linotype-Hell), with their Linotronic series of imagesetters. For the first few years, the PostScript imagesetter business belonged almost totally to Linotype-Hell—to such an extent that many service bureaus named Lino-this and Lino-that appeared, and "to Lino" became a verb.

But so much of a good thing is sure to attract competitors, and Linotype-Hell now shares the market with a variety of established companies and leading-edge startups.

Linotronic imagesetters

The first major product released by Linotype-Hell is the Linotronic 630, which brings together Linotype's unmatched imagesetter experience with the drum technology used on all Hell's high-end film recorders.

The L630 is an internal drum imagesetter using a laser light source and a spinning prism to image on photographic material mounted inside the drum. It has resolutions of 1,219 dpi, 2,438 dpi, and 3,251 dpi, sufficient for color separations with screen frequencies up to 200 lpi.

The L630 is sold with a high-speed RIP 40, which supports the Hell HQS screening angles. Based on a 68040 processor running at 25 MHz, the RIP 40 includes a high-performance Ethernet interface and supports the Apple EtherTalk Phase 1 and Phase 2 protocols, as well as TCP/IP.

The Linotronic 330 imagesetter has a maximum 3,386 dpi resolution, compared with the 2,540 limit of the earlier L300. This enables it to create a tonal range of 256 gray levels at higher line-per-inch screen rulings, both for top quality monochrome work and for four-color separations. When imaging halftones at higher screen rulings, the increased resolution produces somewhat better definition and image clarity, with reduced banding and moiré. Detailed linework and text containing delicate serifs also benefit when more pixels per inch are available. Linotype uses a special coprocessor board called LIRA to handle the halftone screening in hardware.

An advantage of the Linotronic 330 over the L300 is that its film transport system is designed so that each separation begins from the same position within the drive mechanism, and is exposed from the same point in the laser optical system. However, it's still a roller-feed mechanism, as compared to the pin-register systems used in high-end film recorders.

The Linotronic 530 is similar to the model 330 in many respects, but has a top resolution of 2,540 ppi and offers a maximum width of 18", compared with 12" for the L330. This enables two 8.5-by-11 inches pages to be imaged side by side, with printer's marks in position. Using the rotation feature, broadsheets, banners, and signatures can take full advantage of the wide-measure image area.

High Quality Screening (HQS)

In mid-1991, Linotype-Hell introduced the High Quality Screening (HQS) algorithm as a software upgrade to the RIP 30, thereby improving the quality of color separations and significantly reducing the moiré problem. HQS screening has been widely used on high-end color prepress systems for years, and is now available for PostScript output devices.

Figure 10-3
An imagesetter 18 inches wide allows you to print a printer's spread—two full pages side by side, with registration and crop marks in position.

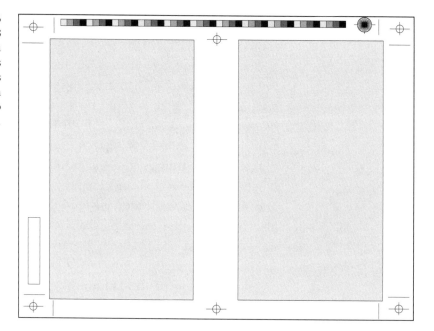

Most current PostScript interpreters use *rational* screen angles, which can't produce the classic separation angles without moiré effects. With rational screens, in order to obtain the desired screen angles, one must often compromise by having different screen frequencies for each color, which can reduce quality. These limitations have been overcome with HQS screening. Specific screen angles and screen rulings can now be achieved with great accuracy.

The traditional high-end prepress vendors all use *irrational* screening—in fact Crosfield, Scitex, and Screen all license Hell's High-Quality Screening algorithms. Scitex was the first vendor to offer this irrational screening in a high-resolution PostScript output device with its Dolev PS.

Figure 10-4
Rational screen angles
used by most current
PostScript imagesetters

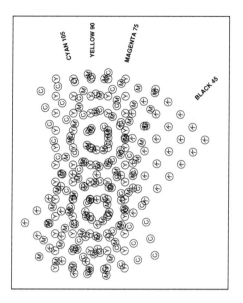

The speed of the RIP 30 is maintained, even with the new screen angles, through the use of a built-in math coprocessor specially designed for screening continuous-tone images. A range of pre-calculated dot shapes for different screen values are loaded into a cache on the RIP 30's Linotype Image Rasterizing Accelerator (LIRA) board at start-up. If other screen values are requested by an application, they are computed at run time and stored in the cache. HQS is a software upgrade to the RIP 30—no additional hardware is required.

The Adobe Accurate Screen algorithms described in Chapter 2 use an *unlocked rational* screen technique, which is in some ways similar to HQS. Both essentially eliminate moiré as a major quality concern.

The Flamenco alternative

One specialized screening solution challenges the conventional notion that each of the four colors needs to be at a different angle. Flamenco screening, developed by Marcel Codrech of Anaya Systems in Spain and distributed by The Color Group, simplifies the way dots are placed. Rather than rotating the color screens, Flamenco places them all at 45° with optimal spacing of the dot centers. The screens are slightly offset from one another. The horizontal and vertical offsets cause the dots to form squares, with a different color at each corner.

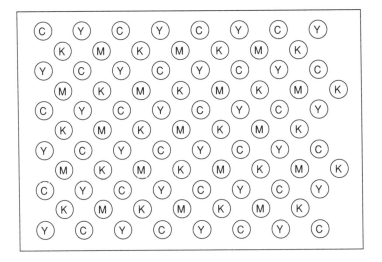

Figure 10-5
Flamenco screens have all four colors at 45°, with each color slightly offset in both directions.

Flamenco screening works with Adobe Photoshop and Separator, and is currently being used at a number of newspapers, as its quality improvement is most apparent at low resolutions. The primary drawback of Flamenco screening is that it requires extremely precise alignment of the dots, because registration problems on press can lead to extreme color shifts.

Agfa Compugraphic imagesetters

Agfa Compugraphic is a major new competitor in the imagesetter marketplace. The strategy of the Agfa Compugraphic ProSet 9000 series has been to separate the raster image processor (RIP) from the writing engine, so that you can configure a system to your particular requirements. Modularity ensures easy upgrading of both RIP and marking engine.

The ProSet 9400 is targeted at service bureaus, typographers, commercial printers, and corporate publishers. For producing both black-and-white and color work, the ProSet 9800 is a better choice—it's faster and offers better repeatability than the 9400. It uses a special imaging system with a dual-beam laser and a prism that minimizes vibration and wobble. It also has a new media transport mechanism that allows output of registered films at up to 150-line screen for commercial-quality color work. Agfa also makes the ProSet 9550, with features and cost halfway between the 9400 and 9800.

Agfa SelectSet 5000 imagesetter

Agfa's high-end imagesetter is the SelectSet 5000, which offers punch registration, rather than using the roll-feed mechanism present in most imagesetters. The SelectSet 5000 uses an internal drum to hold the medium stationary during exposure for maximum image accuracy and to ensure precise registration. The length of the optical path between the laser and the medium remains constant, so halftone dot sizes and densities are consistent across the image area.

The SelectSet 5000 is matched with Agfa's new 5000 PS Star PostScript RIP, which uses the new Adobe Accurate Screen software to help eliminate moiré patterns. Although it's the most costly, this is definitely the model to buy if your primary concern is high-quality color separations.

Varityper imagesetters

Varityper, a subsidiary of Tegra, Inc., offers a mix-and-match approach that permits the client to select the optimal configuration of RIP, low-res proofer, and imagesetter.

Varityper 4000 and 5000 image controllers

Varityper has upgraded its Series 4000 imagesetters with the new Emerald Controller, for even faster throughput of color separations, and has licensed Adobe's Accurate Screen technology. The Emerald Controller is based on the R3000 RISC microprocessor from MIPS Computer Systems, and makes use of static RAM chips (rather than the slower dynamic RAM) for high-speed instruction and data memory.

Figure 10-6
The Agfa SelectSet 5000 is among the new generation of PostScript imagesetters designed specifically for color separations. Photo courtesy of Agfa Corporation.

One interesting Varityper feature is *instant replay*, which lets you re-image a job without re-RIPing. Jobs that require multiple repros, those which the processor ate, or those requiring imaging at another density can be re-run at full recorder speed. Although it may seem like a small detail, the existence of superior job control software can make a significant difference to the profitability of a service bureau.

The Varityper 5000 Image Controller contains the RIP, imaging software, Tegra fonts, and disk storage. It receives data from a front-end system (PC or Mac), generates a raster image of type and graphics, and transmits the data to an output unit. Each controller can drive both a plain paper and a film output unit, with all output units using a common image controller, type library, and command language.

Varityper 5330 and 5510 imagesetters

The Varityper 5330 Imagesetter outputs on film and RC paper at resolutions up to 3,048 ppi, producing screens up to 180 lpi with 256 shades of gray. Its repeatability and accuracy are important, especially for color separations. The 5330 runs with either the Series 4000 or Series 5000 image controllers.

When configured with the Series 5000, the 5330 supports more than 20 front-end type composition systems, as well as Macintosh, IBM-compatible, and other publishing platforms, such as Unix, that support PostScript. If configured with the Series 4000 controller, the 5330 operates in an Adobe PostScript environment that takes advantage of the image controller's page buffer architecture to ensure consistent high-quality output. It supports the complete Tegra library of more than 1,000 typefaces.

Optronics ColorSetter imagesetter

The ColorSetter 2000 is a drum laser imagesetter specifically designed for producing color separations. All page elements—type, line art, graphics, tints, and color and black-and-white photographs—are imaged in position to eliminate stripping. Output formatting options include A4 or 10"-by-12" images positioned four-up (CYMK) on a single sheet of 20"-by-26" positive or negative film, photosensitive paper, or plate material.

System configurations include either an Adobe PostScript RIP or a PostScript-compatible RIP, running in a high-speed on-board Clipper RISC processor. Optronics' proprietary digital screening technique, IntelliDot, controls edge definition and dot shape and size, and provides for optimal gray scales over a range of line screens. Optronics has also licensed the new HQS algorithm from Linotype-Hell. Page layouts can be imaged at resolutions up to 2,000 ppi, with photographs screened at frequencies up to 175 lpi.

The ColorSetter can be connected to a wide variety of color publishing and prepress systems with Ethernet, RS-232, RS-449, parallel, and Versatec interfaces. The server can also handle additional data formats such as DDES, TIFF, CT2T, and I/Script.

Figure 10-7
Optronics™ ColorSetter™ is a drum-based imagesetter with special hardware for creating halftones. Intergraph® is a registered trademark of Intergraph Corporation. ColorSetter™ is a trademark of Intergraph Corporation.

Optronics claims that its drum-based imaging system with precision film mounting eliminates the undesirable banding effect found in flatbed laser imagesetters. The ColorSetter uses an external drum film mounting system, like those used by high-end film recorder manufacturers such as Scitex, Hell, and Screen. Film is mounted on industry-standard Stoesser register pins and is adhered to the drum with a vacuum during imaging.

Many imagesetters perform halftone screening in software, but the ColorSetter is equipped with proprietary screening hardware that intercepts PostScript calls for screening and processes them at high speed.

Scitex Dolev PS

In addition to the proprietary high-end prepress systems described in the previous chapter, Scitex also makes an internal-drum PostScript imagesetter designed for color separations, the Dolev PS.

Version 2 of the Scitex Dolev PS imagesetter can plot color linework and continuous-tone images at resolutions up to 3,556 ppi at sizes up to 14-by-20 inches. Scitex uses proprietary screen generation hardware to output continuous-tone color images at screen rulings up to 250 lpi. The Dolev PS includes an Adobe PostScript interpreter that uses Scitex software installed on an IBM PS/2 computer running under the AIX operating system.

Film loading, feeding, cutting, and unloading into a removable cassette are automatic and completely enclosed, so the image-setter operates in normal room light. An optional in-line processor eliminates the need for a darkroom. A punch for pin registration holes is another option.

Other imagesetter vendors

Mannesmann Scangraphic

The Scantext imagesetters from Scangraphic use a simple but ingenious internal drum imaging system in which a single rotating mirror is used to deflect the beam from the laser to the film. The Scantext 2030PD and 2051PD imagesetters both feature a maximum resolution of 3,232 ppi, and are identical except for their imaging areas (13-by-24 inches for the 2030PD and 20-by-24 inches for the 2051PD).

Both models include a version of the Adobe Emerald RIP, based on the MIPS R3000 RISC processor, plus a MIPS R3010 floating point processor for increased speed of color separations.

The concept of exposing the whole page onto motionless film inside a drum guarantees excellent precision, registration, and repeatable accuracy for producing color separations. The laser beam travels exactly the same distance, and at exactly the same angle, for every point on the film. There are no correction lenses or prisms which would otherwise distort the laser beam and affect its sharpness. The film does not move during exposure, eliminating the possibility of registration errors.

Purup ImageMakers

Purup, a European high-end prepress vendor, now markets its ImageMaker 80/10 in North America. This is a production-oriented imagesetter with a RISC-based PostScript RIP and up to four microprocessors. The ImageMaker uses a stationary internal drum with spinning laser optics, and Purup claims 15-micron accuracy and 5-micron repeatability over the entire 26"-by-20" imaging area. Among its other features, the Purup ImageMaker offers automatic dot size adjustment, and automatic film loading and punching.

Selecting a service bureau for desktop color

While most service bureaus are firmly rooted in the tradition of black-and-white publishing, and some have little if any experience with color prepress, they may forget to tell you that. Other service bureaus started as offshoots of traditional color houses, and have an extensive background in both color prepress and imagesetting.

A good service bureau must be competent in many different areas. Here is a shopping list if you are contracting work to be done by a service bureau—and for use as a standard of quality if you are operating a service bureau.

- **Communication:** Communication with a service bureau is the single most important issue—interpersonal communication, not the bits-and-bytes kind. Over and over again, knowledgeable users emphasize that it is especially important, when color is involved, that the service bureau understand each job well enough that potential breakdowns are anticipated before they occur. When any aspect of a job is not clear, the service bureau personnel must be able to explain the problem clearly, and communicate possible courses of action and their potential advantages and drawbacks. (Simple things, like answering phone messages promptly, are an important aspect of this communications process.)

- **Imagesetter output quality:** The overall quality of a set of separations can be gauged with a densitometer and with a proof, but the real test occurs when the plates are on the press. After running a handful of desktop color jobs through the service bureau and all the way through printing and binding, you will get a better sense of where your negative film stands in terms of density calibration and dot repeatability.

- **Systems:** For quality color separations, up-to-date hardware is essential, especially the imager. The precision and repeatability of its halftone dots will have a significant impact on the overall quality and color fidelity of your documents. If you have a large quantity of pages to separate, look for a service bureau that has more than one imagesetter, and that runs multiple shifts.

- **Technicians:** Crucial but often overlooked is the operator behind the imagesetter, the person who ensures that all the controls are properly set, and that established procedures for maximizing quality are being followed to the letter. Although many service bureau employees are self-taught, there are good reasons for trying to hire someone, if at all possible, with an in-depth knowledge of photochemistry combined with at least three years of hands-on Macintosh and PC experience.

- **Hands-on computer knowledge:** Publishing requires extremely powerful computers and peripherals, and depends to a great extent on connecting diverse people and machines into dynamic networks. Dozens of software programs—PC and Mac—create the PostScript files that are raw material to the service bureau, and the complete technician needs at least passing familiarity with all of them, plus extensive knowledge of five or six key programs.

- **Applications experience:** If the service bureau technician is really knowledgeable about the specific applications programs you are using, such as PageMaker or QuarkXPress, you can send the bureau the original graphics and text files, in addition to the PostScript files output from your application. In the case of a particular graphic that is preventing the job from imaging, the technician will be able to go into your original application and correct or remove the problem, thereby allowing the rest of the job to be processed properly. This would be impossible, or at best very difficult, if they only had the PostScript file.

- **Problem-solving ability:** Pages that should in theory print perfectly are often difficult or impossible to print in practice. The expert service bureau technician should have a diverse repertoire of tricks for coaxing problematic pages to print, including hacking some PostScript code where necessary. Adobe Systems offers a training course in PostScript that most operators will find very useful. Eliminating PostScript errors requires perseverance and ingenuity, as imagesetting is a new field, and today's service bureau operators are pioneers trying to develop standard practices for the future.

- **Price and service equation:** This factor is listed last because it is very difficult to correlate the price paid to the quality of the separations or the service. The successful desktop color service bureau owner must charge for the use of all that expensive equipment, while providing value-added services that in some measure compete against the corner bit-buckets offering imagesetter pages at two bucks apiece.

File transfer issues

To print your job, the service bureau needs your files. There are two distinct problems that must be resolved: the data format of the files and the physical media on which they are transferred between systems.

In most cases, the service bureau requires the application files you wish to output, plus any fonts, data files, and printer description files used. In other cases, you will send along the complete document or graphics in its original applications file format, so that the service bureau technicians can modify the file directly to make it run.

Be sure to write down all the specifications for the job, and include this with the files. Keep a copy for your records. Again, work out the details for file transfer in consultation with your service bureau in advance, and don't experiment with telecommunications when you're working to deadline.

The files can be transferred on various kinds of disks and tapes, or transmitted through modems. Given that color graphics files can be a few megabytes in size, while color image files can be 10 times larger still, you must pay close attention to the size of your files, the capacity of your mass storage drives or tapes, and the compression and decompression of files.

In many cases, individual color graphics or spot-color page layouts will fit on a floppy diskette, so they can be easily copied and delivered to the service bureau. Compression programs such as StuffIt (Macintosh) and PKZIP (IBM-compatible) further extend the capacity of floppies, so that an 800 Kb disk will store 3Mb or more of data. Naturally, the service bureau needs the appropriate decompression program to use the file. Also, these programs are too slow for working with large image files.

For multiple files, the removable 44Mb and 88Mb hard disk cartridges made by SyQuest have become a standard for transporting large volumes of data from the desktop to the service bureau. Be certain the service bureaus you plan to work with have the appropriate drives to read your cartridges.

Portable external hard disk units are another way to get higher capacities, while getting around the device dependency of removable cartridges. Because they are available in 300Mb and 600Mb sizes, they are well suited to applications involving color images. They are much bulkier than cartridges, however, because they contain the entire drive mechanism and power supply.

Portable drives connect to your Mac or PC through an SCSI port, which provides a measure of device independence in moving data from the desktop to the service bureau. Remember that it's not a good idea to cart around all your original data files, so a portable hard disk should contain only a copy of data from your main hard disk, with any required system files.

For transferring color prepress data, one storage medium with incredible potential is digital audio tape (DAT). Digital audio tape is already widely used in home audio systems, where it combines the digital fidelity of the compact disk with the recording ability of a cassette recorder. Indeed, its success in home audio is expected to drive down the price of DAT, making it a cost-effective way to store many gigabytes of image data.

Each tiny DAT cassette, the size of a matchbook and costing less than $10, can store more than 2.5Gb (2,500Mb) of data, the equivalent of a few thousand floppy disks. Further refinements are expected to quadruple this capacity.

Color data communication

Telecommunications can be a significant tool in moving data files from the designers and layout artists to the service bureaus. More and more of this potential is being realized as bandwidth and speed increase, users become more experienced, and color image files shrink through JPEG compression.

In the next few years, telecommunications will become easier and more common, and communications software built around "expert systems" will make connecting with remote computers a background activity. One important factor will be the

Adobe Accurate Screens

The new Adobe Accurate Screen algorithms use a *supercell* consisting of many smaller digital halftone cells in order to precisely create any screen angle.

This image was scanned on an Optronics ColorGetter, and separated on an Agfa Compugraphic SelectSet 5000 imagesetter at 200 lines per inch using Accurate Screens.

JPEG File Compression

These three versions of the same color image show the effects of JPEG image compression. The image on this page is the original.

The top image shows the effect of having been compressed 43:1 then decompressed and printed. The bottom image has been compressed 20:1. At 20:1 compression, there is virtually no visible quality degradation after the picture has been decompressed.

Black Generation

By controlling the amount of black in a CMYK separation, you can often improve print quality and reduce costs. The image below shows a bright, or *high-key* image that has been separated in Adobe Photoshop, with the Black Generation set for light and maximum (left), and black plate (right).

This image below is a dark, or *low-key* image to which the same black generation settings have been applied.

Adobe
Photoshop 2.0

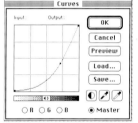

The Curves Feature in Photoshop lets you draw tonal compression curves that can significantly improve the quality of a picture. The original picture is shown above.

Reducing the midtone values while leaving the shadows and highlights untouched produces an even more washed-out image.

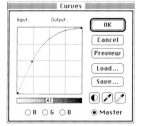

By reshaping the Curve to be convex, the midtones have been punched up without sacrificing loss of detail in the shadows or highlights.

Color Correction

The Cachet color correction program from EFI (Electronics For Imaging) contains a database of color characterizations for every major color peripheral (scanner, printer, monitor).

By comparing the subject image (upper left) with a reference image (upper right), you can quickly apply a global color correction based on your perception of which reference image most closely approximates the desired color values in the original. Adjusting brightness (bottom right).

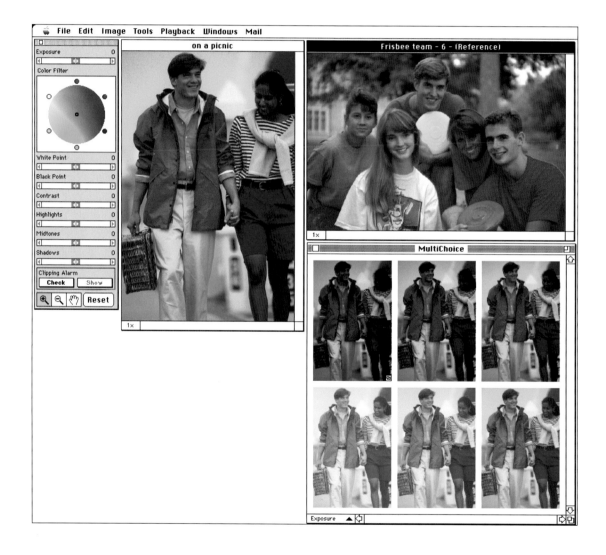

Image Filters

An original image (top left) has been modified in Adobe Photoshop using a variety of filters including (clockwise from top right) Add Noise Gaussian, Solarize, Wind, Pointilize, and Crystalize.

Quantel Graphic Paintbox

The Quantel Graphic Paintbox is a midrange system specially designed for electronic painting. This image was constructed entirely from scratch on the Paintbox.

widespread implementation of the JPEG compression system (see Chapter 7), which will allow the transmission of relatively small files, yet transparently work with high-resolution images within applications.

At the same time, improved modems and error-correcting circuitry will make it possible to quadruple the speed of file transfers over ordinary voice lines. In the latter part of the 1990s, the widespread use of Integrated Systems Digital Networks (ISDN) will provide a data superhighway with sufficient bandwidth to easily handle large image files.

Working with a color service bureau

Once you've selected a service bureau, sit down and talk with its manager about your expectations, project specifications, timelines, budget, and other details. Don't be afraid to ask about their experience or recommendations in any aspect of the job. If they use any terms that you don't completely understand, ask for clarification.

According to service bureau operators, designers new to color work often have unrealistic expectations about how long things take, or how many details must be attended to in order to produce reasonably high quality separations. To keep your friendly neighborhood imagesetter operator happy, do not, for example:

- expect a perfect match between a proof and your monitor;

- plead for a printout of your 25Mb file in 15 minutes;

- insist that computer-specified PANTONE Colors built from four-color inks precisely match the special PANTONE solid inks;

- rely on the service bureau to discover overlooked parameters, such as fonts and image files;

- send files containing complete garbage without printing a low-resolution black-and-white proof, then disclaim responsibility for wasting hours of their time and valuable film and chemicals.

Wherever possible, involve your service bureau operator as early as possible in the creative process, in order to avoid building production constraints into the graphic design. In drawing programs, for instance, the curve flatness settings and the use of grouping, layers, arrays, and other features can dramatically impact the length of time for a given page to print. Other things to watch for include rotated pattern fills, and drawings containing a large number of blends. In some cases a small change to the drawing's structure will not be visible, yet will reduce the print time from minutes to seconds.

Trouble-shooting output problems

At most service bureaus, between five and ten percent of the jobs arrive incomplete, usually as a result of missing fonts or data files. The service bureau technician will sometimes spot the problem before the job is run; otherwise, the first indication of trouble will be when somebody notices that most of the type is set in Courier.

There are also some jobs that are destined not to print, for reasons unknown to mere mortals. Any number of factors, individually or in combination, can prevent a complex page from imaging properly or at all. The fact that a job won't print on a given imagesetter does not mean there is something wrong with the service bureau personnel, even if you are subsequently able to get the file to print at a different service bureau.

Based on conversations with many service bureau operators, the following problems are the most frequently cited reasons for a job not printing.

- Weird files—you are free to use applications programs to construct whatever kinds of graphics and pages you want, even if they might be particularly difficult for PostScript to image;

- Bugs in the imagesetter's PostScript interpreter;

- Insufficient RAM in the imagesetter to store all required downloaded fonts and prep files, or insufficient virtual memory to handle complex graphics;

- Using an outdated version of the prep file, or neglecting to download a prep file;

- Exceeding device limits with an overly complex file or graphic, such as a page layout file containing numerous EPS graphics plus many small cropped images;

- Bugs in the graphics, imaging, or page layout programs used to create the file;

- Device-dependent code (not conforming to the PostScript standard), used intentionally by some applications for image scaling and rotation, or for custom screens or gray response curves.

The problem of device-dependent code is likely to become more severe with the emergence of PostScript Level 2, which offers broader support for device-specific features such as document stapling and binding.

Solutions to common problems

There are a number of things you can do to maximize the quality of the files you send to a service bureau and increase the chances that they will print properly. The most important is to build the files well—be moderate in your use of the applications programs. For instance, don't create a graphic in which each line contains thousands of control points.

You can also avoid many problems by not being obsessed with creating the job as a single piece of film, rather than splitting it into more reasonable chunks that could be put together by the film stripper. By all means, make use of the film stripper's skill, rather than building a composite file that is too complex to image. After all, whatever piece of film you come up with will have to be stripped into flats anyway, and it doesn't take that much longer for the film stripper to drop a few graphics or images into the page.

Wherever possible, do little or no image cropping or resizing in your page layout program. Perform any needed cropping in an imaging program, prior to importing the picture into a page layout. This can have a significant effect in reducing the size and complexity of your PostScript files. In draw programs, simplify all unnecessary detail, reducing graphics elements to the smallest number of points required to maintain the desired level of quality.

The service bureau can also take certain actions to minimize problems when running color separations. Wherever cost-effective, they should purchase the latest and greatest RIP, and pack it with plenty of RAM. In fact, adding RAM makes more of a difference in the speed on an older RIP than on the newer models, as it allows larger cache files. It's also important they use the correct prep file.

In a good service bureau, the technicians will know plenty of tricks to make difficult jobs print, in many cases based on the error messages generated by the PostScript interpreter. These error messages are returned by the printer on the same communications channel on which the program originated. This works fine for a standalone user, but causes big problems on a network. If an application has sent its stuff and then signed off, any subsequent error in processing will not be reported back to the application. The user is left wondering what happened.

Many serious color service bureaus use an *error reporter* to help track down problems that are slowing or stopping a file from imaging. Utilities such as the PostScript Error Reporter from PinPoint and the Advanced PostScript Error Handler from Systems of Merritt provide a detailed interpretation of the error messages, with some suggestions for corrections.

Many service bureaus, and the desktop publishers who keep them busy, also use a handy utility called LaserCheck, which lets a 300 dpi PostScript laser printer mimic an imagesetter, allowing you to proof a file before committing it to film. LaserCheck works by intercepting the low-level PostScript page set-up commands, then scaling the image to fit on the physical page used by the laser printer. Important job information is printed around the edge, including data on the fonts used, allocations of memory and processor time, device parameters, and the list of calls that modify the graphics state.

These clues are often useful for tracking down why a given file might not print properly (or at all). Indeed, the use of a utility like LaserCheck is highly recommended for novice color publishers, to minimize the likelihood of surprises when first color separations are generated. Even experienced color publishers may find it cost-effective to use LaserCheck as a proof before going to the imagesetter.

Halftone accuracy

One potentially explosive issue hidden within the emergence of output service bureaus for desktop color publishing concerns the legal responsibility for substandard film output. A research study conducted at dozens of service bureaus in 1990 found that virtually all of them produce film output that falls short of the film one might expect from a traditional color trade shop.

Even the best service bureaus in the study often produced output samples with at least a 4 percent error at the midtone (50 percent) dot. Most output showed an error in the range of 10 to 20 percent—when a client specified a 50 percent tint, the service bureau typically delivered 60 to 70 percent on paper and 30 to 40 percent on film. These errors, caused by pixel growth due to overexposure, were common across all makes of imagesetters, all common resolutions, and all common line screens.

According to lawyers specializing in product liability issues, the quality-related legal obligations of service bureaus and color houses are essentially identical. Both produce a film representation of a page that will be used for making a printing plate which in turn is used to manufacture large quantities of that page. It is only a matter of time before a service bureau faces an expensive lawsuit from a disgruntled client whose printing job has turned out poorly due to inaccurate halftones.

Figure 10-8
Typical film negative output, showing the effect of overexposure

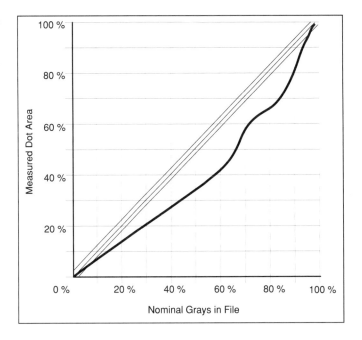

As previously discussed, precise control over the density of halftones is crucial to maintaining quality in color publishing. Unlike most other defects in film negatives, incorrect halftones often fail to show up on visual inspection—the eye doesn't judge density or halftone percentage accurately. This, coupled with a tendency at many service bureaus to boost exposure to increase density, especially in paper output (to make black type look crisper), leads to output that is overexposed, much to the detriment of any halftones this output may contain. This is less of a problem for color separations, which would be output to film, not paper.

Overexposure is all to easy to accomplish: to allow for proper exposure of different types of film, and to allow for the tendency of lasers to vary in output power as they age, imagesetters provide a control (usually labeled "intensity" or "density") that varies the intensity of the laser spot. In theory, once the exposure setting has been determined for a particular kind of medium, it should be adjusted only to compensate for changes in laser output or variations between different batches of film. The control's accessibility proves tempting, however, and it often ends up being used to "fatten" type or increase density for aesthetic reasons.

Figure 10-9
Good film negative output, with a maximum density error of about 5 percent

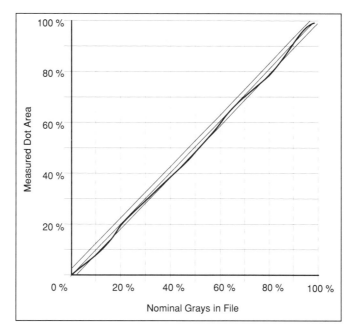

In a halftone, the subjective darkness of any small area is directly related to the coverage of the area by halftone dots, commonly expressed as halftone dot area. Given the tiny dimensions of halftone dots, normally inconsequential size variations in imagesetter pixels become extremely significant when creating halftones for color images or tints. It is the amount of error in pixel size that determines the amount of error in halftone dot size. The problem is that as pixels enlarge, they don't change their center position, but rather grow outward from it.

For the imagesetter operator, the challenge is to find the point at which density is sufficient for proper print production, while keeping the halftone tints relatively accurate. One way to accomplish this is to invest in a "hard dot" imagesetter with a tightly focused laser beam, which offers better exposure-related halftone accuracy than an imagesetter using the older "soft dot" technology.

For most service bureaus, however, a more cost-effective approach involves characterizing and calibrating all the components involved in imaging and developing film output.

Calibrating film output

Calibrating the output system requires careful attention to the processor chemistry, the choice of film media, the use of densitometers, and determination of optimal exposures.

Apparently there are still some low-end service bureaus that never calibrate, figuring that whatever variability they encounter is inevitable, or not worth the trouble of eliminating. In the world of black type and linework you can get away with that approach, but in the color world the cost of re-doing defective jobs will more than exceed the cost and hassle of calibrating.

As previously discussed, stable processing forms the basis for consistent output quality, and requires consistent processor maintenance and careful monitoring of the chemistry in the processor.

To interpret film output, you will need three precision instruments:

- a hand-held microscope or high-power magnifier (with 50x magnification) for close examination of imagesetter halftone dots;

- a transmission densitometer to measure densities and halftone dots on film;

- a reflection densitometer to measure press sheets in order to pre-compensate your negatives for high-quality production.

Once you are satisfied that your processor is sufficiently stable, and that you are using the appropriate media and chemistry, you must determine the optimal exposure setting that will give the necessary densities without creating severe halftone errors.

Most imagesetters have an exposure test, which creates a page composed of lines generated with different intensity settings. The service bureau technicians will run this page through the processor, and measure the results with a densitometer, which will determine the optimal exposure for a given type of emulsion. Every time a test page is run, annotations are kept, where necessary, and filed. Run a test page every time you change a significant variable, such as media, chemistry, or prep files.

Calibrating the imagesetter

Calibrating the imagesetter involves changing the PostScript transfer function to compensate for differences between the gray densities requested by an applications program and those output by an imagesetter.

Calibration will only be effective once the other parts of the system, such as the photo-processor, have been stabilized. If dot densities vary more than 5 percent from required values, it makes no sense to begin the calibration process, because you are locking on to an unstable target. Also, once an imagesetter has been calibrated, it should not need resetting until there is a change in some other part of the system. Calibration, when done properly, is a "set it and forget it" process, except for when film is changed.

The calibration procedure is simple, though it can be time-consuming. First, use an application program or calibration utility to create a test page containing various desired densities, in 1 percent steps from 1 percent to 100 percent. Run the test negative through the imagesetter and processor, and take densitometer readings on the resulting film. Next, apply corrections to revise the PostScript transfer function in the RIP, either by programming it directly or through a calibration utility. Then run the test negative again, and take new densitometer readings. Repeat as necessary until the densitometer values match the desired gray values.

Among the service bureaus and color houses that are striving to build a reputation in the new color desktop prepress business, many use the Color Calibration software developed by Technical Publishing Services, or the Precision program sold by Kodak.

Kodak Precision generates mathematically correct calibration tables for permanent storage on the RIP, which allows the user to define the uncalibrated screen percentages and enter them into the Precision table. Using the data, Precision builds and stores the calibration tables specific to each line screen, resolution, and medium type. Because the tables are stored on the RIP, it automatically selects the correct table based on the specific job being processed. Another significant advantage of RIP resident calibration is the linearization utility, which corrects compatible software applications without intervention—optimizing the output device for any program application sent to it.

**Dot gain
pre-compensation**

The calibration process also allows for pre-compensating the film for the effect of dot gain on press. For example, when your application program creates a tint with a 50 percent dot density, the resulting halftone dot in the printed piece is usually closer to a 70 percent dot.

You can measure the effects of dot gain for any given combination of press, paper, and ink, and commercial printers have available books full of charts and graphs on predicting dot gain. By plotting the error at each density level, you can build a transfer curve that will mirror the error. Be sure to check with your printer before pre-compensating for dot gain; otherwise, the printing company's production people will have a difficult time printing your excessively light negatives.

Also, despite the fact that a number of graphics and imaging programs allow you to customize the transfer function, you're best off not tinkering with it in an application unless you have a clear understanding of the probable density effects on your output.

Printer description files

Printer description files help Macintosh PostScript-language applications communicate with a particular brand and model of PostScript printer. They describe the capabilities of the printer so an application program can take advantage of its special features, and they allow the user to fine-tune the printer's operation to adjust things like grayscale tones.

When a page from a PostScript-language application is printed on a PostScript output device, the content and format of each page are device-independent. However, each model of printer has unique specifications for features such as automatic and manual paper feed, paper trays, film and paper media, and so on. These unique characteristics are stored as printer description files, which make it possible to add printer support by merely adding or updating current files, instead of by changing the application itself. The original Aldus Printer Description files (APDs) were written by Aldus for a large variety of printers, and built into PageMaker and FreeHand.

These have since been supplanted by Adobe PostScript Printer Description (PPD) files, which are shipped with each PostScript output device and built into many publishing and graphics applications programs. The PPD system benefits users who purchase an output device that is not yet supported by their particular application. Instead of waiting for the software publisher to develop a printer description file, you can be up and running immediately by using the PPD file shipped with your printer.

Only the most general printer information is included in Adobe's PPD files, so Aldus places other printer-specific information in a secondary printer description extension file, or PDX.

The PDX is of interest to imagesetter operators because it contains commands that calibrate the printer output (normalized transfer functions) for more uniform gray scales. Calibrating your imagesetter takes fewer steps—you can bypass the PDX file and print a calibration file through the PPD file, then enter any calibration corrections to the normalized transfer function directly in the PDX file.

For those creating PostScript output from IBM-compatible computers, the printer description information is included as part of the Windows driver for any particular device.

The service bureau of the future

The emergence of desktop color service bureaus is a challenge the traditional color houses don't know how to compete against. They have different origins, they work with different technologies, and their customers are printers and typesetters, not independent desktop publishers.

On the other hand, existing color houses possess crucial color skills, and they often have the capital to properly implement desktop color systems. A Macintosh-based color prepress system complete with imagesetter and digital proofer might cost upwards of $200,000 or more, which seems quite expensive to most computer users but sounds like a real bargain to someone planning to use it instead of a high-end color prepress machine costing well over $1 million.

For the new service bureau owner, color is a great opportunity, bringing a broader range of customers to desktop publishing, customers who are willing to pay a premium price for color. A whole new range of services can be marketed alongside color desktop publishing, including film, slide, and paper output, design, training, and consulting.

Color, creativity, and the future

We are in the early stages of a revolution that will surely sweep aside many of the old tools and techniques for color production, and replace them with faster, better tools. The pace of technological change in this domain will be rapid throughout the 1990s.

A growing number of desktop publishers are performing the entire publishing process, including separating color images, on the desktop. However, four main problems remain to be solved:

- desktop scanners must improve their resolution and dynamic range, to compare with high-end rotary drum scanners;

- desktop proofing systems (direct digital proofs) must increase in quality to rival that of traditional film proofs;

- PostScript imagesetters must improve their precision and repeatability to ensure accurate halftone screening;

- computer processors must become even more powerful to speed up the manipulation of large full-color images.

Some of these problems are being addressed by products that have recently come to market, while others won't be completely solved for some years.

As color production migrates to the desktop, it brings a tremendous opportunity for people, especially those without formal design training, to take hold of these bright new tools and use them to express the vibrancy and color of their unique creative impulses.

Vendors

Adobe Systems Corp.
15585 Charleston Road, PO Box 7900
Mountain View, CA 94039

Adobe Photoshop
Adobe Illustrator
Adobe Streamline

Agfa Compugraphic Corp.
200 Ballardvale St.
Wilmington, MA 01887
914-365-0190

ProSet and SelectSet imagesetters

Agfa Matrix Division
1 Ramland Rd.
Orangeburg, NY 10962

TT200 Thermal Printer

Aldus Corp.
Suite 200, 411 First Avenue S.
Seattle, WA 98104-2871
206-628-2396

Aldus PageMaker
Aldus PrePrint
Aldus FreeHand

Apple Computer Inc.
20525 Mariani Ave.
Cupertino, CA 95041

Macintosh computers

Atex Magazine Publishing System
32 Wiggins Avenue
Bedford, MA 01730

Atex PC Page Makeup

Barneyscan Corp.
1125 Atlantic Avenue
Alameda, CA 94501
415-521-3388

Color scanners and control software

Bestinfo, Inc.
1400 North Providence Road
Media, PA 19063
215-891-6500

Wave4

Birmy Graphics Corp.
2244 N. W. 21st. Terr.
Miami, FL 33142

Birmy imagesetters

C-Cube Microsystems Inc.
399-A Trimble Road
San Jose, CA 95134
408-944-6300

JPEG compression chips

Calcomp Inc.
2411 W. La Palma Ave.
Anaheim , CA 92801
Colorview thermal transfer printers

Canon U.S.A.
1 Canon Plaza
Lake Success, NY 11042-1113
Canon Laser Copier CLC-500

Colorocs Corp.
2830 Peterson Place
Norcross, GA 30071
404-840-6500
Colorocs CP 4007 printer

Computer Presentations Inc.
1117 Cypress St.
Cincinnati, OH 45206
Windows Colorlab Imageprep compression program

Computer Support Corp.
15926 Midway Road
Dallas, TX 75244
214-661-8960
Arts & Letters Graphics Editor

Corel Systems Corp.
1600 Carling Avenue
Ottawa, ON Canada K1Z 8R7
613-728-8200
Corel Draw

Crosfield Electronics Inc.
65 Harristown Road
Glen Rock, NJ 07452
617-338-2173
Lightspeed CLS-2
StudioLink

CyberChrome Inc.
P.O. Box 9565
New Haven, CT 06536
203-786-5151

Digital Technology International
500 W. 1200 S.
Orem , UT 84058
801-226-2984
Adspeed and Color Pagespeed

DS America Incorporated
5110 Tollview Drive
Rolling Meadows, IL 60008
Scanagraph and Sigmagraph

Electronics For Imaging (EFI)
950 Elm Avenue
San Bruno, CA 94066
415-742-3400
Fiery color laser controller
Cachet color correction software

Exabyte Corporation
1745 38th Street
Boulder, CO 80301
Exabyte DAT

General Parametrics Corp.
1250 Ninth St.
Berkeley, CA 94710
Photometric Slidemaker

Hell Graphic Systems
25 Harbor Park Drive
Port Washington, NY 11050
516-484-3000
Hell ChromaCom, ScriptMaster

Hoechst Celanese Corp.
3070 Highway 22 West
Somerville, NJ 08876-1252
908-231-5875

Pressmatch DIP

Howtek Inc.
21 Park Ave.
Hudson, NH 03051
603-882-5200

Scanmaster scanners, Pixelmaster color printer

Image-In Incorporated
406 East 79th Street
Minneapolis, MN 55420
612-888-3633
fax 612-888-3665

Image-In-Color

Imapro Corporation
2400 St. Laurent Blvd.
Ottawa, ON Canada K1G 5A4
613-738-3000

QCS Scanners

InSight Systems, Inc.
10017 Coach Road
Vienna, VA 22181
703-938-0250

Publisher's Prism

Iris Graphics Inc.
6 Crosby Dr.
Bedford, MA 01730

Iris Inkjet color proofers

Eastman Kodak
32 Wiggins Avenue
Bedford, MA 01730
617-275-8300

Eikonix Digital Camera

Eastman Kodak
23 Crosby Drive
Bedford, MA 01730
617-259-1400

Prophecy color prepress system

Eastman Kodak
343 State Street
Rochester, NY 14650
800-445-6325

XL7700 digital printer
ColorSqueeze compression software

Lasergraphics Inc.
17671 Cowan Ave.
Irvine, CA 92714
714-727-2651

Mac/LFR, Rascol II/LFR film recorders

Letraset U.S.A.
40 Eisenhower Dr.
Paramus, NJ 07653

ColorStudio, DesignStudio

Linotype-Hell Company
425 Osler Ave.
Hauppauge, NY 11788
516-434-3079

Linotronic series

MacDonald Dettwiler
13231 Delf Place, #501
Richmond, BC Canada V6V 2C3
604-273-7730

FIRE 1000 color film recorder

Micrografx Inc.
1303 Arapaho
Richardson , TX 75081
214-234-1769

Micrografx Designer

Mirus Corporation
758 Sycamore Dr.
Milpitas, CA 93035

FilmPrinter Turbo color film recorder

Mitsubishi Electronics America Inc.
991 Knox St.
Torrance, CA 90502
213-515-3993

G330, G650 thermal transfer printers

Monotype Inc.
2500 Brickvale Dr.
Elk Grove Village, IL 60007

Lasercomp imagesetters

Networked Picture Systems
2953 Bunker Hill Lane, Suite 202
Santa Clara, CA 95054-1131
408-748-1677

NPS Page Express

Nikon Inc. (Electronic Imaging)
623 Stewart Avenue
Garden City, NY 11530
516-222-0200

LS-3500 color scanner

Optronics
7 Stuart Rd.
Chelmsford, MA 01824
508-256-4511

ColorGetter Plus scanner
ColorSetter 2000 imagesetter

Pre-Press Technologies, Inc.
2443 Impala Drive
Carlsbad, CA 92008
619-931-2695

SpectreScan
SpectreSeps PM, SpectreSeps QX
SpectrePrint Pro

Presstek, Inc.
8 Commercial Street
Hudson, NH 03051
603-595-7000

Presstek direct to plate technology

QMS Inc.
1 Magnum Pass
Mobile, AL 36618
205-633-7223

Colorscript 100 series thermal transfer printers

Quantel Inc.
655 Washington Blvd.
Stamford, CT 06901
203-348-4104
fax 203-356-9021

Graphic Paintbox

Quark Inc.
300 S. Jackson Street # 100
Denver, CO 80209
303-934-2211

QuarkXPress

Radius Inc.
1710 Fortune Dr.
San Jose, CA 95131
408-434-1010

Color monitors
PrecisionColor Calibrator

Raster Image Processing Systems Inc.
4665 Nautilus Ct. S.
Boulder, CO 80301

RIPS Image 4000

Rasterops Corp.
2500 Walsh Rd.
Santa Clara, CA 95051
408-562-4200

RasterOps Calibrator display system

Scitex Users Group
305 Plus Park Boulevard, Box 290249
Nashville, TN 37229
615-366-1798

Scitex Visionary
Dolev PS

Screaming Color, Inc.
125 N. Prospect
Itasca, IL 60143-1860
708-250-9500

RIPLINK series

Seiko Instruments USA
1130 Ringwood Ct.
San Jose, CA 95131

CH-5000 series color printers
Seiko ColorPrint

Sharp Electronics Corp.
Sharp Plaza
Mahwah, NJ 07430

JX color scanners
JX-730 color ink-jet printer

Storm Technology
1101 San Antonio Ave, Suite 10
Palo Alto, CA 94306
415-322-0506

ImagePress JPEG compression

SuperMac Technology
485 Potrero Ave.
Sunnyvale, CA 94086
408-773-4403

Superview series color monitors

Tektronix Inc.
P.O. Box 1000 M-S 63477
Wilsonville, OR 97070
800-835-6100

Tektronix Phaser thermal transfer printers

Trumatch, Inc.
331 Madison Avenue
New York, NY 10017
212-351-2360

Trumatch color matching system

Ultimate Technographics, Inc.
4980 Buchan Street, Suite 403
Montreal, PQ Canada H4P 1S8
514-733-1188
fax 514-340-1291

Impostrip imposition software

Varityper Inc.
11 Mt. Pleasant Ave. East
East Hanover, NJ 07936
201-887-8000

Varityper imagesetters

Ventura Software Inc.
15175 Innovation Drive
San Diego, CA 92128
619-673-0172

Ventura Publisher

Wacom Inc.
West 115 Century Road
Paramus, NJ 07652
201-265-4226

Wacom cordless pressure-sensitive digitizers

Videotex Systems, Inc.
8499 Greenville Avenue, Suite 205
Dallas, TX 752331
214-343-4500
fax 214-348-3821

ChromaTools image conversion software

Glossary

achromatic	colors, such as white, gray, and black, that have no hue
additive primaries	red, green, and blue light, which produce the sensation of white light when added together; *see subtractive primaries*
acetate	transparent cellulose sheet placed over a mechanical, on which color separation directions can be written
airbrush	small pressure gun that sprays paint with compressed air, or its electronic equivalent, found in most imaging programs
analog	information in non-discrete values, such as voltages, rather than as numeric digitals
anti-aliasing	a way of averaging the brightness values of adjacent pixels in order to eliminate jagged edges in computer images
AppleTalk	a low-cost local area network, built into every Macintosh and accessible from some other LANs
application	a computer program written to perform a specific function, such as illustration or page layout
art	all visual materials used in preparing a job for printing; any copy to be reproduced
ASIC	application specific integrated circuit — a semi-customized chip made to perform a specialized function
ASCII	American Standard Code for Information Interchange; a common file format for plain text
auto-trace	the ability of a draw program to automatically trace imported bitmap images to create editable lines and curves
baud	a unit of data transmission speed, measured in bits per second

Bézier curve   a line segment that can be interactively altered by moving not only the nodes that define the line, but also the nodes that modify the angle at which the line approaches each node

bit   a *bi*nary digi*t*, the fundamental unit of digital information; a zero or one

bitmap   an array of bits that defines a character or image

black   the absence of all reflected light, caused by printing an ink whose colorant gives no apparent hue; one of the four process inks

black printer   the black plate produced from the four-color separation of an image; used to increase contrast, especially of dark tones

bleed   to extend the printed image beyond the edge of the paper, so it goes right to the edge of the paper after binding and trimming

body type   the main text of a document, as distinct from the headings; also called body copy

brightness   the lightness value of a color or tone, regardless of its hue or saturation; also, the intensity of a light source

buffer   computer memory for storage of data, especially images, awaiting processing

bullet   dot used as an ornamental device

byte   eight bits, equivalent to a single alphabetic or numeric character

CAD   computer aided design, or computer aided drafting

CAM   computer aided manufacture

calibrate   to set up a scanner, monitor, printer, or imagesetter so that it produces accurate and consistent results, such as predictable halftones

CCD array   a row of tiny charge-coupled devices, each of which converts light into electricity

CEPS   color electronic prepress systems

chroma   the saturation or vibrancy of a color

chrome   a color transparency, named after brands such as Kodachrome, Ektachrome, Agfachrome, and Fujichrome

CIE   an international color standard based on definitions and measurements of the Commission Internationale de l'Eclairage

CMYK	the four-color process inks used in printing, composed of cyan, magenta, yellow, and black components
color balance	a combination of cyan, magenta, and yellow that produces a neutral gray
color cast	the modification of a hue by the addition, often unintentional, of a trace of another hue
color correction	a photographic or electronic process used to compensate for the deficiencies of the process inks and the color separation process; also, any color change requested by the client
color gamut	the range of colors that can be formed by all possible combinations of colorants in any color reproduction system
Color Key	an off-press overlay color proof method from 3M
color model	a metaphor that enables a person to imagine what a color space looks like
color proof	a representation of the final printed piece, used for checking color accuracy
color separation	the process of making films from a color original (one for each of the process colors), from which printing plates can be made
color sequence	the order in which inks are applied, usually yellow, magenta, cyan, black
color space	a mathematical abstraction that describes a domain of visible or producible colors
color temperature	the temperature (measured in degrees Kelvin) to which a object would have to be heated before it would radiate a given color; the higher the color temperature, the bluer the light
colorant	dyes and pigments used to color materials
colorimeter	an optical measuring device designed to respond to color in a manner similar to the human eye
colorimetry	the science of measuring and specifying colors
comprehensive	a preliminary version of a design, often created for client input or approval; a comp
continuous tone	images that are represented, not by pure black and white, but by a series of evenly graduated tones, as in a photograph; sometimes called a contone
contrast	the variation between the lightest and darkest parts of an image

Cromalin	a popular off-press color proof from duPont
crop	to select part of an image, discarding the rest
cyan	a subtractive primary, and one of the four process color inks (sometimes called process blue); cyan absorbs red light, and reflects or transmits blue and green
DDES	Digital Data Exchange Specifications, an emerging standard prepress file format
densitometer	an electronic device for measuring the amount of light transmitted through or reflected from a sample, such as the gray percentage values in a halftone
density	a photographic image's degree of darkness or opacity; ranges from 0 (clear) to 4.0 (totally black)
desktop publishing	the use of microcomputers to produce typeset documents
digital	the use of discrete pulses or signals to represent data (as the digits zero and one); see *analog*
digitizer	device used to scan a video input and convert it into a bitmap that can be stored and manipulated in a computer
direct digital color proof	proof made directly from digital data output by a desktop or high-end color prepress systems, without an intermediate film stage
dithering	alternating the values of adjacent dots or pixels to create the effect of intermediate values or colors
DOS	disk operating system; co master control program that integrates the various parts of an IBM-compatible computer
dot area	the proportion of a given area covered by halftone dots, usually expressed as a percentage
dot etching	a manual technique for chemically changing the dot size on halftone films, usually for localized or general color correction
dot gain	the change in size of a printing dot from the film to the printed sheet, expressed as a percentage; an increase in dot size from 50 percent to 60 percent is called a 10 percent gain
dot pitch	the distance between adjacent dots in a halftone screen
doubling	a printing defect in the halftone imaging process, in which a faint secondary image appears, slightly out of register with the primary image

dpi	dots per inch; a measure of the resolution or addressability of a display or output device
drum scanner	a color scanner in which the original is wrapped around a rotary scanning drum
dye	a soluble coloring material, such as those used as colorants in color photographs; as opposed to pigments, which are insoluble
dye transfer	a method of producing color prints by making separation negatives, then transferring cyan, magenta, and yellow images from dyed matrices
EIP	electronic integrated publishing; the use of computer in the publishing process, from concept through to the final printed product
EPS	Encapsulated PostScript, a file format that facilitates the exchange of PostScript graphic files between applications
emulsion	in photograph processes, the photosensitive coating on film
fake color	producing a color illustration, usually from a black-and-white photograph, by specifying tint areas in terms of their four process color components
exposure	the time and intensity of illumination acting upon the light-sensitive emulsion on a film
filling in	in offset lithography, the problem caused by ink filling the areas between halftone dots or plugging up the small spaces in type
filter	a transparent material that selectively absorbs light of certain wavelengths; used to separate the red, green, and blue components of an original during the color separation process
flat	the assembled composite of film for each set of pages, ready for plate-making
flat color	a solid or tint area without tonal variation, achieved with a special ink mixture, overlapping halftone tints, or a single halftone tint
folio	page number that appears at the top or bottom of a page throughout a publication
font	the complete set of characters in a typeface, in a specific size, weight, and attribute

four-color process	method of reproducing full-color artwork and photographs by separating the original into its cyan, magenta, yellow, and black components
frequency	the number of lines per inch in a halftone; also called screen ruling
front end	the hardware on which graphics and documents are created and stored, prior to being output on the back end of the system
Gb	gigabyte, a billion bytes, a thousand megabytes
gamma	a measure of the contrast in a photographic image or display; the ratio of the density range of a negative to the density range of the original
GCR	gray component replacement, a separation technique for replacing cyan, magenta, and yellow inks with black
gradient	a blend between two colors or shades of gray
gravure	printing method based on the *intaglio* principle, in which the image area is etched below the surface of the printing plate
gray balance	the values of cyan, magenta, and yellow needed to produce a neutral gray when printed at normal density
gray scale	the file created by scanning a continuous tone original and saving the information as shades of gray; also, an image containing a series of tones stepped from white to black; a step wedge
halftone	an image composed of dots that vary in size but are constant in spacing, giving the appearance of different shades of gray
hardware	any tangible part of a computer system
high key	a photograph in which the majority of tonal values are higher, or lighter, than a middle gray
highlight	the whitest or brightest parts of a photograph; the opposite of shadow
hints	algorithms contained in some fonts, such as Adobe PostScript fonts, that increase type quality when printing at low resolutions or in small point sizes
hue	the color family or color name, such as green, purple, orange, or red
icon	image on a computer display that graphically represents an object, function, message, or concept in the underlying program

imagesetter	a device for recording high-resolution type and graphics on photographic film or resin-coated paper
imposition	the arrangement of pages in a press form so they will appear in correct order when the printed sheet is folded and trimmed
ink holdout	a characteristic of paper that keeps ink on the surface, rather than being absorbed into the paper's fibers; coated papers have better ink holdout and therefore can reproduce finer halftones
ink jet printing	a printing technology in which dots are sprayed onto the paper to form an image; used for both very low-quality and high-quality output
intensity	another name for color saturation
jaggies	the jagged edges on type and bitmapped graphics formed on a raster device such as a display monitor or laser printer
Kelvin (K)	unit of temperature measurement starting from absolute zero (-273 degrees Celsius)
Kb	kilobyte, a thousand bytes
keyline	thin line around a box containing an image
knockout	the absence of ink in a specified area, so that the color of an object printing on top of it is not altered
laser	an intense light beam, essential for recording digital images
lightness	the variation of a hue along the scale from black to white
line art	artwork consisting of solid blacks and whites, with no tonal values
lithography	a printing process in which the image area is separated from the nonimage area by means of chemical repulsion
local area network	computers connected together within a single building or cluster of buildings
logotype	a graphic used to create an organization's visual identity
lpi	lines per (linear) inch, a measure of screen frequency
luminance	the amount of light emitted by any radiant source
Mb	megabyte, a million bytes
macro	a single keystroke that can play back a complex series of previously performed keystrokes; an essential computer tool for automating repetitive tasks

magenta	a subtractive primary color that reflects blue and red light, and absorbs green; one of the four process colors, sometimes called process red
make-ready	setting and testing of all the press controls just prior to a printing run
mask	a photographic vignette used to isolate one part of an image for color correction, contrast reduction, tonal adjustment, or detail enhancement
memory	a computer's temporary storage area; usually referred to as RAM (random access memory)
metamers	colors that are spectrally different but visually identical for a given observer under specified viewing conditions
micron	one millionth of a meter
microprocessor	an integrated circuit that carries out programmed instructions
modem	a device for transmitting computer files across telephone lines
moiré	undesirable patterns that appear in printed materials when the halftone screen angles of the separations are set to the wrong angles; caused by interference patterns between two or more regular grids
mouse	small hand-held table-top device moved to control the motion of the cursor on screen
multi-tasking	running two or more jobs in a computer at the same time
negative	a reverse photographic image on paper or film
neutral	a color that has no hue, such as white, gray, or black
object-oriented graphic	a graphic made up of distinct objects that can be individually modified
offset	common term for offset lithography, in which the image is offset from the printing plate onto a rubber blanket and from there to the paper
opacity	a material's lack of transparency; for printing ink, the ability to hide or cover up the image or tone over which it is applied
optical character recognition	scanning and electronically converting typewritten or typeset documents into editable text files
optical disk	a high-density mass storage medium using a laser to read and write data

overlay	transparent paper or film placed over artwork to protect it from damage, to indicate instructions to the printer, or to show the breakdown of color in mechanical color separations
overprint	an object that prints on top of other colors; the opposite of a knockout
PANTONE MATCHING SYSTEM	PANTONE, Inc.'s check-standard trademark for color reproduction and color reproduction materials; a system of solid ink color mixing, matched to swatchbook samples
PC	personal computer, especially an IBM compatible
peripheral	an input or output device attached to a computer
photomultiplier	a highly sensitive electronic component, used in many color scanners, that transforms variations of light into electric currents
photon	a bundle of light energy
pica	a unit of measure, about one-sixth of an inch; composed of 12 points
pigment	an insoluble coloring material, used as a colorant in printing inks
pixel	a single picture element, the smallest unit of information in an input or output device
point	a unit of measure for specifying type; about 1/72nd of an inch, or 1/12th of a pica
positive	a photograph reproduction on paper or film in which the tonal values correspond to the original
PostScript	the standard page description language for graphics and publishing
ppi	pixels per inch, a measure of a device's resolution
primary colors	the set of colors that can be mixed to produce all the colors in a color space; in additive systems they are red, green, and blue, while in subtractive systems they are cyan, magenta, and yellow
printing plate	a surface, usually metal, rubber, or plastic, that has been treated to carry an image
process colors	the four ink colors (cyan, magenta, yellow, and black) used in full-color process printing
program	a collection of instructions that activate a computer to perform a task

progressive proofs   a set of press proofs that includes the individual process colors, plus overprints of two-, three-, and four-color combinations in their order of printing

proof   a hard-copy sample designed to approximate how an image or document will appear when printed

punch register   the use of punched holes and pins or studs to hold copy, film, masks, negatives, and plates in precise register

RAM   random access memory; the internal memory chips in a computer

rasterization   the conversion of computerized graphics and images into tiny printer dots, which are often combined into halftone dots

reflective art   artwork, such as photographs or paintings, viewed by reflected light; compare with transparency

registration   the precise alignment of films or plates for printing

registration marks   crosshair targets on color separations to allow precise positioning of the various pieces of film

resolution   the degree to which adjacent small details, can be distinguished visually, photographically, or electronically

retouching   correcting imperfections in a photograph before it is reproduced

reverse type   white type against a black background

RGB   the red, green, and blue color system used for color video display

RIP   raster image processor; the component of an output device that rasterizes the image

ROM   read-only memory; memory chips that hold information permanently in a computer, such as the chips containing its setup parameters; contrast with RAM

rosettes   the patterns formed when halftone color images are printed in register at the correct screen angles

rough   a very preliminary layout or design, often done on tracing paper, to give a general idea of the size and position of various type and graphic elements

saturation   the vividness or purity of a color; the less gray a color contains, the more saturated it is

scale   to increase or decrease in size

scanner   device for converting visual information into digitized data

screen	traditionally, the glass or film device through which a photograph is converted into a halftone; now used to mean the halftone pattern itself
screen angle	the angle at which the rulings of a halftone screen (or its digital equivalent) are set when making screened images for printing halftones
screen ruling	the number of lines per inch on a halftone screen; also called screen frequency
SCSI	Small Computer System Interface, an industry standard for connecting peripherals to computers
secondary color	a color that results from mixing two primary colors; orange (yellow and red), purple (red and blue), or green (blue and yellow)
shadow	the darkest point in an image; the opposite of a highlight
sheet-fed	a method of printing in which the paper is fed into the press as sheets rather than a web
signature	a group of pages printed on a sheet of paper which, when folded and trimmed, will appear in their proper sequence
software	computer programs; either applications programs or operating system software
spot color	a solid color, such as those specified by the PANTONE MATCHING SYSTEM; the opposite of a process color
spread	a pair of facing pages; in printing, the enlargement of a color area to build trap with adjacent areas of different color
stock	paper or other material to be printed upon
stripping	taping together different pieces of film so they can be composed into a single film, prior to making a printing plate
subtractive primaries	yellow, magenta, and cyan, the hues used (with black) for process color inks
Tb	terrabyte, a trillion bytes; a thousand gigabytes
TIFF	Tag Image File Format, a format used for transferring bitmapped and grayscale images between computer applications
tint	a halftone area made up of dots of equal size; a color obtained by adding white to the solid color
tone	the variation in a color or the range of grays between black and white

transparency	any artwork viewed by having light pass through it, rather than reflecting off it
trapping	creating small overlapping areas wherever two colors meet, to ensure that slight mis-registrations on press do not show up as white gaps on the printed piece
wavelength	the physical property of light that determines its color
web	printing method in which paper is fed into the press in continuous rolls, rather than as individual sheets
WORM	write-once read-multiple optical storage device
WYSIWYG	a hypothetical condition in which what you see (on the screen) is what you get (on the printed page)
xerography	an electrophotographic copying process that uses electrostatic forces and toner to form an image
yellow	a subtractive primary, and one of the four process ink colors; it reflects red and green light, and absorbs blue

Bibliography

Books

Josef Albers	*Interaction of Color.* New Haven: Yale University Press, 1975
Nancy Aldrich-Ruenzel, editor	*Designer's Guide to Print Production.* New York: Watson-Guptill Publications, 1990
David Bann and John Gargan	*How to Check and Correct Color Proofs.* Cincinnati: North Light Books, F&W Publications, 1990
Mark Beach, Steve Shepro, and Ken Russon	*Getting it Printed: How to Work with Printers & Other Graphic Arts Services to Assure Quality, Stay on Schedule, and Control Costs.* Portland, OR: Coast to Coast Books, 1986
Stephen Beale and James Cavuoto	*The Scanner Book: A Complete Guide to the Use and Applications of Desktop Scanners.* Torrance, CA: MicroPublishing Press, 1989
Michael Beaumont	*Type and Color.* Oxford: Phaidon Press, 1987
Faber Birren	*Color and Human Response.* New York: Van Nostrand Reinhold, 1978
Faber Birren	*Principles of Color.* West Chester, PA: Schiffer Publishing, 1987
David Blatner and Keith Stimely	*The QuarkXPress Book.* Berkeley, CA: Peachpit Press, 1991
Michael Bruno, editor	*Pocket Pal: A Graphic Arts Production Handbook, 14th edition.* Memphis, TN: International Paper Company, 1989
Tom Cardamone	*Mechanical Color Separation Skills for the Commercial Artist.* New York: Van Nostrand Reinhold, 1980
Hideaki Chijiiwa	*Color Harmony: A Guide to Creative Color Combinations.* Rockport, MA: Rockport Publishers, 1987

Chris Dickman	*Mastering Corel Draw, 2nd edition.* Berkeley, CA: Peachpit Press, 1991
Gary Field, editor	*Color and Its Reproduction.* Pittsburgh: Graphic Arts Technical Foundation, 1989
Karl Gerstner	*The Forms of Color.* Cambridge, MA: MIT Press, 1986
Luigina de Grandis	*Theory and Use of Color.* New York: Harry N. Abrams, 1986
Johannes Itten	*The Elements of Color.* New York: Van Nostrand Reinhold, 1970
Harald Kueppers	*The Basic Law of Color Theory.* Woodbury, NY: Barron's Educational Series, 1982
Rafiqul Molla	*Electronic Color Separation.* Montgomery, WV: R.K. Printing and Publishing Company,1988
Miles Southworth	*Pocket Guide to Color Reproduction Communication and Control.* Livonia, NY: Graphic Arts Publishing Company, 1988
Donna and Miles Southworth	*Glossary of Color Scanner, Color System and Communication Terms.* Livonia NY: Graphic Arts Publishing Company, 1987
Fred Wentzel, Ray Blair, and Tom Destree	*Graphic Arts Photography: Color.* Pittsburgh: Graphic Arts Technical Foundation, 1987
Jan White	*Color for the Electronic Age.* New York: Watson-Guptill Publications, 1990
Paul Zelanski and Mary Pat Fisher	*Color for Designers and Artists.* London: Herbert Press, 1989

Periodicals

Aldus Magazine	Aldus Corporation 411 First Avenue South Seattle, WA 98104-2871 phone 206-343-3205
Bove & Rhodes Inside Report on Desktop Publishing and Multimedia	Bove & Rhodes P.O. Box 1289 Gualala, CA 95445 phone 707-884-4413
Desktop Communications	International Desktop Communications 48 East 43rd St. New York, NY 10017 phone 212-867-9650

Electronic Composition & Imaging

Youngblood Publishing Company Limited
505 Consumers Road, Suite 102
Willowdale, ON
Canada M2J 4V8
fax 416-492-7595
phone 416-492-5777

Desktop To Press

Peter Fink Communications Inc.
2704 Ontario Road N.W.
Washington, DC 20009
phone 202-667-6400
fax 202-667-6512

MacPrePress

Prepress Information Service
12 Burr Road
Westport, CT 06880
fax 203-454-4962

MicroPublishing Report: The
Independent Newsletter for the
Desktop Publishing Industry

Micro Publishing
21150 Hawthorne Blvd., #104
Torrance, CA 90503
phone 213-371-5787

Multimedia Computing & Presentations

Multimedia Computing Corporation
2900 Gordon Avenue, Suite 100
Santa Clara, CA 95951
phone 408-245-4750

Personal Publishing

Hitchcock Publishing Company
191 S. Gary Ave.
Carol Stream, IL 60188
phone 708-665-1000

Pre-: The Magazine for the
PrePress Industry

South Wind Publishing Company
8340 Mission Road, Suite 106
Prairie Village, KS 66206
phone 913-642-6611
fax 913-642-6676

Publish

Integrated Media Inc.
501 Second St.
San Francisco, CA 94107
phone 415-243-0600

Seybold Report on Desktop Publishing

Seybold Publications, Inc.
P.O. Box 644
Media, PA 19063
phone 215-565-2480
fax 215-565-4659

Seybold Report on Publishing Systems

Seybold Publications, Inc.
P.O. Box 644
Media, PA 19063
phone 215-565-2480
fax 215-565-4659

Step by Step Electronic Design:
The How-To Newsletter
for Desktop Designers

Dynamic Graphics, Inc.
6000 North Forest Park Drive
Peoria, IL 61614-3592
phone 800-255-8800

Verbum: The Journal of Personal
Computer Aesthetics

Verbum Inc.
P.O. Box 15439
San Diego, CA 92115
phone 619-233-9977

Professional Groups and Associations

ADEPT—Association for the Development of Electronic Publishing Technique	360 North Michigan Ave, Suite 1111 Chicago, IL 60601
Association of Desk-Top Publishers (AD-TP)	Suite 800, 4677 30th St. San Diego, CA 92116 phone 202-232-3335
Association of Imaging Service Bureaus	5601 Roanne Way, Suite 605 Greensboro, NC 27409 phone 919-854-5697
Berkeley Macintosh Users' Group (BMUG)	1442A Walnut St., #62 Berkeley, CA 94709 phone 415-549-2684 fax 415-849-9026
Electronic Publishing Special Interest Group (EPSIG)	c/o OCLC 6565 Frantz Road Dublin, OH 43017-0702 phone 614-764-6000 fax 614-764-6096
Graphic Arts Technical Foundation (GATF)	4615 Forbes Ave. Pittsburgh, PA 15213 phone 412-621-6941 fax 412-621-3049
Graphic Communications Association (GCA)	Suite 604 1730 N. Lynn St. Arlington, VA 22209-2085 phone 703-841-8160 fax 703-841-8144
Hell Users Group, North America	P.O. Box 1665 Orlando, FL 32802

Institute for Graphic Communication (IGC)	77 Rumford Avenue Waltham, MA 02154 phone 617-891-1550 fax 617-891-3936
IDEA—International Design by Electronics Association	1120 Connecticut Avenue N.W. Washington, DC 20036
International Association of Laser Printers	4828 Loop Central Drive, Suite 50 Houston, TX 77081
International Prepress Association	552 West 167th Street South Holland, IL 60473
National Association of Desktop Publishers (NADTP)	Museum Wharf 300 Congress Street Boston, MA 02210 phone 617-426-2885 fax 617-426-2765
National Composition & Pre-Press Association	730 N. Lynn St. Arlington, VA 22209 phone 703-841-8165 fax 703-841-8178
National Newspaper Association	Suite 400, 1627 K St., NW Washington, DC 20006-1790 phone 202-466-7200 fax 202-331-1403
National Printing Equipment & Supply Association (NPES)	899 Preston White Drive Reston, VA 22091-4326 phone 703-264-7200
Open Software Foundation (OSF)	1 Cambridge Street Cambridge, MA 02142 phone 617-621-8700 fax 617-225-2782
PostScript Imaging Centers Association	c/o CIS Graphics 234 Broadway Cambridge, MA 02139
Professional Prepress Alliance	739 Bryant Street San Francisco, CA 94107
Scitex Graphic Arts Users Association	P.O. Box 290249 Nashville, TN USA 37229

Society for Imaging Science and Technology   7003 Kilworth Lane
Springfield, VA 22151

*Typographers International
Association (TIA)*   262 Hall Place NW
Washington, DC 20007
phone 202-965-3400
fax 202-965-3522

About the Author

Michael Kieran is president of Desktop Publishing Associates, a Toronto-based training and consulting company specializing in electronic publishing.

Desktop Publishing Associates was formed in early 1985, and is an authorized training center for Aldus PageMaker and FreeHand, QuarkXPress, Ventura Publisher, Corel Draw, Micrografx Designer and Charisma, Word for Windows, and FrameMaker.

Michael provides consulting on color publishing systems for a variety of large and small organizations. He also is the Color Editor for Electronic Composition & Imaging, a leading journal in the desktop publishing field.

He has been a guest speaker at many industry associations and conferences, including Color Connections, the Seybold Electronic Publishing Conference, the International PrePress Color Conference, the Electronic Desktop Publishing Association, the Association for Systems Management, the Canadian Computer Show, ComGraph, VICOM, and others.

Michael worked for eight years researching and writing educational television programs at TV Ontario, and has won awards for his television writing in Canada, the United States, Europe and Japan. He also spent three years as a science and technology reporter for The Globe and Mail.

Michael lives in Richmond Hill, Ontario with his wife Jane and his sons Christopher and Andrew.

Colophon

This book was written on an IBM-compatible computer running the obscure GonzoWrite word processing program. Screen shots of PC-based applications were captured with Tiffany Plus, and of Macintosh applications with ScreenShot.

The illustrations were created in SuperPaint, Aldus FreeHand, Adobe Illustrator, QuarkXPress, and Micrografx Designer. Photographic effects were generated in Adobe Photoshop.

Except where otherwise noted, the color pages were created in Adobe Illustrator and separated in Adobe Separator. Color images were scanned from 35mm slides on an Optronics ColorGetter, and, except where noted, film separations were output to an Optronics ColorSetter Plus.

Color page 17 was output on an Agfa Compugraphic SelectSet 5000 imagesetter by Graphics Express of Boston. Color pages 6 and 7 were output on Linotronic imagesetters, and the images on Color Page 8 were stripped in traditionally

Index

The Optronics™ division of Intergraph®
is proud to have contributed the scanning and laser imagesetting for the color pages in *Desktop Publishing in Color.*

Images were scanned from transparencies by Optronics' Bob Janukowicz using an Optronics ColorGetter Plus desktop scanner linked to a 32 MB Macintosh IIfx computer.

After designer Donna Chernin, of Computer Graphic Design, manipulated the images in Adobe Photoshop, she laid out pages in QuarkXpress and gave the files to Bob for film separations. Bob generated the color separation films on the Optronics ColorSetter at 175 line screen, with type and page geometry set at 2,000 dpi.

ColorGetter Plus is a high resolution tabletop color scanner that scans transmissive or reflective artwork ranging from 35mm to 10" x 14" in a single pass. Three photomultiplier tubes (PMTs) simultaneously capture red, green, and blue data from the original, ensuring precise registration of the RGB information. Color is captured up to a full 12 bits (4096 gray levels) per color. Unlike CCD-based light sensors used in most of today's desktop color scanners, the PMTs used in the ColorGetter support a broad dynamic range - from 0.0 to 3.8 D Max - to capture brilliant highlights to deep shadows.

The ColorGetter Plus consists of a desktop scanner and an intelligent controller. The scanner features removable drums for off-line mounting.

ColorSetter 2000 is a drum-based laser imagesetter that accepts input in a wide variety of formats and records high resolution output of fully made-up pages. All page elements are imaged in position, eliminating manual assembly. The ColorSetter's format size of 20" x 26" allows imaging of 4-up A4 or 8 1/2" x 11" pages including bleed on a single sheet of positive or negative film or photosensitive paper.

Optronics' proprietary hardware screening technique, IntelliDot, controls edge definition, dot shape and size, and optimizes gray shades over a range of screen frequencies. IntelliDot screening is performed in dedicated hardware for fast image screening. Plate ready films are imaged at a resolution of 2,000 dpi with photographs screened at frequencies up to 175 lpi.

For more information about how Optronics' ColorSetter family of imagesetters and ColorGetter and ColorGetter Plus desktop color scanners can improve your performance, please photocopy, then fill out the form below and mail or fax it to: Optronics, An Intergraph Division, Marketing Services Department, 7 Stuart Road, Chelmsford, MA 01824. Fax: (508) 256-1872.

Please send more information on: ____ColorSetter 2000

____ColorSetter 4000

____ColorSetter XL

____ColorGetter

____ColorGetter Plus

Name_____

Title_____

Company_____

Address_____

City_____

State_____Zip_____

Phone_____Ext._____

Optronics
An Intergraph Division